Many Pathways to Literacy

This unique and visionary text is a compilation of fascinating studies conducted in a variety of cross-cultural contexts where children learn language and literacy with siblings, grandparents, peers and community members. Focusing on the knowledge and skills of children often invisible to educators, these illuminating studies highlight how children skillfully draw from their varied cultural and linguistic worlds to make sense of new experiences.

The vastly experienced team of contributors provide powerful demonstrations of the generative activity of young children and their mediating partners – family members, peers, and community members – as they syncretise languages, literacies and cultural practices from varied contexts. Through studies grounded in home, school, community school, nursery and church settings, we see how children create for themselves radical forms of teaching and learning in ways that are not typically recognized, understood or valued in schools.

The book challenges readers to examine assumptions and cultural stereotypes about literacy learning as well as their own teaching practices and beliefs. Presenting some of the first Syncretic Literacy Studies of young children, it sets a new direction in literacy research. The book will be invaluable reading for teachers, teacher educators, researchers and policy-makers who seek to understand the many pathways to literacy and use that knowledge to affect real change in schools.

Eve Gregory is Professor of Language and Culture in Education, Goldsmiths College, University of London.

Susi Long is Associate Professor in Early Childhood Education and Language and Literacy at the University of South Carolina.

Dinah Volk is Professor of Early Childhood Education, College of Education, Cleveland State University.

Many Pathways to Literacy

Young children learning with siblings, grandparents, peers and communities

Edited by

Eve Gregory
Susi Long
Dinah Volk

RoutledgeFalmer
Taylor & Francis Group

NEW YORK AND LONDON

First published 2004
by RoutledgeFalmer
270 Madison Avenue, New York, NY 10016

Simultaneously published in the UK
by RoutledgeFalmer
2 Park Square, Milton Park, Abingdon, Oxon, OX14 4RN

Reprinted 2005

RoutledgeFalmer is an imprint of the Taylor & Francis Group

Typeset in Baskerville by
Keystroke, Jacaranda Lodge, Wolverhampton
Printed and bound in Great Britain by
MPG Books Ltd, Bodmin, Cornwall

Library of Congress Cataloging in Publication Data
A catalog record for this book has been requested

British Library Cataloguing in Publication Data
A catalogue record for this book is available from the British Library

ISBN 0–415–306–167 (Hbk)
ISBN 0–415–306–175 (Pbk)

For our families:
Charly, Klara, Jan, Kelli, Steve, Jonah, Anna and Miriam

The editors contributed equally to this book

Contents

Figures

Notes on contributors

Martha de Acosta has taught and conducted research in several Latin American countries and in the United States. Since the early 1990s, she has focused on studying collaborations and partnerships between families, communities and schools to support children's learning and development. At present she directs the Full-Service Community School Initiative at the Milton S. Eisenhower Foundation, Washington, DC.

Donna Bell is a kindergarten teacher in Columbia, South Carolina. She consults regularly in local schools focusing on literacy learning in 4- and 5-year-old kindergartens. Her work is published in the National Council of Teachers of English journal, *Primary Voices*.

Jim Brown is a doctoral student in the Department of Educational Leadership and Policies, University of South Carolina, Columbia. He also works as an instructor at Mars Hill College in North Carolina.

Janet Carter-Black is a doctoral student and teaching assistant in the School of Social Work, University of Illinois, Urbana-Champaign. Her research interests and publication topics include racial socialization, impact of gender-specific modes of socialization on achievement outcomes, storytelling and family narratives and the influence of African culture on parenting strategies in African American families.

Yuangguang Chen is Professor of Education at Fujian Teachers University in PR China. She is currently completing her PhD study into bilingualism in education at Goldsmiths College, University of London. Her books include *Curriculum Theory and Curriculum Design* (Fujian People's Publishing House 1998) and *A Comparative Study of School Curricula in US, UK, Japan and China* (Fujian Educational Press 1996).

Manjula Datta is a senior lecturer in Language Education at the London Metropolitan University, UK. She specializes in bilingual children's language and literacy education and has published on the subject widely. Her book *Bilinguality and Literacy: Principles and Practice* (Continuum 2001), has been well received on both sides of the Atlantic. Recently she has co-authored *A World of Languages! Developing Children's Love of Languages* (with Cathy Pomphrey: CILT 2003).

Rose Drury is Principal Lecturer in Early Years Education at the University of Hertfordshire, UK, where she is programme leader for the BA (Hons) in Early Childhood Studies and other Early Years Education courses. She has extensive experience of teaching bilingual children in the early years. Her research and publications relate to this field.

Alessandro Duranti is Professor of Anthropology and Director of the Centre on Language, Interaction and Culture (CLIC) at the University of California, Los Angeles (UCLA). He has studied Samoan communities in Samoa and Southern California, focusing on political discourse and literacy practices. His books include *From Grammar to Politics: Linguistic Anthropology in a Western Samoan Village* (University of California Press 1994), *Linguistic Anthropology* (Cambridge University Press 1994) and *Linguistic Anthropology: A Reader* (Blackwell 2001).

Patricia A. Edwards is Professor of Language and Literacy at Michigan State University where she teaches, writes and conducts research in the areas of family/intergenerational literacy and connections between home and school literacies. She is the author of *A Path to Follow: Learning to Listen to Parents* (Heinemann 1999) and *Children's Literacy Development: Making it Happen Through School, Family, and Community Involvement* (Allyn & Bacon 2004).

Eve Gregory is Professor of Language and Culture in Education, Goldsmiths College, University of London. Her books include *Making Sense of a New World: Learning to Read in a Second Language* (Sage 1996), *One Child, Many Worlds: Early Learning in Multicultural Communities* (David Fulton and Teachers' College Press 1997) and *City Literacies: Learning to Read across Generations and Cultures* (with Ann Williams: Routledge 2000).

Wendy L. Haight is an Associate Professor and Director of the doctoral programme in Social Work at the University of Illinois, Urbana-Champaign. She received her PhD in developmental psychology at the University of Chicago. Her research interests include parent–child interaction in diverse cultural contexts focusing on play, narrative and religious practices.

Clare Kelly is a Lecturer in Language and Literacy at Goldsmiths College, University of London; formerly she was an assistant director at the Centre for Language in Primary Education in London. Her main areas of interest are early literacy development, the teaching of reading and social and cultural literacy practices at home and school.

Charmian Kenner is a researcher on bilingualism and literacy, based at Goldsmiths College, University of London. She recently led an ESRC-funded project on early biliteracy and is currently directing another on intergenerational learning between children and grandparents in East London. Her publications include *Home Pages: Literacy Links for Bilingual Children* (Trentham 2000).

Susi Long is an associate professor in Early Childhood Education at the University of South Carolina, Columbia. Her research interests include language and literacy learning, particularly for children in marginalized communities, and teacher education. Her articles include those published in *Research in the Teaching of English*, the *Journal of Teacher Education*, *Primary Voices*, *Reading, Language and Literacy* and *Studies in Educational Ethnography* (JAI Press).

Gwendolyn Thompson McMillon is an assistant professor of Literacy in the Reading and Language Arts Department, Oakland University, Rochester, MI. She was a recipient of the Spencer Dissertation Fellowship for Research Related to Education. Her current research project is entitled *Crossing Cultural Borders: Urban Teachers Examining and Responding to African American Students' Literacy Experiences at Church and at School* for which she received the Oakland Faculty Fellowship Award.

Melissa Mosley is a doctoral student in Education at Washington University in St. Louis, MO. Her research focuses on how children accelerate as readers and writers within a social justice framework. Prior to her doctoral work she was an elementary teacher in the Midwest USA.

Elinor Ochs is Professor of Anthropology and Applied Linguistics at UCLA. Her research focuses on the nexus of language, culture and society across settings and communities. She is a MacArthur Fellow, member of the American Academy of Arts and Sciences and currently directs the UCLA Sloan Centre on Everyday Lives of Families.

Irma M. Olmedo is an associate professor at the University of Illinois, Chicago. Her research interests include exploration of aspects of children's bilingual development, the use of oral history and family narratives as a way of examining Latino cultures in the United States and preparation of teachers for urban classrooms.

Leena Helavaara Robertson is a senior lecturer and teaches on the undergraduate and postgraduate teacher training and Early Childhood Studies courses at University College Northampton, UK. Currently, she is completing doctoral research into bilingual children's early literacy at Goldsmiths College, University of London. Previously she worked as a class teacher in multilingual schools in England and is bilingual herself (Finnish/English).

Rebecca Rogers is an assistant professor of Literacy Education at Washington University in St. Louis, MO. Her research focuses on the contexts in which struggling readers become proficient and believe in themselves as capable readers and writers. She teaches courses in literacy education, sociolinguistics and research methodologies. She is the author of *A Critical Discourse Analysis of Family Literacy Practices: Power in and out of Print* (Lawrence Erlbaum 2003).

Mary Eunice Romero is from Cochiti Pueblo, New Mexico. Currently, she is serving as a research assistant professor/programme coordinator for the Native Language Shift and Retention Project, a three-year research study funded by the Institute of Education Sciences and sponsored by the University of Arizona. In 2001, she received her PhD from the University of California, Berkeley.

Elia K. Ta'ase is a graduate of the University of California, Los Angeles. At the time of writing the article that is reprinted as a chapter in this book, he was a teacher in American Samoa.

Dinah Volk is Professor of Early Childhood Education, Cleveland State University, Cleveland, OH. She is co-author of *Kaleidoscope: A Multicultural Approach for the Primary School Classroom* (with Leslie R. Williams and Yvonne DeGaetano: Prentice Hall 1997). Her research on the literacy practices of bilingual children and families has been published in *Research in the Teaching of English*, the *Journal of Early Childhood Literacy*, *Reading, Language and Literacy* and the *Early Childhood Research Quarterly*.

Ann Williams is a research fellow at Goldsmith's College, University of London. She has worked on several funded projects in the fields of language change, variation in British urban dialects and literacy in inner city communities. She is co-author of *City Literacies: Learning to Read across Generations and Cultures* (with Eve Gregory: Routledge 2000).

Foreword

Barbara Rogoff and Maricela Correa-Chávez

Psychology Department, University of California, Santa Cruz

How can researchers and practitioners understand and assist young children in the complex process of learning to read and to use language? This engaging volume examines down-to-earth case studies of young children from a wide variety of cultural communities, mostly in the United States and the United Kingdom. The book reveals that literacy and language development is far richer and more multidimensional than is often presumed, especially for children whose home communities are new to literacy in English.

Using sociocultural approaches, the authors provide windows on young children's everyday lives and their participation in multiple communities. They represent children's actual worlds in ways that do not flatten them or reduce them to one or two causal variables, helping to elaborate culture as dynamic practices in which even the youngest children participate and shape through engagement in varied events and institutions.

A major contribution of this book is the idea – discussed and beautifully illustrated – that people contribute to cultural and individual change by syncretically melding ideas from a variety of cultural traditions (see also Rogoff 2003). This idea is a refreshing acknowledgement that many children in today's world engage simultaneously with hybrid traditions of several communities. It contrasts with assumptions that people can be represented in terms of one static cultural category or of membership in several distinct worlds.

The authors illuminate the fusion of many traditions as they show how ethnic and language minority children build on their participation in multiple communities. Many of the case studies show the resourcefulness and skill of children in everyday language and literacy. For example, a Pahari- and English-speaking boy of Pakistani heritage in England used the participation structures and learning approaches of both his English and Qur'anic (Arabic language) schools in learning how to read and speak in Urdu in his fourth-language Urdu class. The 6-year-old children in this Urdu class were able to understand complicated aspects of language such as the arbitrary nature of alphabets and different modes of teaching and learning for distinct literary systems (Robertson, Chapter 13 in this volume). They understood that recitation is appropriate for learning the Qur'an and used that skill in learning the Urdu alphabet and also understood that questions about text are important in English literacy and used those as well.

At the same time, many of the chapters reveal minority children's challenging structural position *vis-à-vis* society at large. Several chapters show that children may not demonstrate literacy in school-sanctioned ways at school, but at home or in other community settings they demonstrated a metacognitive understanding of language and literacy and engaged skillfully in early literacy activities. For example, African American children articulated important literacy skills that they learned in Sunday School, impressively articulating what they learned and its relevance to school (McMillon and Edwards, Chapter 14). Yet, as Haight and Carter-Black (Chapter 15) point out in their study of African American children's participation in a Baptist church, the same child who was able to recite the 27 books of the New Testament from memory also failed a spelling test the same week.

An important conclusion is that literacy learning could be improved in schools with greater recognition of the everyday language and literacy practices that children engage in skillfully at home and in their communities. A key principle for instruction is to start where the learner is (National Academy of Science 1999). This requires an understanding of the skills and knowledge that children meet school with and the contexts in which their strengths show – information that is often unavailable to teachers and school administrators serving children from backgrounds different from their own. The authors argue that such children have far greater language and literacy skills than often presumed and their chapters begin to show researchers and teachers how to look in the right places to find them.

The authors point out that despite the usual assumption that parents are children's primary support in language and literacy learning, many children have other resources that are often overlooked by schools, such as siblings, peers, grandparents and community elders. For example, children learned from stories that elderly Latina women told them (Olmedo, Chapter 6) and connected the stories to what they had been studying in their fourth grade science, geography and literature studies.

Researchers and educators can use this volume's illumination of children's syncretic blending of traditions to connect these resources with the traditions of classroom learning, building on the multiple traditions that young children bring to the classroom.

Acknowledgements

Grateful acknowledgement is made to the following publishers for permission to reprint publications or excerpts from publications:

Caddo Gap Press for permission to reprint: A. Duranti, E. Ochs and E. K. Ta'ase (1995) 'Change and tradition in literacy instruction in a Samoan American community', *Educational Foundations*, 9.4: 57–74.

Cambridge University Press for permission to use portions of the book by W. Haight (2002), *African American Children at Church: A Sociocultural Perspective*.

Cambridge University Press for permission to use M. Cole's Table 1: Psychology and anthropology: conceptual polarities, in J. A. Wertsch (ed.) *Culture, Communication and Cognition: Vygotskian Perspectives*.

Syncretic Literacy Studies
Starting points

Eve Gregory, Susi Long and Dinah Volk

This book originates in the stories exchanged between Early Years educators in Britain and Early Childhood educators in the US during the last decade of the twentieth century about children whose learning challenged commonly held expectations. In other words, these were children who defied existing paradigms of what counted as successful learning in school or whose accomplishments contradicted the deficit perspective that many applied to them. Children, for example, like 5-year-old Tony, who puzzled his teacher when he did not flourish in his relaxed, play-oriented classroom in a small town in England, preferring instead the structured learning and repetition of ideograms in his Saturday Mandarin class. Or Samina and Shahina, also 5, whose ability to draw sophisticated comparisons between English and Bengali grammar and lexis before they could understand the content of their book made traditional early literacy assessment, based on talking about texts, meaningless. Or 5-year-old Mónica, who was Puerto Rican, for whom any judgement on *parental* involvement would exclude the complex network of family and community 'teachers' in her literacy life. Or Nelson, also 5 and Puerto Rican, whose introduction to literacy was through family Bible readings and reading with his siblings rather than one-on-one interactions with his mother and picture books. Or 4-year-old Samia, whose skill in translating from English into Urdu for her 2-year-old brother at home was disguised by her silence in class. These children were typical of many who puzzled teachers in both the US and Britain since they did not fit into accepted frames of what early literacy teaching and learning in school were all about.

Paradigms do not shift easily or quickly. Our stories built on those of others – William Labov, Shirley Brice Heath, Denny Taylor, Luis Moll, Lisa Delpit, Gloria Ladson-Billings and Sonia Nieto, among others – who for years have argued for the value of home and community languages and literacies. Like their work, our stories were sometimes met with consternation by educators who worked with young children, since they seemed to undermine commonly accepted stages of early literacy learning as well as question the popular vision of parental involvement in literacy activities embodied in the bedtime story. Other educators, unsure how to translate our stories into practice, often focused on superficial features of children's cultures. Still others explained that the children *they* taught lacked the ability to use language in complex ways and had few literacy resources and little support at home.

To a certain extent the educators' concerns were justified, since our stories suggested that practices and beliefs relevant to the learning and development of young children which most viewed as universal might, indeed, be cultural, limited to the western and middle-class values of a group to which we also belonged. Our stories added to the ongoing challenge to Piagetian theory, long a foundational perspective in our field, as well as to accepted notions about literacy and appropriate teaching practices. We searched for existing examples and accounts of early literacy taking place at home and in communities which would explain the progress of children such as those outlined earlier. We found ourselves caught within a web of understandings defined by psychologists, sociologists, linguists and anthropologists who were each interested in a separate strand of the literacy learning task. Briefly, psychologists focused on *methods* of teaching and learning, sociologists on the *economic disadvantage* experienced by our children, a disadvantage fleshed out in longitudinal studies by anthropologists and linguists who insisted on a certain *threshold of bilingual competence* needed in order for cognitive advantages to accrue. We realized that our children's literacy practices were invisible and excluded from these accounts. Likewise 'invisible' were the mediators or unofficial 'teachers' in these children's lives – their siblings, grandparents, friends and other community members.

How we began

In 1995, Eve and her colleague Ann Williams were studying the home literacy experiences of Bangladeshi British children. Along with others whose work had also begun to uncover the wealth of 'invisible' literacies in young children's lives, Eve initiated a language and culture research support group based at the University of London. Susi, having just completed a study of peers and cross-cultural learning in Iceland, was living in England and joined the group. Several years later, Dinah, on professional leave in London and writing about her research with mainland Puerto Rican children learning at home with parents and siblings, joined too. Once back in the US, Susi and Dinah worked with Eve on several joint projects that explored young children's skillful negotiation of new cultural worlds, studying contexts, strategies, resources and mediators.

Our starting point was the conviction that the teaching and learning skills of young children living between and within different linguistic and cultural settings had largely been omitted from the Early Years/Early Childhood educational context. Nor did we fit precisely into recent work in social literacies (Baynham 1995; Barton and Hamilton 1998; Street 2003) where studies focused largely on older children or adults. From our perspective, two crucial aspects were missing in this work: the remarkable cognitive, cultural and linguistic flexibility of young children and the crucial importance of the mediator in young children's lives.

Our discussions and presentations were particularly informed by socioculturally situated developmental psychology, especially work by Michael Cole, James Wertsch and Barbara Rogoff in the US and Judy Dunn in Britain. Work by Barbara Rogoff and her colleagues (Rogoff 1990, 2003; Rogoff *et al.* 1993) was important in enabling us to convince teachers that, although families and communities across the world give equally finely tuned support to children's learning, the nature of the curriculum given, i.e. what counts as learning, will be different. Rogoff's photograph of an 11-month-old infant cutting a breadfruit with a machete in the Democratic Republic of the Congo (Rogoff 1990: 131) was studied with excitement and delight by teachers beginning themselves to uncover the hidden skills of young children in their classrooms. Gradually, then, many teachers realized that building on children's home literacy experiences was much more difficult than they had originally believed and that they could not simply assume that children shared their own literacy lives. A familiar cultural practice or parental relationship to a White middle-class British or US child might be very strange for a child who was African American, Bangladeshi British or Puerto Rican.

The principle underpinning all our work was that of the extraordinary capacity of young children across cultures to 'read like butterflies and write like bees . . . only then can they make honey' (Robertson 2002: 125): in other words, recognizing children's ability to pick and choose from their home, community and school languages and literacies to make sense of texts. Our meetings attracted educators interested in language and literacy in cross-cultural contexts from countries as different as Israel, Brazil, Japan, China, Macau, Luxembourg, New Zealand, France, Australia and Germany as well as Britain and the US. A number of our language and culture research group (Chen, Drury, Kelly, Kenner, Robertson, Williams) have joined us in contributing chapters in this book. Members of the group have gradually refined and illustrated in their writing a new approach to early literacy which we refer to as *syncretic*. Within the array of references to literacy at the start of the twenty-first century (multiple literacies, multiliteracies, literacy practices and events etc.) readers may well ask: what are *Syncretic Literacy Studies* and how do they differ from other approaches? We shall outline briefly our definition of syncretism and crucial characteristics of Syncretic Literacy Studies.

Syncretism and Syncretic Literacy Studies

In the 1920s and 1930s, the term syncretism was used by anthropologists studying religion in Caribbean cultures to describe the interactions of African and European Christian religious traditions. Many considered the new practices that were created to be degraded forms of a so-called authentic Christianity. Over the years, however, syncretism has taken on a broader and more positive connotation as the contemporary study of cultures in contact and conflict has flourished. Though syncretism is often seen as 'slippery' (Shaw and Stewart 1994: 21) and hard to define because it embodies contradiction, it has come to mean the creative transformation of culture (Kulick 1992).

Two related characteristics of this redefined syncretism are relevant here. First, syncretism is understood to be more than a mixing of existing cultural forms (Apter 1991). It is, instead, a creative process in which people reinvent culture as they draw on diverse resources, both familiar and new (Shaw and Stewart 1994). The focus is on the activity of transformation, not on fossilized cultural forms. Second, syncretism is described as an inherent feature of cross-cultural encounters and negotiations (Solsken et al. 2000) and is, thus, often characterized by contradictory elements arising out of disparities in power. The reinvention of new forms is generated by the juxtaposition of these elements.

When syncretism was first developed in the anthropological literature, it was used to analyze contact between 'officially recognized culture units' (Rosaldo 1993: 29). More recently, researchers have used it to illuminate the 'mundane practices of everyday life' (Rosaldo 1993: 217). Along these lines, Duranti and Ochs (1997) 'extend syncretism to include hybrid cultural constructions of speech acts and speech activities that constitute literacy' (p. 173), defining syncretic literacy as 'an intermingling or merging of culturally diverse traditions [that] informs and organizes literacy activities' (p. 172). In their work together and with Ta'ase (Duranti et al. 1995 and reprinted in Chapter 12 in this volume), Duranti and Ochs analyze the ways in which Samoan and North American cultural practices and tools are reinvented in syncretic literacy events in Samoan American contexts.

Contemporary researchers, working in school classrooms and a computer club, have investigated the ways that children and teachers appropriate resources from various contexts in children's lives for use in learning activities (Gutiérrez et al. 1999; Solsken et al. 2000; Dyson 2003). Such work explicitly explores the challenges and conflicts created when resources from home and popular culture are juxtaposed with those from school. The activities that result can disrupt established power relationships and have the potential to create more equitable practices and possibilities for learning because they provide 'Third Spaces or zones of development' (Gutiérrez et al. 1999: 286) where teachers can value and build on what children know and where children can help shape learning.

Some of these recent studies have their roots in the writings of Bakhtin (1981) and his theory of the social origin of language and his description of the generative dialogue of voices within any utterance. They use his term *hybridity* to refer to the 'polycontextual, multivoiced and multiscripted' (Gutiérrez et al. 1999: 287) nature of the learning zones where cultures come in contact.

It is important to acknowledge that the definitions of syncretism and hybridity in the literature lack clarity and have changed over the years. Sometimes a distinction is made between the two concepts, at other times they are used synonymously. In this volume, we use the term syncretism because of its traditional use to describe the creation of new forms, not just complex blended ones. Our emphasis is on the fluid and creative interaction of words, ideas and practices to create a dynamic, fruitful and positive whole.

Syncretic Literacy Studies in this volume share the following beliefs:

- Young children are active members of different cultural and linguistic groups and appropriating membership to a group is not a static or a linear process.
- Children do not remain in separate worlds but acquire membership of different groups *simultaneously*, i.e. they live in 'simultaneous worlds' (Kenner 2003, forthcoming).
- Simultaneous membership means that children *syncretize* the languages, literacies, narrative styles and role relationships appropriate to each group and then go on to transform the languages and cultures they use to create new forms relevant to the purpose needed.
- Young children who participate in cross-linguistic and cross-cultural practices call upon a greater wealth of metacognitive and metalinguistic strategies. These strategies are further enhanced when they are able to *play out different roles and events*.
- Play is a crucial feature of children's language and literacy practice with siblings, grandparents and peers.
- The mediators, often bicultural and/or bilingual, play an essential role in early language and literacy learning. Studies investigate different forms of 'scaffolding', 'guided participation' or 'synergy' as young and older children or adults work and play together.

Syncretic Literacy Studies, therefore, go beyond issues of method, materials and parental involvement towards a wider interpretation of literacy, including what children take culturally and linguistically from their families and communities (*prolepsis*), how they gain access to the existing *funds of knowledge* in their communities through *finely tuned scaffolding* by mediators and how they transform existing languages, literacies and practices to create new forms (*syncretism*). This whole process takes place within the wider sociocultural framework outlined in Chapter 1 and is brought to life in the contributed chapters.

Chapter 1

A sociocultural approach to learning

Eve Gregory, Susi Long and Dinah Volk

> We come to every situation with stories, patterns and sequences of child-hood experiences which are built into us. Our learning happens within the experience of what important others did.
>
> (Bateson 1979: 13)

What are these stories and where and why do they originate? Who are 'important others' and what role might they play in our learning? How do we express these stories to ourselves and to other people? In this chapter, we outline a sociocultural approach to literacy and learning and the theoretical framework it provides to respond to each of these questions.

A sociocultural approach draws from and synthesizes insights from two traditionally very different disciplines: psychology and anthropology. Cole (1985) summarizes these polarities neatly in Table 1.1.

In western societies, children's learning was historically the domain of psychologists. Focus was on children's *individuality* as well as the *universality* of learning and learning practices across cultures. Cognitive development was viewed as largely independent from the different influences of particular social and cultural

Table 1.1 Psychology and anthropology: conceptual polarities

Anthropology	Psychology
Culture	Cognition
Higher functions	Elementary functions
Products	Process
Content	Process
Group	Individual
Independent variable	Dependent variable
Observation	Experimentation
Field	Laboratory
Holistic	Analytic
Description	Explanation

Source: Cole 1985: 147. Reprinted with permission from Cambridge University Press.

environments (Piaget 1926). In contrast, work by Soviet psychologists and particularly by Vygotsky (1962, 1978, 1981) argued that all thinking and learning was *social and historical* in origin:

> Any function in the child's cultural development appears twice, or on two planes. First, it appears on the social plane and then on the psychological plane. First it appears between people as an interpsychological (interpersonal) activity and then within the child as an intrapsychological (intrapersonal) activity. This is equally true with regard to voluntary attention, logical memory, the formation of concepts and the development of volition.
>
> (Vygotsky 1981: 163)

Studies taking a sociocultural approach integrate the fields of developmental, cognitive and cross-cultural psychology with those of cultural, social and cognitive anthropology. Additionally, work from linguistics, cultural history and philosophy can also share the same approach. Indeed, a sociocultural approach *transcends* academic disciplines and focuses on the inextricable link between culture and cognition through engagement in activities, tasks or events.

What do sociocultural studies across academic disciplines share? Basically, all 'put culture in the middle' (Cole 1996: 116). All tackle the complex relationship between culture and cognition, believing mind to be interiorized culture and culture exteriorized mind. The anthropologist Geertz (1973: 5) refers to culture as the 'webs of significance' humans have themselves spun and describes the location of culture as being in the minds and hearts of people who are at the same time actors and creators of social interactions. As a cultural historian, philosopher and literary scholar, Bakhtin (1981) argues for the *dialogicality* of the utterance as the real unit of communication. Bruner's (1986) work in social psychology examines the nature of a joint culture creation between teacher and child and, in linguistics, Nelson (1981) shows ways in which knowledge of the culture might be revealed through children's shared schema (knowledge structure) and scripts (ways in which shared knowledge is expressed). Longitudinal ethnographic studies of families and classrooms in both the US and Britain provided finely tuned studies on the nature of the culture–cognition link in everyday life. Young children in both contexts are shown to possess a wealth of language and literacy knowledge that can be very different from the knowledge demanded by the school (Heath 1983; Gregory 1996).

Within a sociocultural framework, young children learn as *apprentices* alongside a more experienced member of the culture. Crucial to a sociocultural approach, therefore, is the role of the mediator (a teacher, adult, more knowledgeable sibling or peer) in initiating children into new cultural practices or guiding them in the learning of new skills. Vygotsky (1978: 86) uses the term 'the zone of proximal development' to describe 'the distance between the actual development level as determined by independent problem solving and the level of potential development as determined through problem solving under adult guidance or in collaboration with more capable peers'.

While agreeing that mediators are essential to children's learning, the extent to which the child also takes control has been viewed in different ways. Early studies concurred with Vygotsky's focus on the adult or more experienced member of the culture in scaffolding a child's expertise, gradually removing the structure as the novice grows more competent (Wood *et al.* 1976; Bruner 1981). More recently, this focus has shifted more towards viewing children as playing an active role in their own learning. In 'guided participation' (Rogoff 1990; Stone 1993) children actively participate with others – 'more skilled partners and their challenging and exploring peers' (Rogoff 1990: 8) – who serve as both guides and collaborators. Together they draw on cultural resources and build on what children know and can do to co-construct learning. Throughout this process, children take on and are given more responsibility and 'appropriate an increasingly advanced understanding of and skill in managing the intellectual problems of their community' (Rogoff 1990: 8). Still other research on reciprocal teaching and learning between siblings describes a synergy taking place in which children play active, complementary and more balanced roles in building on what they both know and in fostering their mutual learning, not just the learning of the one who may be a novice (Gregory 2001).

The research on young children's play conducted from a sociocultural perspective suggests that it is a context in which children are the active creators of their own development, that is, they provide their own scaffolding (Berk and Winsler 1995; Bodrova and Leong 1996). Vygotsky (cited in Berk and Winsler 1995: 52) argued that 'play creates a zone of proximal development in the child', providing the opportunity for imaginative work that is rule governed. There is no universal form of play; it is a culturally mediated activity that has universal as well as developmental elements (Goncu *et al.* 1999; Haight *et al.* 1999). Within the context of play, children often create rich, syncretic worlds, drawing on the many resources in their lives (Long *et al.* 2001).

Although the studies presented in this volume are very different in content and context, all work within a sociocultural approach to literacy learning. Within this frame, they adhere to three key principles summarized below:

- *Recognizing that culture and cognition create each other:* authors aim to uncover the language and literacy knowledge and practices as well as ways of learning held by people in their communities and how these may contrast or complement those which count in formal schooling.
- *Acknowledging that a joint culture creation between teacher and child in classrooms is crucial for learning:* authors aim to document the role of important mediators of language and literacies in different contexts and how this takes place.
- *Giving a voice to those whose voices would otherwise not have been heard:* authors aim to celebrate participants' voices as well as recognizing their own voice as events are interpreted.

Ultimately, then, 'a sociocultural approach concerns the ways in which human action, including mental action (e.g. reasoning, remembering), is inherently linked to the cultural, institutional and historical settings in which it occurs' (Wertsch 1994: 203). Authors in this volume begin to uncover both the multitude of different settings in which children learn as well as the complexity with which they interpret these settings to themselves. In the sections following, we unpick different strands important to understanding Syncretic Literacy Studies within a sociocultural framework. First, we outline ways in which we see young children as active members of *communities of learners* working and playing in the context of meaningful activities with others. We show the importance of recognizing *prolepsis* and *funds of knowledge* as inherent within intergenerational learning processes. We then focus more specifically upon early literacy learning, investigating *literacy as a social and cultural practice, emergent literacy* and *critical literacies* within our framework of interpretation. Finally, we show how ethnography can be used as a research approach to investigate and analyze interaction within a syncretic literacy framework.

Learning communities

In the field of education, the focus of attention traditionally has been on the mind of the individual learner and his/her accumulation of the valued information and abilities transmitted by a teaching adult. As noted earlier, research and practice grounded in sociocultural theory (Wells *et al.* 1990; Lave and Wenger 1991; Rogoff *et al.* 1996) shift and broaden that focus to the learner's active appropriation of valued cultural practices and knowledge within a social context. Learning, from this perspective, occurs in coparticipation and is mediated by others. It is embedded in social relationships and is constructed by and distributed across members of learning groups. Research on communities has much to contribute to an understanding of this perspective on learning.

Lave and Wenger (1991) propose the concept of *communities of practice*, 'a set of relations among persons, activity, and world, over time and in relation with other tangential and overlapping communities of practice' (p. 98). A community is defined by more than just relevant skills and knowledge, but is understood to consist of both cultural practices and 'the interpretive support necessary for making sense of its heritage' (p. 98). Learning 'is a process of social participation' (Wenger 1998: i) in the community as a newcomer engages in and helps construct cultural practice with peers as well as masters. As learning develops, the newcomer moves from 'legitimate peripheral participation' (Lave and Wenger 1991: 29) to 'full participation' (p. 37) in ways defined by the organization of the community.

Brown (1994; Brown and Campione 1994) developed the concept of a *community of learners* as part of an effort to describe and advocate practice in classrooms in which children and teachers engage in joint inquiry and generate group understanding. This concept is interpreted and implemented by Rogoff *et al.* (2001) within the specific context of formal and informal interactions in a school for young children. For these teachers and researchers, learning is grounded in an understanding of the ways that children in many cultures learn in the context of meaningful and productive activity with others. As a consequence, they define learning as 'a community process of *transformation of participation* in sociocultural activities' (Rogoff *et al.* 1996: 388). In their school, children, parents and teachers explicitly collaborated, 'transforming their understanding, roles, and responsibilities as they participate[d]' in significant, joint activities (Rogoff *et al.* 1996: 390). While adults were recognized as more knowledgeable in many ways and as the primary guides, all participants were learners and took leadership in the ongoing reinvention of their practice.

Research on communities continues to work to balance a broader perspective on the group with an in-depth view of individual learning interactions (Toohey 2000; Linehan and McCarthy 2001) and to reject the reification and essentializing of the communities studied (Guerra 1998; Moje 2000). Individuals are understood as community members and communities are described as inherently dynamic and heterogeneous, characterized by change, differences and conflict as well as stability, commonalities and consent.

While there has been a great deal of research on children as individuals learning from parents or teachers in either homes or schools, there has been little on young children as learners in communities or networks that include people in their schools, neighbourhoods and extended families. The chapters in this book begin to fill the need for work that illuminates this community-centred view of literacy (Willett and Bloome 1993; Rogoff *et al.* 2001; Compton-Lilly 2003) by taking as their starting point the child as a member of many interwoven communities.

Prolepsis and funds of knowledge

Within communities, the process of *prolepsis* represents one kind of intergenerational link. The concept has evolved over the years, as has the meaning of the word itself. In the 1970s, *prolepsis* was taken up by Rommetveit, a psycholinguist, to refer 'to a communicative move in which the speaker presupposes some as yet unprovided information' (Stone 1993: 171). This initiating move, if it works, sets in motion a process in which the listener recreates the speaker's presuppositions. In the 1990s, the meaning of prolepsis was further explored by researchers using a sociocultural perspective to analyze scaffolding in the zone of proximal development (Stone 1993) and intersubjectivity (Goncu 1998). In both cases, the focus was on the dynamics of communication, as the speaker looks forward with certain presuppositions, the listener works at recreating them and the two are drawn together in a creative process of joint meaning making.

Cole (1996), in a sociocultural explanation of the cultural mediation of development, further elaborates our understanding of prolepsis as 'the cultural mechanism that brings "the end into the beginning"' (p. 183). The adult – the mother in Cole's example – brings her idealized memory of her cultural past and her assumption of cultural continuity in the future to actual interactions with the child in the present. In this nonlinear process, the child's experience is both energized and constrained by what adults remember of their own pasts and imagine what the child's future will be. Cole's conceptualization of the adult–child relationship is further expanded by researchers (Goncu 1998; Long 1998a) looking at children's play in which the roles of expert and novice can be exchanged. In cross-cultural play interactions, either the cultural insider or the newcomer may project a future that they must construct together.

The concept of *funds of knowledge* was developed by Moll and his colleagues (Moll and Greenberg 1990; Moll 1992; Moll and González 1994) during a research project with teachers that included ethnographic analyzes of the working-class, Mexican American communities of the children in their classes. As is widely known, the team of researchers and teachers identified many 'material and intellectual resources' (Moll 1992: 214) within the communities that were crucial to the families' survival. They called these *funds of knowledge*, the 'historically accumulated and culturally developed bodies of knowledge and skills essential for household or individual functioning and well-being' (Moll *et al.* 1992: 133). These funds were then used by the teachers as resources to develop units of study that were contextualized and meaningful to the children.

Less well known is the team's finding that the knowledge and skills were transmitted within a social matrix, a community of social networks based on reciprocity and *confianza* or mutual trust. Community members shared what they knew and were assisted when necessary in what the researchers refer to as 'extended zones of proximal development' (Moll and Greenberg 1990: 344). That is, the funds of knowledge are not just the bits of useful information and handy skills but also represent the human activity of assistance and sharing in a meaningful context.

Contrary to the deficit perspective that defines some children and their families by their so-called 'deficiencies', the funds of knowledge perspective defines them as skillful and resourceful teachers and learners. In their ordinary lives they facilitate their own learning and that of others and, as a consequence, they have much to teach classroom teachers. This perspective is an essential part of three approaches to early literacy learning that underpin studies in this book: social literacies, emergent literacy and critical literacy. Each is now outlined further.

Literacy as a social and cultural practice

Imagine a box of Persil clothes-washing detergent. Covering the whole of one side is a caption 'The bedtime story' with a photograph of a White, expensively dressed mother reading a bedtime story to her little girl. All are in immaculately white outfits. Everything seems perfect. What we see portrayed symbolizes a culturally specific image of what counts as both 'valid' and 'valuable' home reading in Britain at the start of the twenty-first century. The 'bedtime story' reading practice here is cleverly equated with 'cleanliness'. Likewise, for the parent, participation in the practice itself is shown as being as important as making sure you care for the cleanliness of children's clothes. Such an advertisement will have little currency in many parts of the world; nor would it have been meaningful in Britain or the US before the mid-twentieth century when children's books were not so easily accessible and notions of 'good parenting' not intimately tied to books. This simple advertisement, therefore, demonstrates very clearly that what 'counts' as literacy is not neutral but is historically and locally specific.

Until the 1970s, literacy was largely studied as an intellectual skill that had far-reaching implications for cognition and the mind. Researchers working with 'schooled' and 'unschooled' children argued that *literacy itself* advanced the formation of concepts, self-consciousness, abstraction and cognitive flexibility (Greenfield 1984). Such research studies led to a number of historians and anthropologists positing what Street (1984) terms the 'great divide' theory or the 'autonomous' model of literacy. Quite simply, this meant that 'literate' people were seen to be able to engage in context-independent thought, think logically and in abstract terms and see things from 'variable points of view' (Street 1984: 33) and that this was due to the possession of literacy itself (Goody 1968; Olson 1977; Greenfield 1984). From the start, however, the boundaries between literacy and illiteracy were left very unclear, particularly in relation to young children who were still at the early stages of learning to read.

In 1981, a research study by Scribner and Cole provided evidence that seriously questioned the argument for literacy as an autonomous skill. Their work set in train a wider and more complex interpretation of literacy that was later to link researchers from linguistics, psychology, sociology and anthropology in a common interest. Their work took place with the Vai people of Liberia who were becoming literate in different contexts and languages: Vai literacy (the vernacular) which was used for poetry and personal letters and English which was used for formal schooling. A third group was not literate in either Vai or English. Crucially, their work showed that it was the *type of literacy practice* that led to particular cognitive skills, not literacy *per se*. In other words, knowledge of the Vai script facilitated explicit verbalization skills and western schooling in English led to superior performance in western tests, for example, completing syllogisms. Scribner and Cole (1981) used the term 'literacy practices' to distinguish their interpretation from that of literacy as an overarching autonomous skill as previously accepted. Their findings were further developed during the early 1980s by Street. Drawing upon research conducted in Iran, Street (1984) similarly observed the very different skills utilized by people engaged in English, Qur'anic and 'maktab' or commercial literacy, used in the fruit markets.

Scribner and Cole's and Street's work had taken place with adults or older teenagers, who were already literate in different scripts. Until the 1980s, early literacy education was largely dominated by a focus on *methods* and the 'great debate' as to whether literacy was best approached through phonics (the bottom-up approach: Chall 1967) or through whole language/'real books' (the top-down approach: Meek 1991; Goodman 1996). Early childhood teaching methodology generally was considerably influenced by Piagetian ideas stressing the importance of 'starting from the child' (child-centredness) that resulted in an emphasis on individuality at the cost of considering the child as member of a cultural group (see earlier in this chapter).

However, during the early 1980s a comparative study of families from different racial and economic groups living in the rural Piedmont area of the Carolinas in the US, revealed that even very young children entered school as active members of specific language and literacy practices. In *Ways with Words*, Heath (1983) carefully documented ways in which three groups of families (White working class, Black working class and White middle class) living in close proximity, socialized their children into very different language and literacy practices. Heath then showed ways in which teachers responded to these, recognizing as valid only practices that corresponded closely to their own and those taking place in the school. Heath's work provided a starting point for others across the US, Britain and Australia who, during the 1990s, began to uncover the wealth of language and literacy practices in young children's lives even before they enter formal schooling (Gregory 1994b; Volk 1997a; Luke and Kale 1997; Kenner 2000b).

These studies fit closely within recent anthropologically oriented views of literacy that have become known as the *New Literacy Studies* (NLS). An overview of the principles common to authors whose writings fall within this remit is outlined by Street (2003). He explains the term as referring to:

> a series of writings in both research and practice that treat language and literacy as social practices rather than skills to be learned in formal education. Research within this frame requires language and literacy to be studied as they occur in social life, taking account of the context and their different meanings for different cultural groups.
>
> (Street 2003: 79)

He and others (Collins 1995; Gee 1996) go on to explain that NLS studies are premised on two major tenets: social literacies and the dialogic nature of language. Crucial to the definition of 'social literacies' is first, the understanding that literacy is not a single essential phenomenon with consequences for cognitive and social development, but that there are multiple literacies which vary according to time and place and that are embedded in specific cultural practices and second, that literacy is ideological in nature. Crucial to the understanding of language as dialogic is the interpersonal sense of both language and literacy 'the word . . . exists in other people's mouths . . . it is from there that one must take the word and make it one's own' (Bakhtin 1981: 294).

The studies in this volume all call upon principles of the New Literacy Studies. However, they also acknowledge crucial differences relating to work taking place with young children, differences that also exist between the earlier model of 'literacy practices' put forward by Scribner and Cole (1981) and that of those within the NLS. As Hull and Schultz (2002) point out, 'practice' as coined by Scribner and Cole (1981) and later used by Cole (1996), explicitly includes notions of skill, technology and knowledge as well as patterned activity, while the NLS studies focus upon ways in which literacy is 'infused by ideology' (Hull and Schultz: 25) and there is little or no interest in the cognitive dimensions it might have. Authors in this volume, however, acknowledge the different nature of learning by young children whose minds are highly flexible, open to influence by others and in the process of development. We hope that this work will provide the foundation to the social view of literacy learning by young children we refer to as Syncretic Literacy Studies (SLS). Such a view steps beyond early literacy learning, described below, as focused on school and parental methods and materials to a wider perspective of the young child as an active member of different language and learning communities.

Emergent literacy

Since the late 1970s, an emergent literacy perspective has been the dominant view in the field of early literacy learning. Research that supports this view comes largely from work done in naturalistic settings in homes and schools (Holdaway 1979; Harste *et al.* 1984; Wells 1986; Hall 1987; Rowe 1994) and from studies done by parent-researchers in their own homes (Bissex 1980; Baghban 1984; Schickedanz 1990). A common finding across studies is that literacy learning is a social process through which meaning is negotiated when learners are engaged with more knowledgeable others in meaningful transactions with texts. Typically, these studies describe the more knowledgeable other to be a parent or a teacher but some also describe the role of peers (Harste *et al.* 1984; Rowe 1994).

In western societies, young children's initiation into literacy is often demonstrated as most effectively supported through shared reading and writing experiences: parents reading to and with children, asking and answering questions and demonstrating reading in their own lives (Durkin 1966; Ninio and Bruner 1978; Wells 1986). Researchers identify specific aspects of literacy knowledge that are acquired when adult and child interact regularly around books. Holdaway (1979), for example, demonstrates that children who have frequent shared reading experiences with adults develop conceptual understandings about what readers do orthographically, motivationally, linguistically and operationally. Clay's (1973) work identifies specific early reading behaviours or understandings of concepts about print (directionality, book orientation, page matching, one-to-one matching, locating words, locating letters within words, the structure of written language) that are acquired as children interact with adults around texts. Goodman (1965) identifies readers' orchestration of semantic, syntactic and graphophonemic cue systems as learners' transactions with text are scaffolded by interactions with more experienced readers.

Based on these and other studies of early literacy and her own work, Sulzby (1986) used the term 'emergent' to describe how literacy knowledge grows over time when human beings are engaged in purposeful literacy experiences in the company of more experienced readers and writers. The view of literacy learning as emergent provides a direct response to readiness perspectives that view children as ready to learn to read only after they have demonstrated competency in prerequisite skills such as small and large muscle control and auditory and visual discrimination. An emergent literacy perspective provides an alternative to what Freire (1993) called a 'banking concept of education' – education based not on communication and negotiation of meaning, but on a view of teacher as depositor of information 'which the students patiently receive, memorize and repeat' (p. 53). According to Freire, this banking view of learning removes the learner as 'conscious being' (1993: 60) from an active role in the learning process.

The emergent literacy emphasis on reading and talking about books as the most significant factor affecting early literacy growth in school-oriented western societies (Wells 1986) prompted other researchers to look beyond the bedtime story and to conduct studies in homes representing other than the middle-class English-speaking populations that typically engage in story-reading experiences. Findings from these studies reveal literacy used extensively and expertly in a variety of ways including sharing oral histories, reading the Bible and reading and writing letters (Heath 1983; Taylor and Dorsey-Gaines 1988; Volk 1997a; Hicks 2002; Compton-Lilly 2003). Homes traditionally assumed by educators to be lacking in literacy were found to be filled with print in many forms. Research in those settings provide windows into literacy worlds not previously acknowledged as legitimate, effective and valuable. Second language researcher Nieto's (1999) description of experiences in her own family life captures the richness and range of literacies identified by these studies:

> As a young child in a working-class family where no one had even graduated from high school, I do not remember any books or reading activities taking place in our apartment . . . but this does not mean that we had no experiences with literacy. I remember sitting around our kitchen table listening to stories in Spanish . . . or tall tales of family exploits. I also recall my mother repeating the rhymes and riddles (in Spanish) that she herself had learned as a child and my aunt telling us scary stories (in English) in the dark. These too were literacy experiences and although they generally were not known or acknowledged by my schools, they could have been used to extend my learning.
>
> (Nieto 1999: 7)

In spite of differences in forms of literacy found in homes, strong commonalities exist across studies that focus on storybook reading and those that investigate other forms of literacy. In all settings, data illuminate the act of reading and learning to read and write as social processes; children as active, competent and intentional participants in those processes; and the emergence of literacy from birth. Children are described not as passive recipients of literacy knowledge, but as active seekers of meaning who construct knowledge about literacy as they work to make sense of the literate world around them.

This thinking parallels similar findings from studies of first language acquisition. Moving beyond the behaviourist belief that language is learned through imitation and reinforcement and the innatist view of language learning as primarily grounded in biology, sociolinguists consider language learning in terms of the interplay between biological predisposition and learners' transactions within linguistic worlds. Engaging in activity that is meaningful to both parties, learner and more knowledgeable partner negotiate meaning in a sort of communicative dance (Bruner 1983). Conversational partners provide demonstrations and scaffolds that create contexts for learners to make approximations, receive feedback and take responsibility for their own learning (Cambourne 1988). Key to this perspective is the notion that learning occurs as the child uses language to be able to function in his or her worlds (Halliday 1975; Wells 1986).

Although Piaget's view of children as active constructors of knowledge provides a foundation for these understandings, sociolinguists draw heavily from the work of Vygotsky to think more specifically about the roles of the learner and the communicative other. According to Vygotsky (1978), child and partner interact within a communicative relationship that, because of (a) the partner's language knowledge and sensitivity to the child's capabilities and (b) the child's innate desire to become a part of the communicative world, extends the learner's knowledge within zones of proximal development – those 'particularly promising area[s] just beyond the child's reach' (Lindfors 1999: 20). In these contexts, language is used to explore complex concepts before relegating them to internalized thought (Wertsch 1985). Form follows function, as children acquire both linguistic and communicative competence (Brown 1970; Halliday 1975; Cazden 1988) 'in the pursuit of other ends' (Hall 1987: 13).

Current theories of second language learning also draw from the work of sociolinguists who question once-held notions such as Lenneberg's (1967) critical age period hypothesis. By looking at situational and contextual factors, we now understand the acquisition of a second language to be dependent not on age or stage, but on opportunities to develop relationships and interact purposefully with native speakers (Wong Fillmore 1976; Dulay et al. 1982; Hakuta 1986; Long 1998a). Strategies used by second language learners as they observe, experiment and receive feedback through meaningful interaction with communicative partners are similar to those used by first language learners. In co-created zones of proximal development, developing bilinguals learn about language structure, pronunciation and cultural usage as they use language in contexts where they feel safe enough to risk experimentation. They play with sounds and words, use objects to scaffold communication and construct approximations by code-mixing phrases, gesture, facial expression and physical demonstration (Wong Fillmore 1976; Levine 1990; Long 1998a).

In much the same way that findings from studies of second language acquisition have many parallels to findings in first language research, the process of learning to read in a second language has similarities to learning to read in a first language. A key difference, however, is that the second language learner's world knowledge, including his or her definition of literacy, is often very different from the cultural knowledge that underlies the new language. This can make comprehension difficult and literacy events confusing (Urzua 1986; Gregory 1994a). The act of reading in a new language can become focused on the pronunciation of isolated words rather than on making meaning.

Issues of equity, power and social justice: a critical literacy stance

The study of early literacy and language learning in homes and schools prompts the consideration of findings in relation to issues of equity, power and social justice. If we indeed value home and community languages and literacies, then we must consider how to use our knowledge and appreciation of home cultures to promote learning and to broaden worldviews for all children. The current practice of devaluing non-mainstream language and literacies perpetuates a deficit perspective that limits learning potential for all students. When educators refuse to accept as valid the kinds of knowledge and experiences with which some students come to school (Nieto 1999); when they do not value, understand or even acknowledge the legitimacy of children's lives beyond the classroom, 'nowhere is the student's very personhood acknowledged or celebrated [and, too often] children whose language is considered defective are themselves viewed as defective' (Delpit 2002: 41). When children are taught through worksheets, textbooks, or activities that make no reference to their lived experiences, 'instruction is stripped of children's cultural legacies' (Delpit 2002: 44). Moll (2001) writes:

> This dual strategy of exclusion and condemnation of one's language and culture, fostering disdain for what one knows and who one is, has another critical consequence in terms of schooling – it influences children's attitudes toward their knowledge and personal competence. That is, it creates a social distance between themselves and the world of school knowledge.
>
> (Moll 2001: 13)

Such practices are destructive not only for the children outside the mainstream, but also for all children. Teachers' failure to recognize and value home language and culture tragically limits learning and worldviews for children from privileged cultures who receive messages sent about the superiority of their language and culture rather than an appreciation for the richness of many languages and cultures (Wynne 2002).

Though it is crucial for teachers to value home cultures, they also have a responsibility to help children become successful in the mainstream. Based on her study in a blue-collar White community in the Appalachian area of the US, Purcell-Gates (2002) describes the importance of supporting home culture and language while helping students develop the ability to code-switch into the dominant language and culture:

Nonstandard, socially marked dialects do prevent people from succeeding in the middle-class world, but they do not prevent people from learning to read and write. If we insist that learners learn a different way of talking and communicating before, or as a condition of, learning to read and write, we leave them irrevocably behind . . . Speakers will use the appropriate language register (or 'type' or form) to fit the social context they find themselves in.

(Purcell-Gates 2002: 137–8)

Current discussions of validating home and community literacies are interwoven within a broader literacy pedagogy – critical literacy – that assumes 'an increasingly critical attitude toward the world' (Freire 1973: 34). From this perspective, educators view literacy learning as directly tied to purpose – learning to read the word and the world critically for the purpose of affecting change in the lives of those who are marginalized. Building on the work of Dewey (1916), who envisioned education as experience based in action and reflection for the purpose of promoting democratic practice, educators extend commonly held models of learning by tying them fundamentally to issues of social justice. In the field of early childhood education, Cannella (1997) suggests that we deconstruct what we understand about learning and build a new framework grounded in the pursuit of social justice. In the field of language and literacy, Harste (2001) proposes an extension to Halliday's (1984) language learning model – learning language, learning about language, learning through language – by adding a fourth dimension, learning language to critique, 'to question what seems natural and normal as well as to redesign and create alternate social worlds' (Harste 2001: 2). Shor (1999) applies a Freirian focus to Vygotsky's zone of proximal development suggesting that, as learners interact with and learn from one another, they lay the groundwork for affecting social change.

Ethnography

In the final section of this chapter, we share a brief outline of ethnography, the research approach on which many of the authors in this volume draw. Originating in the field of cultural anthropology, ethnography is a way of learning about and representing 'the culture of groups of people' (LeCompte and Schensul 1999: 21). Ethnography is 'an interpretive act of "thick description"' (Geertz 1973, cited in James 2001: 246) that conveys a rich, in-depth and contextualized portrait of actions and events and the 'locally specific' (LeCompte and Schensul 1999: 1) meanings that shape them from the multiple perspectives of the participants. All interpretations are understood as 'partial and historical' (Agar 1996: 36), never fixed but constructed by participants in interaction with researchers. This complex challenge of rigorously constructing the *emic* or insider perspective embedded in context is at the heart of the ethnographic endeavour (Agar 1996; Atkinson and Hammersley 1998).

Ethnography has been used in various fields and, despite dissension about what ethnography *should* be, there is some agreement about general characteristics (Van Manen 1990; Denzin 1997; Atkinson and Hammersley 1998; Massey and Walford 1998; LeCompte and Schensul 1999). First, ethnography always involves fieldwork carried out in a natural setting, usually over a sustained period of time. Committed to studying lived experience (Van Manen 1990), the researcher acknowledges and accounts for the ways his/her presence and decisions about observing, recording and interpreting data may alter these natural settings (Denzin 1997). Second, the researcher is the primary instrument of data collection. This means that the researcher's developing relationship with participants is of central concern and that his/her own conceptual frames must be identified and considered as the data are collected and interpreted. Third, the researcher uses multiple techniques to collect data from multiple sources. These techniques may include participant observation, audio- and videotaping, taking field notes and photographs, conducting interviews and collecting artifacts. Fourth, the researcher uses inductive strategies synthesized with deductive ones to analyze the data collected. This analysis is always qualitative but may also include quantitative means. It is developed in multiple iterations throughout the research process to build 'local cultural theories' (LeCompte and Schensul 1999: 9), tentative interpretations of the specific culture being studied that can be used to build patterns or hypotheses.

Beginning in the 1960s, anthropology in general and ethnography specifically were criticized as instruments of those in power. Ethnographers' claims to objectivity were exposed as a fiction and the notion of homogeneous and static cultures was labelled a reductionist distortion of the complexity of real lives that facilitates the separation of the 'simple' natives from the 'civilized' researcher (Rosaldo 1993). These tensions within the field have not been entirely resolved, with some ethnographers advocating a critical stance, others a scientific stance and many others combining elements of both with other theoretical perspectives (Atkinson and Hammersley 1998).

Today, most would agree that ethnography is an interpretive and primarily qualitative approach, a means of making visible cultures that are close to home and distant, that are complex and internally varied, that change, that merge and re-emerge syncretically and that are shaped in creative ways by participants. Its strength

> lies in the ways in which, through close attention to the everyday and familiar through which the social world is both created and sustained, it has enabled the voices of those who would otherwise be silent to be heard.
>
> (James 2001: 255)

Conclusion

In this chapter we have presented a sociocultural framework within which Syncretic Literacy Studies are situated. Crucially, it is a framework wherein culture and cognition are intimately intertwined. Young children learn to become members of different cultural practices, involving different languages, literacies, materials and ways of interacting together. In appropriating membership, they gain access to different ways of thinking, of seeing the world. Along their pathways, even very young children step simultaneously into very different literacy lives, taking materials, methods or interaction patterns from each practice and transforming these to create new meanings. In all of this, the cultural and linguistic mediator plays a vital role. All the chapters in this volume examine ways in which young children become literate through interaction with a number of 'invisible' teachers in their literacy lives. These may be siblings, grandparents, friends or other important cultural and linguistic mediators in their communities. The metaphor of young children flitting like butterflies but making honey like bees aptly sums up the fleeting and productive workings of young minds in context.

As educators and researchers, we are only just beginning to understand the multiple pathways to literacy in young children's lives. In order to extend this understanding, we conclude the volume with implications for practice and questions for researchers that draw on chapters from the sections following. We hope that these provide guidance for future work and that this book will be the first of many others to investigate what has hitherto remained 'invisible'.

The family context

Siblings and grandparents

Introduction to Part I

Young children's learning interactions outside of school occur within 'organized, flexible webs of relationships that focus on shared cultural activities' (Rogoff 1990: 97). These webs include, among others, family members and fictive kin. In many cultures, siblings play an important role within this supportive web, mediating children's learning and syncretizing literacies and languages drawn from home, school and community contexts as well as from popular culture with impressive skill. Little is known about the mediating role of grandparents and the funds of knowledge they represent. The chapters in this part analyze learning with siblings and grandparents, describing a range of literacies and abilities that are rarely visible or valued in classrooms. They illustrate some of the many ways that guided participation may be constructed and reveal the value of understanding literacy as a social and cultural practice for fostering collaborations between homes and schools.

In Chapter 2, Dinah Volk and Martha de Acosta analyze sibling teaching in literacy events in the homes of two mainland Puerto Rican 5-year-old girls. These syncretic events took place within the girls' networks of support, often with their mothers' guidance. Volk and de Acosta explore the varying skills of the older siblings as mediators as well as differences in the aspects of literacy co-constructed. They also raise important questions about the characteristics and practices of sibling teachers and about the dynamics and contexts of children's networks of support.

Chapter 3, by Rose Drury, is an analysis of the informal school play of a Pakistani, Pahari-speaking 4-year-old and her 2-year-old brother at home. She compares the older child's interactions in a nursery (preschool), where her abilities were largely unknown to the teachers, with her interactions at home in which she took control as her brother's teacher, displaying her knowledge of English and school procedures while syncretizing home and school learning contexts. Drury provides an insightful discussion that interweaves issues of bilingual language learning with children's social development and play in school and at home.

Chapter 4 by Ann Williams compares and contrasts the sociodramatic play of Anglo-British and Bangladeshi British siblings, each family with a younger child between 4 and 8 years. As the children played school together at home, older and younger siblings displayed their abundant knowledge of school practices and scripts. Williams highlights key differences in the children's play that reflected differing cultural constructions of literacy as well as the relation of their communities to British schools and society. Current emphases in British schools on a national curriculum and on standardized tests could also be seen in the children's play.

In Chapter 5, Clare Kelly focuses on a 4½-year-old White working-class child and his 'guiding light', his grandmother, who has been influential in introducing him to texts and literacy practices common to their family and community. In school, Jamie did not see himself as competent and seemed uninterested in books despite the expertise with oral and visual narratives and with technology that had been nurtured within learning relationships at home. Kelly explores the critical and interrelated issues of what counts as literacy at home and at school and of the importance of tapping into funds of knowledge constructed by families.

In Chapter 6, Irma Olmedo broadens the perspective on literacy in her description of an intergenerational collaboration between 9 year olds in a Spanish–English dual language fourth grade classroom and their fictive kin, Latina *abuelitas* (grandmothers) in a centre for the elderly. Olmedo provides an analysis of the *abuelitas'* oral narratives and performative style and the children's construction of knowledge using those narratives to write their own accounts in Spanish and English. Her work points to funds of knowledge within many communities where the storytelling of elderly people is typically valued. She advocates the use of such interactions with community members as the basis for authentic multicultural experiences that integrate content areas across the curriculum.

Chapter 2

Mediating networks for literacy learning

The role of Puerto Rican siblings

Dinah Volk with Martha de Acosta

It was an observer's nightmare and a moment of insight: one participant observer in the Torres[1] family living room eating the overflowing plate of food provided by Sra Torres while keeping an eye on the receiver and tape recorder, taking notes and observing the family; 5-year-old Julializ, one of the children we were studying, wearing the transmitter; three simultaneous literacy events with siblings as teachers and learners plus a parent and a church 'brother' in teaching roles; two languages; and one Super Mario game on television. The following excerpt from the field notes describes this literacy event.

> Francisco (brother, 9 years old) asks his mother to help him spell some words from his spelling list. She sits on the couch with him and goes through the list, telling him to correct his spelling when he is wrong. They speak Spanish and spell the English words in English. At the same time, the three girls have started to play with the Super Mario game. Julializ and her older cousin (6) sit on either side of the little cousin (3) on the floor. They take turns and argue a bit, helping the little one . . . Eventually they are happily screaming directions at each other and the screen – in Spanish with some code-switching into English. When print in English comes on the screen, the older one points to it and reads it out loud to the others. At the same time, Fernando (brother, 12) is sitting at the kitchen table working on some maths homework with the young man from their church. They work for about 40 minutes or more completing several worksheets . . . in English. They speak Spanish and English.
>
> (Field notes, 12/3/98)

At that moment, it was clear that our recording arrangements were based on a model of literacy events at home that included only one child with a text and, perhaps, one adult. Later we began to understand the complex networks that mediated learning in this home and the others we were studying. We began to see literacy events there as social and jointly constructed, dynamic, multigenerational and syncretic.

These observations were part of a broader study of the literacy practices of three bilingual, Puerto Rican 5 year olds in their bilingual kindergarten, their homes and communities. In that study, we found that the children's developing literacy was mediated by a network of people that included their teacher, parents, peers, siblings, extended family members, family friends, Sunday school teachers and pastors. In this chapter, we focus on sibling teaching in the homes of two of the children, Julializ and Fidelia. In their homes, older siblings supported their literacy learning, often with great skill, as together they drew on beliefs, practices, languages and literacy resources within the immediate context established by their parents and the broader context of their culture.

Conceptual framework

Literacy as a social and cultural process

Our work is grounded in a sociocultural perspective (Rogoff 1990) and we understand literacy to be a social and cultural process that exists in multiple forms (Baynham 1995). These *multiple literacies* (Barton and Hamilton 1998) vary within and across settings. School-identified literacy is privileged in most contexts while other literacy practices may be invisible to educators, labelled irrelevant or even detrimental to young children's developing competence with text (Gregory 1999; Street 1999; Compton-Lilly 2003).

Literacy and learning in Latino families

Patterns in educational beliefs and practices emerge from a number of studies of Puerto Rican and Mexican American families, all working class or poor (Delgado-Gaitan 1994b; Valdés 1996; Hidalgo 1994, 2000). Many of these beliefs and practices are attributed to both cultural groups. In reviewing these studies, we should remember that people create culture as they are shaped by it. Thus, the Latino homes we describe should be understood as 'complex sites of cultural production rather than as representatives of a self-contained, homogeneous culture' (Rosaldo 1993: 217).

The literature indicates that Latino families typically value education highly, though the ways and the frequency with which parents support their children's schoolwork vary (Valdés 1996; Volk and de Acosta 2001). Some studies propose that Latino parents rarely engage in deliberate teaching, a task they see as the teacher's job. Others observe that when Latino parents help their children with literacy, they stress accurate word and letter recognition at the expense of meaning, as their own teachers did. Still other work describes both deliberate instruction and learning interactions embedded in daily activities, balancing a focus on accuracy with an interest in meaning.

The work on Latino families' funds of knowledge (Moll and Greenberg 1990) describes how abundant information and skills are exchanged in many Latino communities. Community members contribute to the survival of others by sharing what they know and are, in turn, assisted when necessary through relationships built on trust and reciprocity.

Siblings across cultures

Older siblings play an important role in the care and education of children in most cultures (Weisner 1989). Typically, older siblings act *with* parents, not as substitutes for them. Described as cultural and linguistic mediators, older siblings introduce younger ones to valued knowledge and skills in familiar contexts, syncretizing the familiar and the new.

The cross-cultural literature indicates that the definition of *sibling* can vary (Zukow 1989; Cicirelli 1995). In industrialized societies, siblings tend to be defined by a specific biological relationship while in many non-industrialized societies, cousins, aunts, uncles as well as fictive kin may be included in the sibling group. In Latino families (Valdés 1996; Volk 1999), sibling caretaking and teaching are typically valued aspects of family life. Depending on their national origin and whether their roots are urban or rural, Latino families lean towards one or the other interpretation of *sibling*, often blending elements of both.

Families' networks of support

Studies of families and their resources use various conceptual models to describe the links people create to share resources. The work on funds of knowledge (Moll and Greenberg 1990) explains that valued information is shared through a 'social matrix' (p. 326) consisting of 'social relations of exchange that are multistranded and flexible' (p. 344). Both the content of these exchanges and the process of sharing mediate community members' learning. Moje (2000), discussing the concept of community, defines it as 'circles of kinship, friendship, position and power' (p. 106) to make explicit the complexity and fluidity of such supportive, multiple associations. Wallman (1984), in a study of urban households, combines aspects of both perspectives and uses network maps consisting of concentric circles to chart the human resources accessed by families. With households at the centre, the maps display resources in terms of both geographic and affective distance from the perspective of the participants at one moment in time.

Studying literacy in context

We used an ethnographic approach to study literacy as a culturally embedded practice combined with an ethnomethodological approach to study discourse patterns in individual interactions. Using a multilayered analysis, we studied teaching strategies and related aspects of literacy within the context of the focal children's literacy interactions, which were in turn situated within the wider social contexts of the homes, community and classroom (Gregory 1998).

Fieldwork in the kindergarten was initiated in August with participant observation during weekly, day-long visits. From January through to June, we conducted observations and audiotapings in the classroom twice a month and in each home once a month. We also conducted observations and informal interviews in the churches and Sunday schools. In all sites, we collected data on reading and writing and on oral and written texts.

In March, the parents helped us complete network maps based on Wallman's (1984) model to chart the multiple relationships around each child that mediated his or her developing literacy. Each map had a focal child at the centre and rings indicating the closeness of the relationship plus the frequency of interactions. Working together with the parents, we filled in the people who interacted with their child during that kindergarten year; they then profiled the interactions that were literacy related. We also used these maps to select literacy events for data collection during the subsequent three months.

Semi-structured interviews in June with the teacher, the parents and some siblings explored their literacy histories and descriptions of how and why they support the children's literacy development. To further understand the participants' perspectives, we also worked with two Puerto Rican cultural insiders.

Literacy events, 'observable episodes which arise from [literacy] practices and are shaped by them' (Barton and Hamilton 1998: 7), were our unit of analysis. Within events, we analyzed literacy practices, 'what people do with literacy' (Barton and Hamilton 1998: 6) as well as the ways in which people understand and value literacy. In particular, we were interested in the teaching practices or strategies used and the aspect of literacy that was the focus of each strategy. Aspects of literacy studied included:

- *oral language development:* the ability to use spoken language to communicate meaningfully
- *concepts of print:* knowledge about the conventions of print as well as letter-name knowledge and phonemic awareness
- *word identification:* the ability to immediately recognize a familiar word
- *word analysis:* the ability to use knowledge of specific letter–sound associations to figure out unfamiliar words
- *comprehension:* the understanding of text as a source of information and the ability to construct meaning from texts
- *fluency:* the ability to identify words rapidly (Vacca *et al.* 1991; Hiebert *et al.* 1998).

Julializ, Fidelia and their mediating networks

Julializ and Fidelia's school and homes were located in two adjacent working-class neighbourhoods with substantial Puerto Rican populations in a large Midwestern city. Both girls attended the same bilingual kindergarten. The network maps in Figures 2.1 and 2.2 illustrate the circles of family and friends that surrounded the children. The people who were identified as participating in the networks that mediated the girls' developing literacy are indicated in bold. The following discussion will concentrate on Julializ Torres, her 9- and 12-year-old brothers, Francisco and Fernando, and her 6-year-old cousin, Zoila, as well as Fidelia Ugarte and Felicidad, her 6-year-old cousin. In both families, the cousins were raised with the focal children and were described as *como hermanitas* (like sisters).

Julializ Torres lived with her mother, two brothers and a 'church brother and a sister', a couple from their church. Another 'church brother', a young man from the neighbourhood, visited frequently. Sra Torres had graduated from high school in Puerto Rico and was receiving government assistance while earning a few dollars caring for children at home. Her brother and his wife had two daughters, Hilary (3 years old) and Zoila; the three adults shared in the care of the three girls.

Fidelia Ugarte lived with her aunt, uncle and cousin who she referred to as her mother, father and sister. (We will refer to them using her terms.) Felicidad, her sister, was the Ugartes' adopted niece. Fidelia was the birth daughter of Sra Ugarte's brother, who visited her weekly. Her birth mother and siblings lived in Puerto Rico. Sr Ugarte's brother, his wife and their two toddlers were living with the family during the study as was his elderly father. Both the Ugartes had graduated from high school in Puerto Rico and were working in local factories.

Both families spoke primarily Spanish though the children were learning English and used it with siblings and friends. For all the parents, learning to read meant learning the letters and putting them together, an understanding informed by how they had learned to read. They talked about the *Cartilla fonética* (*Phonics Primer*), still in use in Puerto Rico, which draws on the regular phonetic characteristics of Spanish and teaches reading through sound patterns in syllables. This emphasis on letter sounds and names was balanced in the girls' literacy interactions at home with meaningful experiences with text.

When asked about their role in their children's education, the parents described how they responded to their questions and helped them complete homework. Julializ's mother spoke about teaching her children letters and numbers and how to write their names. She and her brother often read to their three girls together. Julializ got books in English from the library and used workbooks in English her mother had purchased. For Fidelia's mother and father, a key part of their role was getting the children to school on time, clean and well fed. They saw teaching as the teacher's job and Fidelia's mother noted that it was hard to remember information learned in school long ago. There were a few children's books in English in their home which Fidelia's father read to her, in translation, with gusto. He also recited a favourite poem in Spanish to her at bedtime.

Siblings as mediators

Literacy events were embedded in the daily life of the families and most were social interactions with text rather than individual ones. That is, participants usually used texts in the small public spaces of their homes in interaction with others. The vignette shared at the start of this chapter describing literacy events in Julializ's home is a good example of the social nature of these literacy interactions. The families also read the Bible together, adults and children participating.

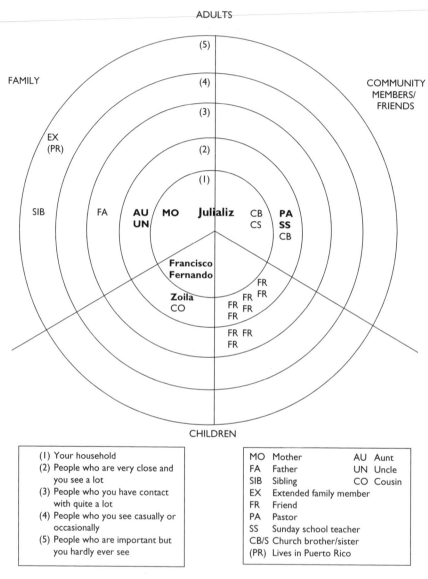

Figure 2.1 Network map of Julializ's home/community
            (bold indicates members of literacy network)

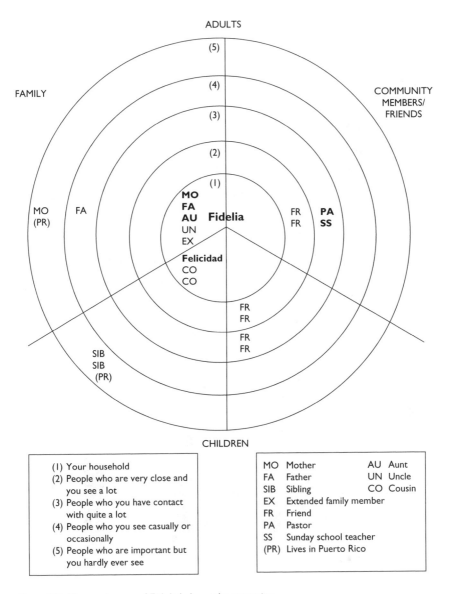

ADULTS

(5)

(4)

FAMILY

(3)

(2)

(1)

MO
FA
AU **Fidelia**
UN
EX

Felicidad
CO
CO

FR **PA**
FR **SS**

MO
(PR)

FA

COMMUNITY
MEMBERS/
FRIENDS

FR
FR

FR
FR

SIB
SIB
(PR)

CHILDREN

(1) Your household	MO Mother AU Aunt
(2) People who are very close and you see a lot	FA Father UN Uncle
(3) People who you have contact with quite a lot	SIB Sibling CO Cousin
(4) People who you see casually or occasionally	EX Extended family member
(5) People who are important but you hardly ever see	FR Friend
	PA Pastor
	SS Sunday school teacher
	(PR) Lives in Puerto Rico

Figure 2.2 Network map of Fidelia's home/community
(bold indicates members of literacy network)

Literacy events involving siblings often included more than two children and at least one adult. Some of these events were embedded in play as when the children played the Super Mario game or played school or church. Particularly in these events, the role of teacher tended to be negotiable, with the younger *or* the older sibling taking the lead. The examples shared in this chapter are instances of deliberate instruction that occurred when younger children worked on homework or practised school-related skills with the assistance of more capable older siblings.

In Julializ's home

Sra Torres reported that Julializ was, according to her teacher, the best reader in her class. She understood basic concepts of print and was putting her energy into word identification, word analysis and comprehension. She knew many sight words in both Spanish and English, used invented spelling in both languages and worked hard at sounding out new words using her knowledge of letter sounds.

As shown in Figure 2.3 and the transcript excerpts following, there were characteristic differences in the ways the siblings constructed literacy events with Julializ. When Julializ read with Francisco, over half of the literacy strategies they used aimed at developing basic concepts of print while only a third that

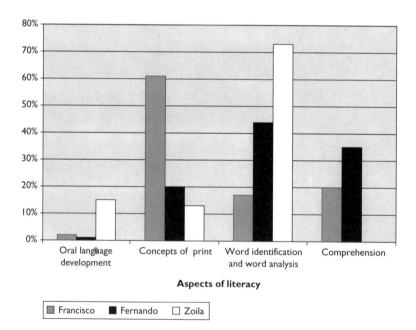

Figure 2.3 Aspects of literacy constructed by Julializ and siblings (as percent of literacy strategies used)

many strategies involved comprehension. Only when his mother insisted, did he ask her about what she had read. Fernando and Zoila, in contrast, worked with Julializ on comprehension and word identification and analysis in a way that matched her level of competence and provided scaffolding for her to move ahead. Neither Julializ nor Fidelia had opportunities to develop their fluency with siblings; interactions emphasizing this aspect of literacy were all constructed with adults.

Excerpt 1 comes from an event in which Francisco helped Julializ read in a workbook. Francisco was an impatient teacher who insisted on speaking only English. He had struggled in school until his mother transferred him out of the bilingual programme in his school where both English and Spanish were used for instruction. In this case, Francisco helped Julializ by saying each word for her to repeat and then moving to the next word without a contingent response. In reaction to this method of merely providing text, Sra Torres prompted Francisco to use what she believed were more appropriate teaching strategies. In turns 2 and 14 she told him to go more slowly and attend to the meaning of the words. She then asked Julializ if she had understood the story, modeling a comprehension question. Francisco followed with his own comprehension question in turn 19 and confirmed her response in turn 21.

Excerpt 1: Julializ and Francisco work on concepts of print with mother's assistance

1	*Francisco:*	One day a pig and a dog met a frog //on a log.//[2]
2	*Sra Torres:*	//Pero papi suave.// [But slowly dear.]
3	*Julializ:*	One.
4	*Francisco:*	Day.
5	*Julializ:*	Day.
6	*Francisco:*	A.
7	*Julializ:*	A.
8	*Francisco:*	Dog. I mean a fro-I mean a pig.
9	*Julializ:*	A pig.
10	*Francisco:*	And a dog.
11	*Julializ:*	And a dog.
12	*Francisco:*	Met.
13	*Julializ:*	Mmmat.
14	*Sra Torres:*	Enseñale la palabra nene, si no, no aprende. [Teach her the word boy, if not, she doesn't learn.]
15	*Francisco:*	Dog. I mean frog.
16	*Julializ:*	Frog . . .
17	*Sra Torres:*	Mami //¿tú entiendes// la historia? [Dear do you understand the story?]
18	*Julializ:*	Yes.
19	*Francisco:*	All right. ¡Espera! ¡Espera! Primero antes que tú escribas. ¿Qué era la historia aquí? [Wait. Wait. First before you write. What was the story here?]

20 *Julializ:*   Um de un pig, de un dog, de un frog, de un . . . log. [About a pig, about a dog, about a frog, about a . . . log.]
21 *Francisco:*   Mhmh.

Excerpt 2 comes from another literacy event that began with Julializ reading a picture book with her mother's assistance. Fernando, a confident, biliterate student, joined as the mother stepped away, starting with a cue that helped Julializ analyze the words. He then focused on comprehension by giving Julializ Spanish translations of the English words and directing her attention to a picture in turn 24. Unlike Francisco, Fernando responded contingently with corrections and confirmations. In turns 6, 19 and 21, Julializ read several words together on her own, participating more actively and with a higher level of competence than she displayed when she was reading with Francisco.

Excerpt 2: Julializ and Fernando work on word analysis and comprehension
 1 *Fernando:*   Recuerda la W hace 'wh'. [Remember the W says 'wh'.]
 2 *Julializ:*   Wa.
 3 *Fernando:*   Mhmh. No. We.
 4 *Julializ:*   We. //Are.//
 5 *Fernando:*   //Went.// Went.
 6 *Julializ:*   Went. To. The. Zoo.
 7 *Sra Torres:* Mhum.
 8 *Julializ:*   It. Whhhas . . . A.
 9 *Fernando:*   Grande. [Big.]
10 *Julializ:*   Big. Park. Www//www// . . .
11 *Julializ:*   . . . With.
12 *Fernando:*   Mucha. [A lot.]
13 *Julializ:*   A lot.
14 *Fernando:*   Mhum.
15 *Julializ:*   Animals.
16 *Fernando:*   Mhmh. Of.
17 *Julializ:*   Of.
18 *Fernando:*   Diferente. En inglés. [Different. In English.]
19 *Julializ:*   Different animals.
20 *Fernando:*   Mhum . . .
21 *Julializ:*   The lllions wwwear.
22 *Fernando:*   Mhmh. Cubs.
23 *Julializ:*   ¿Qué? [What?]
24 *Fernando:*   ((points to picture)) ¿Qué son éstos? . . . [What are these? . . .]
25 *Julializ:*   Cubs.

In Excerpt 3, Zoila helped Julializ read a list of English words while they spoke Spanish together. Just a year older, Zoila considered herself a successful English reader. Throughout this event, she allowed Julializ to read the words she could and, when she hesitated, provided two kinds of scaffolding: cues using Spanish vowel sounds to help with the troublesome English vowels and demonstrations of how to blend sounds into words. For example, in turn 1, Zoila provided a cue for the O sound in *to* using the sound of U in Spanish. Julializ read *to*, then read *go* correctly on her own. In turn 5, Zoila provided a cue for another English O, this time using the Spanish A sound. Demonstrations come in turns 7 and 9 when Zoila drew out the sounds of the letters as she blended them together.

Excerpt 3: Julializ and Zoila work on word analysis

1	*Zoila:*	La O (ō) es U (ōō). [The O is U.]
2	*Julializ:*	To. Go.
3	*Zoila:*	P. A. (ā) //P.//
4	*Julializ:*	//P//lay.
5	*Zoila:*	La O (ō) es. A (ŏ). [The O is. A.]
6	*Julializ:*	Nnnn ot. Not.
7	*Zoila:*	U (ŭ). I-U (ĭ-ŭ). Ruuuuuun.
8	*Julializ:*	Run.
9	*Zoila:*	Oo (oo). Ll ook.
10	*Julializ:*	Look . . .

In Fidelia's home

Fidelia struggled through most of the school year to understand a basic concept of print: the consistency of letter–sound relationships. She worked hard at literacy activities at home and in school, learning the sounds of some letters and related words. Fidelia's strength was in oral recitation. She often made up poems and stories or recited memorized ones from school. When she read a book, she leafed through the pages, telling a story based on the pictures.

Fidelia constructed literacy events with Felicidad, a beginning reader who received tutoring in school because of her slow progress. At home, Felicidad instructed Fidelia in how to do her homework, sometimes taught her songs from school and often addressed her as *nena* (girl) or *m'ija* (my daughter) as an older person might a younger one. Figure 2.4 shows that Fidelia's literacy interactions with Felicidad emphasized concepts of print and, to a lesser degree, oral language development. The excerpts following illustrate how Felicidad scaffolded Fidelia's developing understanding of literacy.

In Excerpt 4, Fidelia practised writing the vowels at the suggestion of her mother. Felicidad soon took over and the mother stepped back. This excerpt represents a common pattern in the literacy events the girls constructed: they wrote and named letters and connected the sounds with words memorized in school. Throughout, Felicidad responded contingently, providing a cue to the letter sound in turn 12, naming the vowels and explaining that there are not two Es. The role played by Sra Ugarte in this excerpt is also typical as she joined Felicidad in providing the correct names of the vowels in turns 7, 13 and 17.

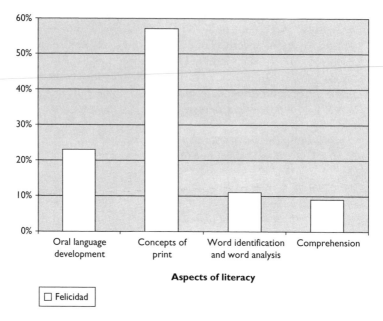

Figure 2.4 Aspects of literacy constructed by Fidelia and siblings
(as percent of literacy strategies used)

Excerpt 4: Fidelia and Felicidad work on concepts of print with assistance

1	*Sra Ugarte:*	Dale ( ) las vocales las escribiste. . . . [Do ( ) the vowels that you wrote. . . .]
2	*Fidelia:*	((FI writes)) A.
3	*Felicidad:*	U. O. OU. A E I O U. (vowel sounds in Spanish)
4	*Fidelia:*	((writes)) Yo sé. [I know.]
5	*Felicidad:*	U. U.
6	*Fidelia:*	Felicidad ¡yo sé! . . . ((holds up paper)) Las cinco vocales . . . A. I. [Felicidad I know! . . . The five vowels . . .]
7	*Sra Ugarte:*	//E.//
8	*Felicidad:*	//No.// E.
9	*Fidelia:*	I. O. O.
10	*Felicidad:*	No. U. Empieza con la U. [No. U. Begin with the U.]
11	*Fidelia:*	¿Ese? [That one?]
12	*Felicidad:*	No. Uuu. Empieza con la de u-uva. Empieza con la uva . . . [No. Uuu. Begin with the one for g-grape. Begin with the grape.]
13	*Sra Ugarte:*	La U. [The U.]
14	*Fidelia:*	Sí sí. A. A. I. //O.// . . . [Yes yes.]
15	*Felicidad:*	Esta es una E. [This is an E.]
16	*Fidelia:*	¡Ah! Uh-pero un-. Sabe la que está la A. Esa. A. E. I. O. [Ah! Uh but a-. You know the one that is the A. That.]

17 *Sra Ugarte:* U.
18 *Fidelia:* U. E.
19 *Felicidad:* ((chuckles)) Otra vez la E. Tienes dos E. [The E again. You have
two Es.]
20 *Fidelia:* //E.// //Grande.// [E. Big.]
21 *Felicidad:* Esas son las cinco vocales. [Those are the five vowels.]

On another occasion, Felicidad produced a replica of a typical school worksheet for Fidelia with words aligned with pictures to aid the beginning reader.
But instead of a picture of a mother for the word *mamá*, Felicidad wrote the name
of the girls' mother, transforming the generic worksheet into a meaningful text
for these two girls, both separated from their birth mothers. In response, Fidelia
wrote a message to Felicidad, her first effort at invented spelling and evidence of
her understanding of letter–sound relationships. Using Spanish letter sounds,
she wrote *Alebiu* for 'I love you'.

Insights for research and practice

Many educators approach children's learning at home with a school-based model
of valued learning interactions and, as a result, judge homes to be deficient when
their expectations are not met. As suggested by the vignette opening this chapter,
we need to set that model aside and observe literacy practices in homes from diverse
cultures. Our analysis of what we observed points to several related insights about
these practices. Taken together, these insights contradict stereotypes of Latino
families and show that many may be 'people rich', with substantial funds of
knowledge relevant to literacy teaching and learning shared through mediating
networks.

Our first insight is that literacy events were co-constructed by multiple
participants and were syncretic. Julializ and Fidelia, along with their siblings
and parents, drew on Spanish and English, their own experiences with school
and religious texts, both oral and written and texts encountered at home and in
the community, on the US mainland and in Puerto Rico. Different literacies
and languages were blended and reinvented as the children built on what they had
learned in school and developed new skills to take back there. These reinvented
literacy practices stand as a challenge to impoverished images of learning at home
and conceptions of literacy as an individual task. They are potentially subversive
to classroom practices grounded in single approaches to literacy prescribed top-
down by teachers, administrators and legislators.

Second, our findings confirm other research describing older siblings from
diverse cultures (Farver 1993; Gregory 1998) as skillful mediators who work
together with younger ones in ways that can advance the literacy learning of both.
With some exceptions, siblings sensitively attuned their teaching to the younger
children's levels of literacy competence. In contrast, siblings in mainstream
American families are portrayed in the literature (Ellis and Rogoff 1986; Farver

1993) as less skillful teachers. Possibly because they are not socialized to play this role, they tend to focus on finishing a task rather than on communicating concepts or attending to the learner's ability level.

Third, the findings begin to problematize our understanding of sibling teaching by describing differences in the ways the four older siblings mediated literacy learning. The aspects of literacy they emphasized seemed influenced in complex ways by their differing abilities to gauge the level of assistance needed, their age and school experiences, the focal children's competencies as developing readers in relation to their own literacy competencies in both languages, family and cultural perspectives on literacy and sibling teaching and the assistance *they* received from more capable readers. This suggests that, as researchers and educators, we are just beginning to understand the relevance of individual, but socially rooted, characteristics for the co-construction of learning in children's interactions, particularly in diverse families (Hogan and Tudge 1999).

Fourth, our work illustrates just one aspect of the multistranded networks of relationships that mediated the children's developing literacy. The sibling teachers acted *with* their parents, not as substitutes for them, within a mediating network (Volk 1999). Sra Torres' interactions with Francisco provide a glimpse into a process through which siblings may learn how to provide assistance with literacy. Developing mediators such as Francisco might also learn by observing others in the characteristically social literacy events in their homes. Overall, our work highlights the importance of identifying and understanding both the content and form of mediating networks and how they are created in children's homes and communities. Using this knowledge, teachers can tap into such networks as classroom resources (Moll and Greenberg 1990) as well as nurture networks of teaching and learning as resources within classroom communities.

Building on these insights, we plan to extend our research on the ways young bilingual children construct their own literacy learning and that of others as they participate in mediating networks. We shall look closely at how children develop as learners and teachers within sociocultural contexts in relation to characteristics such as competence and age and to the assistance they receive. We shall explore issues of change and conflict as well as commonalities within these networks and in the 'contact zones' between the networks in children's communities and their schools (Guerra 1998; Moje 2000). To do so, we shall continue to observe in homes and listen to families, working to develop methods that capture the meanings and complexity of teaching and learning literacy at home. We urge other interested educators to immerse themselves in these networks in order to learn about them at first hand. And we caution them to be aware that the more they learn about the literacy lives of the children they educate and study, the more likely they will be to challenge accepted notions of what literacy learning, teaching and research look like.

Acknowledgements

We would like to thank Julializ and Fidelia and all the members of their networks of support as well as their teacher, Mrs. Martin and our research assistant, Zulma Zabala. Our work was supported by grants from the Graduate College and the Urban Child Research Center, Cleveland State University.

Notes

1   Pseudonyms have been used for all participants.
2   Transcription conventions include: empty parentheses (   ) for unclear speech; double slashes //   // for overlapping speech; translations in brackets.

Chapter 3

Samia and Sadaqat play school
Early bilingual literacy at home

Rose Drury

The Early Years (Early Childhood) curriculum has a long-established tradition in the UK, but until recently there has been little guidance at a national level to inform practice for practitioners working with bilingual children. Since the early 1990s, a number of documents have sought to incorporate principles of equal opportunities and inclusion of all children in mainstream classrooms (School Curriculum and Assessment Authority (SCAA) 1996; Department for Education and Employment/Qualifications and Curriculum Authority (DfEE/QCA) 1999). One of the ways these have been related to bilingual children has been through a limited acknowledgement of the principle of supporting children's home languages. However, it is not clear how this support is to be delivered. Little research has taken place, for example, into which language bilingual adults should use with young bilingual children and under what circumstances. Equally, while the need to support bilingual children in the process of their learning of English as an additional language (EAL) has gradually been recognized (SCAA 1997), official documents have not discussed how practitioners should provide this support.

There may be several reasons for this situation. One may be the widespread view that young children pick up English by osmosis very quickly (Crystal 1987; Browne 1996). Many children do acquire sufficient English in a relatively short time to enable them to catch up with their peers. But this is not the case for all children and it is, in any case, doing a disservice to all children learning EAL not to give specific attention to their distinctive learning situation. Another reason may be that few contributors to official documents have expertise in teaching young bilingual children, or are able to draw on such expertise. And a further factor may be that there have been relatively few research studies to inform policy-makers and practitioners about the strategies that will best assist children with EAL in the Foundation Stage (National Curriculum level for 3–5 year olds).

More recently, the UK government's emphasis on inclusion of all children in mainstream classrooms has led to rather stronger references in official documents to children learning EAL. The Curriculum Guidance for the Foundation Stage (DfEE/QCA 2000) is the first official statutory document to include consideration of EAL since the National Curriculum was introduced in 1989. A central aim for the new Foundation Stage for early learning is to 'foster personal, social and emotional well-being' through 'promoting an inclusive ethos and providing opportunities for each child to become a valued member of that group and community so that a strong self-image and self-esteem are promoted' (DfEE/QCA 2000: 9). However, while practitioners who are informed about the education of bilingual children would not disagree with the statements set out in the section entitled 'Children with English as an additional language', which recognize the importance of home languages, the guidance is at a highly generalized level. The one statement which refers to learning English as an additional language states: 'providing a range of opportunities for children to engage in speaking and listening activities in English with peers and adults' (DfEE/QCA 2000: 19). Because this does not suggest on a specific level how practitioners can support English language learning, it implies that all that is necessary are opportunities for speaking and listening.

Recommendations of general principle which are unsupported by more detailed guidance on provision or by training, signal a weak priority and create a culture in which practitioners have to rely on their own resources. This may lead to a situation in which some bilingual children do not have the opportunities to display their abilities which greater knowledge and understanding of their distinctive position might provide. In order to fill what is effectively a vacuum of informed guidance at a national level, research studies are needed which provide further insights into the ways young bilingual children learn EAL. It is hoped that the study highlighted in this chapter contributes to this process.

This chapter is concerned with the experience of one bilingual child as she starts nursery (preschool). Although current educational policy views such children's cultural and linguistic diversity positively, how are teachers and other early years educators able to respond to these children's needs if all that is visible in the nursery is their performance in English?

Language socialization

Since the late 1970s studies have examined a number of related aspects of second language learning and socialization. From a language acquisition perspective, studies have drawn attention to the early developmental stages of learning a second language in early years settings (Wong Fillmore 1979; Saville-Troike 1988; Tabors and Snow 1994; Clarke 1996; Tabors 1997). Wong Fillmore (1979) shows how the minimal resources of formulaic speech can be used by second language learners to participate in interactive situations with peers, while Saville-Troike (1988) examined the way the early stage learner rehearses speech very quietly during the 'silent period'. Tabors (1997) identifies four stages of development. The research examining the early stages of development has not been widely acknowledged in the United Kingdom. However, the value of recognizing these stages is that they provide a framework against which practitioners can exercise their judgement about an individual child's progress and provide appropriate learning opportunities.

Social interaction within specific settings is significant not only for language learning but also for discovering what counts as valued social behaviour by both the peer group and by adults. Thompson (1996) has examined social interaction between peers and Hirschler (1994) has shown how native speakers may be instructed to assist second language learners in the preschool context. Attention has also been given to sociocultural aspects of the educational setting. For example, Willett (1987, 1995) takes account of social interaction and examines how the setting constructs the 'desirable identities, social relations and ideologies' (Willett 1995: 499) of the bilingual learners. Following Agar, Willett uses the term 'Languaculture' as a means of showing that language and culture are inseparable and should be considered together. Haste (1987) draws on Vygotsky's (1978) distinctions between intrapersonal, interpersonal and sociohistorical domains as a framework to explore the ways children come to understand culturally and socially encoded rules. For bilingual children, who may experience a significant discontinuity between the home and classroom settings, this process of 'growing into rules' is of particular importance.

Other studies have focused on the continuities and discontinuities between home and school (Heath 1983; Weisner *et al.* 1993; Volk 1997b). These studies consider the use of language in the home and in school and relate their findings to school success. Research has also been undertaken on literacy. Heath (1983) and Gregory (1994a, 1996), for example, examine home and school literacies arguing that literacy needs to be understood in a wider context than the classroom if a deficit view of children from ethnic minority backgrounds is to be avoided.

Finally, studies have pointed to the importance of the development of the first language for the second language learner (Cummins 1981; Wong Fillmore 1991; Ramirez 1992; Collier 1995). Wong Fillmore examines the cost of losing first language competence in favour of second language development. Other studies draw on research which shows the long-term benefits for academic achievement of learning through both first and second languages. Some work has been undertaken on code-switching and the roles of bilingual staff in early years classrooms (Martin-Jones 1995). Drury (1997) also highlights the importance of the role of bilingual classroom assistants in promoting learning for children at a very early stage of English language acquisition.

These studies all have relevance to the learning situation of Samia, a 4-year-old British Pakistani child whose first language is Pahari. She is in the early developmental stages of learning English; she uses her first language and code-switches appropriately; she is unable to successfully interact with the peer group at this stage; and she is learning the social rules of the classroom setting, a process which will remake her identity and influence her future attainment. However, what is lacking in existing literature is evidence of the way in which children take control of their learning in informal settings, as well as finely tuned analyses of the way in which children syncretize home and school learning. Within a language socialization perspective, this chapter examines Samia's learning situation from two particular points of view. The first shows how she is subject to the 'double bind' which Tabors (1997: 35) identifies: 'in any language-learning situation in natural circumstances, communicative competence and social competence are inextricably interrelated; the double bind is that each is necessary for the development of the other'. It then goes on to show how the child herself may play a critical role in enabling a move beyond the double bind associated with the early stages of second language development when she provides her own opportunities for rehearsing and practising classroom learning in the home.

In this chapter, I ask what influences a child's progress through the double-bind situation of early stage learners of EAL? I then ask what may a child do herself to actively influence her progress? How does she syncretize home and school learning? In order to answer these questions I shall draw on transcripts of Samia's language use at the end of her first term in formal schooling, during one session at nursery and one afternoon at home playing with her younger brother.

Methodology and data collection

The case study presented is part of a larger study which aims to describe the learning situation for bilingual children as they enter formal schooling. Using ethnographic approaches, I studied three Pahari-speaking girls in three different multiethnic nursery classes in Watford, near London, over the period of one school year. The children were randomly selected in consultation with bilingual outreach assistants who work in the homes of the focus families, the nursery staff and the children's parents. The largest ethnic minority group in the community originates from Azad Kashmir in northeast Pakistan and the mother tongue spoken by the majority of these families at home is Pahari, a Punjabi dialect. The nursery staff in the schools are monolingual English speakers who do not share the first languages of their bilingual pupils.

My data come from three sources. Audio-recordings were made of the three children using radio-transmitter microphones in the home and nursery contexts. I recorded the 2½-hour nursery session six times; first, when the child started nursery and subsequently once every half term until she entered the Reception class for 4 to 5 year olds. I conducted six tapings of between thirty minutes and one hour in each home. In both settings I recorded naturally occurring interactions, when the children engaged in normal activities. The tapes are transcribed by working with a bilingual informant who is a native speaker of Pahari and a respected member of the community. Second, observations were carried out to record the children's behaviour in the nursery and the activities in which the children engaged in conversation. Third, I conducted two interviews each with the nursery teacher and the child's parents in addition to informal conversations.

Analysis of the data takes account of explanations of the stages of early second language development and of the classroom as a sociolinguistic and sociocultural setting (Hymes 1974). Using this perspective, observation of a nursery session was analyzed in order to construct an integrated description of the child's participation in the classroom context (Willett 1995). The analysis of the child's language use in her constructed play setting at home draws on Halliday's view of language in social context which stresses the interdependence of learning a language and learning a culture in a social context (Halliday 1975: 120). Thus the child's near monologue as 'teacher', with her little brother cast in the role of 'learner', can be seen in terms of Halliday's 'formulation of language as social semiotic' (Thompson 1996: 9), just as the child's distance from the social setting (the classroom) she draws upon and is engaged in, can also be seen in second language learning as social semiotic. 'This presents language as functioning as an expression of, and a metaphor for, the social processes which it creates and the social contexts in which it occurs' (Thompson 1996: 9).

The developmental stage of English acquisition

Samia entered nursery speaking Pahari, her mother tongue, and was just beginning to learn English as a second language. During these early days in nursery, Samia was silent, listening to and watching what the English-speaking children were doing and saying in their play. She engaged in rehearsing and echoing the English she heard (Saville-Troike 1988). By the end of her first term, Samia is at the formulaic stage in the developmental sequence for acquiring a second language (Tabors 1997).

Samia has sufficient confidence to use mainly one or two word utterances which she uses telegraphically to stand for a more complete meaning. Examples of her use of English at this stage are: 'go back', 'I making', 'I teacher', 'you pushing', 'give me that', 'lot of'. In the following sequence Samia has moved onto the carpet where children are playing with a wooden train set. She is silent while playing on her own.

Samia: No, mine.
          Not yours [to another child].
Samia: No [indistinct] big boy.
Samia: Look [to another boy].

There is no response. There is talk going on around her while she is playing, but not addressed to Samia.

Child: No, this is mine.
Samia: It's mine.
Child: You're hurting me, get away from me.
Samia: That's mine.
Child: Hey, you're breaking mine.

Samia's use of formulaic speech helps her respond in play situations with a minimum of language. However, she is not yet able to use English to communicate in terms which the other children can relate to. When she protests to a child playing near her who has taken a piece of her model by saying, 'no, mine, not yours', this is ignored by the other child. She makes two further attempts and this interaction helps her to engage in a limited way with her peers (in this case, to protect her play materials). However, it also illustrates her social isolation in the nursery. The other children playing near her are talking to each other, but she is mostly ignored. As her restricted formulaic utterances are not responded to by her peers, she has very limited opportunities to develop her second language and to become socially accepted in the nursery.

The double bind of language learning and social interaction

The dependence of language acquisition on social interaction and social interaction on the use of appropriate language is referred to by Tabors (1997) as a double bind which many early stage learners of EAL experience for a period of time.

Thus, during her first few months in nursery Samia is socially isolated from other children. She spends long periods of time playing on her own and for much of the time she is silent. The other children in the nursery do not include her in their play or initiate conversations with her. Throughout the nursery session she interacts in English with other children only six times and, with the single exception of the word 'look!', each one involves asserting possession. Such apparently negative responses may not be unusual (Tabors 1997: 34). They reflect the social imperative to acquire English which can express self-assertion. In the context of Samia's experience of the double bind, her assertiveness may be seen as a stage in her progress towards social integration.

There are also a limited number of interactions with adults in the nursery setting during the whole session. In a one-on-one basis, there are two interactions in which Samia responds to five questions with single word responses and she makes one three-word contribution ('lot of green'). Apart from these examples, she attracts the teacher's attention once, is instructed to tidy up several times and she is asked five questions during two group teaching sessions; she is able to provide single word responses to four. Despite the limited interactions with adults, it is noticeable that they are more productive than those with other children. In a study of two children, Willett (1987) found that one child did not start using English until she was accepted by her peers, whereas the other child responded to interaction with adults. In Samia's case, at this stage, the double bind constrains her interaction with children whereas she is able to respond to adult-initiated exchanges. This would suggest that increasing the opportunities for her to interact with adults would build on the social context in which she has the greater confidence.

Samia's teacher comments at the end of her first term at nursery: 'Samia was confident from day one and is now settled in nursery. She can follow activities at worktime, but sometimes won't say anything at recall. I hope she will begin to mix more socially now and speak more English.' The double bind is reflected in these comments. How can Samia gain sufficient English to become a social member of the group when she spends much of her time playing on her own silently and is largely ignored by her peers? What can the nursery staff do to help Samia to begin to speak the new language and to be socially accepted?

Samia as active agent in her learning

Although Samia is not yet able to generate productive speech for social interaction with her peers, in private speech she may use rehearsal strategies which indicate that she is developing an understanding of structures by using substitution. In the following example, she echoes the commentary of a peer sitting near her and repeats this with variation four times. This rehearsing behaviour has been described in other studies (Saville-Troike 1988) and shows how private speech contexts enable children to experiment.

Child: I making a box.
Samia: I making ears? [to herself]
          I making ears?
          I making.
          I making wheels.

In a study of a 2-year-old child in a daycare centre, Karniol (1990) notes that because the setting provides input primarily in the form of imperatives and interrogatives, children of this age adopt the strategy of practice language in doll play. She observes that 'the most remarkable aspect of this behaviour is that at 2:1 it TOTALLY [original capitals] replaced doll play in the dominant language (which had started at 1:11) and prevailed in spite of the obvious difficulty of engaging in this activity with such limited linguistic and syntactic competence' (Karniol 1990: 159). This suggests the importance which the learner attaches to mastering second language acquisition.

The need to successfully engage in the nursery and to learn English is a powerful force in Samia's life which, as Willett (1995) points out, will reshape her identity. It is a force which Samia takes into her life at home. This is illustrated in a transcription of her play with her 2-year-old brother, Sadaqat, which she uses as a means of practising language.

Samia is the middle child in a family of three children. She speaks Pahari, a dialect of Punjabi, to her younger brother, mother and grandmother, but her older brother speaks some English at home. The recognized community language is Urdu and Samia has started to attend Qu'ranic classes in Arabic after school.

(The italicized text indicates English and the plain text indicates Pahari.)

Samia: Sadaqat, stand up
          we're not having group time now

group time
you can play, Sadaqat

shall we play something?

you want to do painting?

[noise from Sadaqat]

OK get your water
let's get a water
let's get a water
let's get a paper

baby didn't cry
hurry up [whispering]
you want paper
and put in the painting
do that and what are you
choose colour
black

Sadaqat: *back*

Samia: *no, there's a black*
                                                              did you finish it?
                                                              painting
                                                              you make it

Sadaqat, do it with this finger
do it like this, do it like that

                                                              wash

which *colour* are you going to choose?

                                                              next thing

don't do it, Sadaqat
orange *satsuma*[1]
I'm doing it *satsuma* colour
[clapping, knocking]
you are having your . . .
[crying]

                                                              like it?

Sadaqat: mummy [calling to mummy]

Samia: let's do some painting
do it like this, Sadaqat

                                                              red

don't do it

now you can do it
now we've done it

finish
I have

Sadaqat, put it over there
and let's do some painting

wash up

Sadaqat, give it to big sister

give paper and I'll do
wash up
put paper over there

now it's story time

In Samia's 'school game', we can recognize the routines of nursery in her play. For example, she refers to story time and group time and the sequence of the painting activity from her nursery experience. She is practising these familiar routines and sequences in the role play with her little brother and displays considerable confidence. At this stage, Samia's use of English does not enable her to extend it so that it conveys meaningful purpose. It does not carry the continuity which comes with the natural expression of thought or sequence which her use of Pahari might do. She appears to be at a stage when she is approaching being able to use English as the direct expression of thought, for example to express intention, but in the main she uses chunks of English. However, as was the case with the one example of extension used in the nursery setting, repetition of a phrase may lead to trying a variation or extension. For example, in a sequence not shown in the transcript above, she says 'there's a bag', repeats it and then tries the variation 'there's some bag'. Shortly after she says,

little bit
things back
little bit back

Given the greater freedom to experiment in the play situation, Samia tries new combinations as she progresses towards a more productive use of English. In the context of her home, Samia's language shows a wider range of lexis, structures and knowledge in English than at school. She is clearly rehearsing the language she has heard at nursery by repeating chunks or formulaic phrases in familiar situations.

When she wants to draw Sadaqat into the game or when she wants to give him a real instruction, one that she wants her brother to follow, she uses Pahari. Thus there is a distinction between the game, which is to play the school game in English and what she needs to do to make the game work with her brother which requires the use of Pahari. The transcript starts with an invitation from Samia to her brother to enter the game in Pahari:

Sadaqat, let's go downstairs.
Come on into school. Yes you can come into school.
Sit over there on a chair.

But there are times when the distinction between engaging her brother to enable the game to work and the use of English to play the school game breaks down and Pahari is used instead of English within the game ('I'm doing it satsuma colour'). This merging of purpose is reflected in the code-switching and code mixing ('what *colour* are you going to choose?'). Samia code-switches into Pahari to keep Sadaqat engaged ('Sadaqat, do it with this finger'). There is a smooth transition between languages and the same lexis is used in both mother tongue and second language during the conversation, for example, group time, painting, colour, satsuma. There is some evidence to suggest that English is fast becoming an alternative to Pahari as a functioning language for communicative use.

Samia draws on the two main language learning contexts from her experience in the nursery. One of these is the language of social interaction which children use when they play together. The other is the language used by adults to children. It is noticeable that much of this relates to the routines rather than to language learned in personal interaction arising from focused attempts by adults to support English language learning. For example, in a different section of the complete transcript she says 'change your *planning board*' and '*tidy up time*'. It also reflects the language of instruction: '*read your book*', '*colour that one*', '*choose a story*', '*wash up*'.

Samia's school game reinforces the culture as well as the language of the nursery. She is learning English for school purposes – that is the English she knows. In this example we have insights into her learning of English which are not observed in the nursery context. First, the social context of her home and her younger brother as a willing participant, provides a supportive environment to rehearse her newly learned English. The play situation enables her to use her brother almost as if he were the respondent of private speech, in much the same way as Karniol's (1990) 2-year-old used doll play. Thus she is freed from the constraints of appropriateness that apply in the nursery and can apply herself with greater confidence. Second, the significance of the routines of the nursery is evident in Samia's role play. We can see the influence of adult language use. The predictability and pattern of the language used at certain regular times and places in the nursery is helpful to her learning of English. Third, Samia uses her mother tongue with considerable fluency in her interactions with Sadaqat. In the nursery, there are very few opportunities for mother tongue use and there are indications that Samia's use of English, at the end of one term in nursery, will soon overtake her Pahari (Wong Fillmore 1991).

Implications for practice

Educators need to ensure that early stage learners of English have opportunities to adjust to the nursery as a sociocultural setting and to be as fully supported as possible in their learning of English. What will assist children like Samia in the double-bind situation in which they find themselves and how can educators support them in their own highly motivated and active learning?

- *Provide opportunities for one-on-one interaction with adults:* early stage learners will benefit from responsive adult interaction which is adjusted to the child's language level, uses repetition and gives time to assist response, enables known patterns to be practised, extended and expanded and models language in the contextualized situation.
- *Provide opportunities for language learning in teacher-led small group work:* teacher-led group work helps bilingual children develop their confidence through joining in choral responses, responding in turn-taking discussions which repeat patterns of language and listening to the interactions of other children with the teacher.
- *Reduce the potential for stress in the new learning environment and maximize opportunities for participation:* one significant way of providing a stress-free environment (Krashen 1985) is to provide bilingual adults who can support early stage learners' understanding of what is expected of them, as well as support their language development. Nurseries which build on children's home experience, facilitate meaningful interactions and understand that bilingual learners need more positive interventions for language learning than is implied by 'osmosis', will be positive settings for children like Samia.
- *Seek ways of supporting social interaction:* contexts which encourage English-speaking peers to interact with bilingual children will support English language learning and assist early stage learners to move beyond the double bind so that they learn the social language required for interaction (Hirschler 1994).
- *Make the rules and routines explicit:* children like Samia will find it easier to adjust to the nursery setting if the rules and routines are consistent and predictable, if they are made explicit and if account is taken of the values and cultural norms of the home.

Conclusion

In this chapter, I have argued that young bilingual children are able to take control of their own learning and, through the example of Samia's play situation with her brother at home, that the early desire to learn English and to adapt to the new sociocultural setting is very strong. In order for educators to capitalize on this, they need to take account of such factors in their responses to young bilingual children even though they may not always be apparent. This will be the basis for the positive acknowledgement of progress, for giving encouragement and for providing positive feedback which supports learning and reflects the expectation of development.

However, there is another side to the impact of participating in the nursery. Being allowed to use the mother tongue and having other speakers of the mother tongue in the setting does not mean that second language learners will necessarily use their mother tongue. They quickly learn that their efforts need to be put into the learning of English if they are to succeed. It follows that any serious desire on the part of educators to avoid first language loss would require a much more formalized commitment to it. Hoping that this will not happen merely by allowing the first language to be used as the child desires, or by providing some hours of adult bilingual support, will do little to counteract the powerful desire to learn English. Planned time and the explicit recognition of the importance of first language development would be necessary. While this aspect of bilingual children's experience is not the focus of this chapter, it is an integral aspect of bilingual children's learning situation. Given the pressure, both internal and external, for English to become the dominant language, it is important that educators and policy-makers are aware of the impact of early formal education on children's lives (Wong Fillmore 1991). Equality of opportunity should include a more determined attempt to prevent language loss than is presently shown in education policy.

Acknowledgements

I would like to thank all the nursery staff involved in this study for their generosity and patience, Asmat Majeed for her interpretation and transcription of the recorded data and the Hussain family for their involvement in the project.

Note

1   Satsuma is a Japanese word commonly used in Britain for a seedless type of mandarin orange.

Chapter 4

"Right, get your book bags!"
Siblings playing school in multiethnic London

Ann Williams

I don't remember my parents reading to me though I suppose they must have done. My sister read fairy stories and poems to me and I especially remember *La Belle Dame Sans Merci* and *Old Meg*. She was nearly seven years older and to my eyes hugely competent and confident. To ape and impress her I had been pretending for some time that I could read by going through the physical motions with stories and rhymes I knew by heart. She knew what I was doing and refused to believe until I had coped more or less effectively with an unseen text! From then on, hooked as I was on what books make possible, I became increasingly in control of what I read.

(Eric Bolton [ex-Professor of Teacher Education, ex-Head of
HM Inspectorate, Chair of 'The Book Trust'] 1998: 1)

Eric Bolton's memories of learning to read with his sister highlight many of the essential characteristics of sibling relationships. A caring and much admired older sister supervises the learning of her younger brother in a warm and secure home setting, with highly successful results. Although such interactions are commonplace in families around the world (Gregory 1998; Volk 1999; Gregory and Williams 2000), the literacy activities in which children engage at home and the role of siblings as mediators of learning have until recently received little attention. It has generally been assumed by educators, politicians and policy-makers that parents, and mothers in particular, are the primary educators and caregivers in the home. Yet research indicates that children spend much more time interacting with people other than their mothers (Rogoff 1991). Moreover, some 65 percent of child–child contacts are between non-age mate peers such as siblings (Barker and Wright 1955). Until recently however, 'the influence of siblings in general and as caretakers in particular has been viewed as negligible' (Bryant 1990: 143).

Background

The importance of parents in a child's early literacy learning, on the other hand, has long been recognized and well documented in the research literature (Wells 1985; Snow and Ninio 1986). The UK Labour government for example, having introduced mandatory daily numeracy and literacy hours in primary schools,[1] have lately turned their attention to the home context. In order to promote in all homes the kinds of learning experiences provided by educated middle-class families, they have established adult numeracy and literacy classes, family literacy schemes (programmes) and websites offering educational advice. Home–school contracts or agreements in which parents agree to supervise homework have been introduced in UK primary schools and all parents are urged to read for 20 minutes per day with their children. Such government schemes, however, are directed solely at parents. Moreover, they are dedicated to promoting 'mainstream' or 'schooled' literacy, whereby parents are encouraged to use materials and methods taken from school into the home. Little account has been taken so far of the informal literacy interactions between children that are a daily occurrence in most homes and which contribute to the multiple literacies which inform children's learning both in and out of school.

Siblings as mediators

Crucial in all these encounters are those who facilitate the process for the young learners, the mediators of literacy. Recent research has highlighted the important role played by grandparents and other family members, friends and mentors (Baynham 1995; S. Long 1997; Volk 1999; Kelly, Chapter 5 in this volume). In the nuclear family context, however, the role is often taken by older siblings. Weisner (1989) points to the value of a familiar and unthreatening relationship in which young children can practise their emerging skills. 'Most children will rehearse, display and experiment with language capacities and cognitive skills with their siblings well before they do so with other people' (p. 11). In his work in Hawaii, he found that children were more talkative, used more Standard English and more complex language with other children than they did with their mothers for example (Weisner *et al.* 1993). In Bangladeshi British families in East London, it is older siblings rather than parents who carefully scaffold the early home reading experiences of their younger brothers and sisters (Gregory and Williams 2003). Siblings are responsible for passing on much more than language and literacy skills, however. As playmates and facilitators, they 'show a capacity for empathy, nurturance and a subtle understanding of elaborate social relationship patterns' (Weisner 1989: 11). Importantly, then, they act as socializing agents, passing on knowledge about what it means to be a member of their particular culture to less expert members. The exact mechanism by which such subtle patterns that are outside conscious awareness are transmitted, however, is still largely unexplored.

Children's play and their development and learning

Vygotsky (1978) proposed that such processes occur in the social interactions in which more competent members of the culture engage with younger members who would be unable to engage in such activities alone. Such encounters permit learning to take place in the zone of proximal development (ZPD). An optimum context for exploiting the ZPD is in play and in particular in collaborative dramatic play, an activity in which many siblings engage enthusiastically from their earliest years. Vygotsky saw symbolic or dramatic play as central to a child's social, emotional and cognitive development. At an elementary level, he maintained, it encourages abstract thought. In play with a more competent playmate it permits children's capabilities to be extended via the ZPD. In addition, it can be a self-help tool, permitting children to 'create their own scaffold, stretching themselves in such areas as self-control, cooperation with others, memory, language use and literacy' (Roskos and Carroll 2001: 4). In play then, children are able to act developmentally ahead of themselves; they can 'realize the unrealizable'.

Vygotsky's claims have been supported by several research studies. In terms of cognitive development, correlations have been found between sociodramatic play activity and high levels of syntactic maturity (David Lewis, cited in Smilansky 1990), classification ability (Rubin and Maioni 1975) and divergent thinking measures (Johnson 1976). Sociodramatic play has also been found to correlate with social skills such as acceptance by peers, frequency of language use, number of friendly interactions and independence from teachers (Marshall 1961). In addition, Smilansky and Feldrhan (1980) found higher than expected correlations between sociodramatic play and scholastic achievement such as reading comprehension and arithmetic. In general, children who are good at sociodramatic play tend to be successful in other areas of their lives.

One of the reasons why sociodramatic play appears to enhance cognitive and social skills lies in the very complex nature of activity (Brian Sutton-Smith, cited in Bretherton 1984: 30; Monighan Nourot 1998). Children begin to engage in role play at a very early age. Dunn (1990) describes second-born 2 year olds engaging in joint role play with older siblings and beginning to make their own innovative contributions as early as their third year. By age 4 children are operating with complex scripts or schemata, the 'skeletal frameworks of everyday events' (Roger Schank and Robert Abelson, cited in Bretherton 1984: 5). Such 'event scripts' rehearse the mundane experiences of life: going to school, meal-time routines etc. More complex are the socioemotional scripts which incorporate insights into relationships and emotions such as quarrels between family members. In older children, media and popular culture often form the basis of the script. Dramatic play is also a useful vehicle for attempting to make sense of the world and for constructing meaning outside the boundaries of reality. Children move easily between the real and the imaginative and 'derive satisfaction from not only the ability to imitate but also from make-believe play which provides unlimited access to the exciting world of adults' (Smilansky 1990: 19). Thus children interweave schemata, incorporating both elements of real life and of fantasy.

The complexity of such scripts necessitates considerable skill in planning and negotiation. For example, players have to signal 'this is play' and indicate that the material within the frame is different from the surround. This is accomplished by a range of metacommunicative devices such as prompting, storytelling, underscoring and ulterior conversation (Monighan Nourot 1998). In addition, each player has to keep track of four prototypical positions: actor, co-actor, director and audience (Sutton-Smith, cited in Bretherton 1984). The result is a seemingly effortless blending of multiple levels of representation, the complexity of which would confound many adults. In short, sociodramatic play provides opportunities for older siblings to initiate younger members of the family into new discourses, new ways of behaving and new fields of knowledge. We shall illustrate how they might accomplish this with reference to two play sessions recorded in the course of a project conducted in 1998–9 in the East End of London.[2]

The context, the children and methods for studying play

While most studies of sociodramatic play have been organized by researchers in school classrooms, we were able to obtain recordings of spontaneous, unsupervised play in children's homes. The neighbourhood where the children lived was familiar to the research group: one member had lived there as a schoolchild, a second was an active member of the Bangladeshi community and the third had already worked in a local school. We worked with Bangladeshi British and Anglo-British children in a district which in terms of health, housing and income is one of the poorest in the country. Eight families from two schools each with an older child in Years 4, 5 or 6 (aged 9–11) and a younger child in the nursery or infants school (aged 4–8) took part in the research. The families, whose sizes ranged from eleven children to two, lived in rented accommodation in tower blocks (apartment buildings) or in small houses in the ethnically mixed neighbourhood. A wide range of data types was collected including interviews with children, parents, teachers and headteachers, recordings of class literacy hour sessions, group discussions and children's literacy diaries. Possibly the most interesting data, however, consisted of home recordings. Each family was provided with a tape recorder and the children were asked to record themselves at home, taking part in a play activity that involved reading or writing. They chose a range of activities: singing songs, reciting rhymes, reading to younger siblings and crucially, playing school.

Playing with siblings

All the project children spent most of their out-of-school time in the company of their siblings and a good deal of that time playing. Cops and robbers, playing house and playing school were listed as favourite role play games (all names are pseudonyms):

Ali: What do you do after school?
Nasima: Play out.

Ali: What sort of games do you play?
Nasima: Hide and seek.
Ali: Do you play any Bangladeshi games?
Nasima: Yes we play house. We wear saris and cook and stuff.

Clear gender differences emerged, especially in the Anglo group, where the older girls spent a good deal of time playing with their younger siblings. Zarah (aged 11) played with Barney (aged 4):

> We play this number . . . maths game . . . and we've got this abacus . . . and we have these little cards that we made out of paper . . . and we're making a new game with the dictionary . . . and it's got all pictures in it.

Older brothers, in contrast, were often reluctant playmates:

AW: What about playing schools?
Rich: My sister [aged 7] does it with my brother [aged 3].
AW: Does she ever try to get you to play?
Rich: She did once and I told her I didn't want to.

AW: What about playing schools?
Jon: Sometimes with Sally cos my mum tells me to. Sally normally be's the teacher and calls out the register and has to do everybody's name.

Playing school in the Anglo community

Boys did occasionally play school, however. The following recording was made by Lee (aged 9), Cathy (aged 7) and their little sister Lizzie (aged 5). The children are playing school in the living room of their flat on the ninth floor of a tower block. Lee, as the eldest with the highest status, is the teacher and his two sisters are pupils. The 35-minute play session loosely follows events in a school day, beginning with 'Show and Tell' in which both girls read out from books they have brought into school. Then the day formally begins:

Lee: Quickly. Just wasted fifteen minutes. Right then, I'm going to do the register. Cathy, Ben, Cameron, Jemal, Lizzie . . . OK, then Class 7, you've got a worksheet on your table so quickly go and sit on your tables.

The 'day' continues with science, story reading by the teacher and 'literacy', followed by a swimming lesson.

Lizzie is pretending to swim.
  1 *Lee:*   Front crawl! Breast stroke!

2	*Cathy:*	Sir, sir.
3	*Lee:*	Right girls, get out and get changed.
4	*Cathy:*	Sir, sir.
5	*Lee:*	Yes?
6	*Cathy:*	She needs armbands she . . .
7	*Lee:*	No she doesn't, she's a good swimmer.
8	*Cathy:*	Oh, she was at the bottom of the pool though . . .
9	*Lee:*	Now we're going to make plantpots.
10	*Cathy:*	Plantpots! I made some sir put them all around there and I got the busy lizzies.[3]
11	*Lee:*	What you got to do, you got to mould them with clay.
12	*Lizzie:*	Ugh!!

. . .

17	*Lee:*	But first in your literacy diary I want you to write what you've done today in literacy.
18	*Cathy:*	But we do da di da dooh.
19	*Lee:*	Right, in a minute it's time for football practice.
20	*Cathy:*	Sir, do we have to stay for football practice?
21	*Lee:*	Yeah, only a penalty shoot-out.
22	*Cathy:*	Sir, do we have to do a penalty shoot-out?
23	*Lee:*	Yeah. Right Lizzie take the penalty.
24	*Cathy:*	Sir, that's what I brought you. That's for your girlfriend.
25	*Lee:*	Very nice.
26	*Cathy:*	[singing] La la la.

. . .

29	*Lee:*	Right then Cathy, it's time for your choir singing practice.
30	*Lizzie:*	And mine?
31	*Lee:*	And Lizzie it's time for your football practice.
32	*Lizzie:*	Football practice.
33	*Lee:*	Ooooooooh what a goal!!
34	*Cathy:*	[singing]
35	*Lee:*	Second penalty! Oooh saved it.
36	*Cathy:*	Sir, sir.
37	*Lee:*	Lizzie, on your head! On your head!
38	*Cathy:*	Sir, sir!!
39	*Lee:*	Yeah well done Lizzie!!!
40	*Cathy:*	Sir, sir.
41	*Lee:*	Yes Cathy?
42	*Cathy:*	Rex [the dog] was just getting on to this chair and it fell down head first and it was broke.
43	*Lee:*	Oh Rex, what's the matter? You hurt yourself?
44	*Lee:*	What a goal Lizzie!
45	*Cathy:*	[still singing]
46	*Lee:*	Right, get your book bags!

It is clear from the beginning that this is an event script. Activity follows activity in quick succession: science, story reading, several playtimes, swimming, football, plant-pot making, school trip in a coach, bedtime and physical education (PE). We have occasional glimpses of the children's 'real school' life. Lee's school friends and fellow pupils, for example, make fleeting appearances:

Lee: Oi, Jemal, Jemal!!! Don't push Cameron off the diving board. Silly boy!!
Lizzie: [whispers to Cathy] Reckon he pushed you . . . [Cathy falls over]

Topical events are incorporated including 'Red Nose Day', a national fund-raising event for charity which was taking place at the time of the recording:

Lee: Right, here's a gift from the school of red noses. [the girls put them on]

Recent innovations in the primary school curriculum are woven into the script. The literacy hour, for example, is mentioned (line 17) and recurs at intervals throughout the text:

Lee: Right, now it's literacy. Right Cathy, your group's going to be reading and
        Lizzie, your group's going to be reading . . .
Lee: Right then, you can have some children's time instead of literacy.

A further recent initiative, the discussion of 'learning objectives', also surfaces:

Lee: What it is [a ruler], it's used to draw triangles better than anything so we're
        going to be learning about that in the next couple of weeks.

This is also a fantasy play session, however, with the children trying out new roles. Lee, as teacher, remains in the frame throughout, yet manages to metamorphose into his hero, his Saturday football coach, in order to engineer his favourite pastime into the script. Cathy, who in real life is a model pupil and star of the school choir, takes on the role of naughty pupil with gusto, using every opportunity to thwart her teacher.

Lee: Right, next we'll do a mother's day card.
Cathy: Sir, we made one already.
Lee: Well we're going to do another one.
Cathy: No!!
Lee: Right, we'll go swimming then.
Cathy: We don't like swimming. We don't even know how to swim.

She constantly challenges the teacher's decisions, at times involving the other pupil, Lizzie, in her rebellious behaviour:

Lee: Come on quickly, science now.
Cathy: [whispers] Boring.
Lizzie: Boring.
Lee: Cathy, be quiet. [Cathy pretends to cry]
Lizzie: Boring.
Lee: Lizzie, you be quiet as well.

Worst of all, she makes frequent references to a totally taboo subject, her teacher's private life (line 24), at one point asking him:

Cathy: Sir, sir, what's your real name sir? I've never known it.
Lee: Lee.
Cathy: All right Lee, nice to meet you.

Lee skillfully negotiates his way through the script, coping with his naughty pupil in a variety of ways: gracefully accepting the present for his girlfriend; redirecting the action, by suggesting she goes off to singing practice instead of playing football and occasionally putting her firmly in her place:

Lee: We're going on a trip tomorrow.
Cathy: Where?
Lee: Danelaw Barn.
Cathy: Been there. It's really good, you see frogs, you can go fishing and there's a park.
Lee: OK Cathy, we don't need to know everything.

The script unfolds effortlessly, constantly changing direction as new items and new moves are introduced. Cathy, for example, brings in a snack from the kitchen which is smoothly incorporated. When Lizzie threatens to leave, Lee acts swiftly in order to maintain the momentum:

Lee: We've got RE [religious education] now.
Cathy: Oh, I forgot to tell you. It's my birthday tomorrow and I brung something.
Lee: OK, everybody. Sit down. We won't do RE today.
Lizzie: Boring.
Lee: We're going to have a little tea party.
Lizzie: Bor . . . Good.
Lee: Can you please hurry up Cathy!!
Lizzie: I'm not playing!
Lee: Lizzie ! Lizzie! When is it *your* birthday?

This is a collaborative play script, co-constructed by children who have a shared history and warm relationships within the family. Although the motivation is play and enjoyment, for little Lizzie in particular, it provides a valuable learning experience. She is being socialized into the language, routines and rituals of 'big school': she is introduced to a curriculum that has science, literacy hours and swimming lessons: she learns that male teachers are addressed as Sir, that many lessons are 'boring' and how naughty pupils behave.

Lee and Cathy use their roles to practise language skills. We see Lee using 'teacherly' language such as 'Perfect timing!', 'Well, that's fascinating' and, when the class finally agrees on a name for the hamster, 'So the class is all agreed'. Cathy also adopts new discourses and accents. For example, we hear her in the role of anxious mother:

Lee: [pretending to phone] Hello Miss Rhodes?
Cathy: [talking with an upper-class accent] Yeees.
Lee: Your daughter's gone on a trip and she won't be back until about six o'clock tomorrow night.
Cathy: Has she now! Not again!!
Lee: I imagine she stayed overnight at school so I'm very sorry about that.
Cathy: She said she was writing a story.

As players, Lee and Cathy are experts. Lee wavers only once when he is concerned about the family dog (line 43). Cathy occasionally has to step outside the frame:

Lee: Who wants some playtime?
Cathy: [sotto voce] Lee, can we really choose? [in pupil's voice] Oh is it playtime sir?

Little Lizzie, however, as the least expert player with the lowest status, frequently has to resort to prompting in order to get her suggestions adopted:
They are going on a trip

Lizzie: Lee, I have to get my swimming costume cos there was . . . Pretend there was a sw . . .
Cathy: Shhhhh.
Lee: Come on Lizzie, just sit down!
Lizzie: Pretend there was a swimming pool.

While it is clear that this play session provides a learning experience for all three players, the improvised and spontaneous nature of the script makes it difficult to isolate the literacy learning taking place. The knowledge acquired here appears to be 'dynamic and synergistic, assembled from informal bits at hand' (Roskos and Carroll 2001: 8). Although all three children practise formal literacy in the form of reading aloud in the course of the play, the session is possibly most valuable in terms of informal learning experiences. The play setting permits them to take on roles, experiment with language, test the boundaries of reality and explore how the world works, in a context that is unthreatening and tolerant. Literacy in this context then

> does not appear structure-like but soft assembled in relation to the play setting . . . essentially a process – a network that varies as a joint function of player, setting and the larger circumstances that give rise to the play environment.
>
> (Roskos and Carroll 2001: 8)

Literacy learning was very different in the neighbouring community, however, as the following section will illustrate.

Playing school in the Bangladeshi British community

For the bilingual children, play and home literacy were sharply differentiated. Although they too played house, played school and rode their bikes after school, they also spent several hours a week engaged in formal literacy activities. Speakers of Sylheti, an unwritten dialect of Bengali, they all attended classes to learn to read and write Standard Bengali either in the local community centre or in neighbours' homes. As members of a deeply religious Muslim community, they also attended Qur'anic classes in the mosque or at home, where they read the Qur'an and related books in Arabic. In addition, most of the Bangladeshi British children attended homework clubs run by the school or the local community centre (Williams and Gregory 2001).

Two sets of Bangladeshi British siblings chose playing school as their home recording. The following extracts are taken from the tape made by Wahida (aged 10) and Sayeda (aged 8). They are playing school in the family sitting room, in a small flat a few hundred yards from that of Lee and his sisters. Wahida, the teacher, has a small blackboard and Sayeda, the pupil, has a notebook. Wahida's friend, Kadija, is also present. The day's 'teaching' begins with the register (attendance):

Wahida: Good morning class.
Sayeda: Good morning Miss Wahida. Good morning everyone.
Wahida: I want to do the register. So . . . Sayeda?
Sayeda: Good morning Miss Wahida.

A 45-minute recording of a school day follows. Although they attend different schools, Wahida's playing school script has a good deal in common with that of Lee and his sisters: both follow a varied timetable with maths, literacy, science, art, choir and assembly. Intriguingly, both groups engage in what we must assume are salient activities for young children, namely going on a trip, celebrating a birthday and naming the class pet. Just like Lee, we see Wahida rushing from activity to activity and 'thinking on her feet' as she incorporates new items into the script:

Wahida: Me and Miss Kadija, we went out and we decided . . . Got a new . . . such a cute guinea pig, a pet for our class. OK, she's just going to get it out of the cage. So, hold on . . . Come on . . . [muffled squeal] . . . Did you hear that? Oh, such a cute . . . OK you can put it in the cage now.

Sayeda: What shall we call it?

Wahida: We'll call it . . . we're going to call it Sue because it's female, OK? OK, we don't want to mess about with the guinea pig all right? So OK, that hasn't got anything to do with education . . . we just wanted to show you. Now we want to do geography.

In spite of the similarities in 'school timetables', however, there are fundamental differences in the way in which the two groups of children conceptualize their play and in particular in the way the role of teacher is interpreted. Whereas Lee rushes through the day, including as many activities as possible in the script, Wahida enacts the role of teacher with a care and meticulousness reminiscent of a highly experienced professional. The following are extracts from her maths and literacy lessons:

Maths

1 *Wahida:* What's 24 times four? If you can't do it, there's another easier way to do times. We do lattice. Yes Sayeda? Good girl for putting your hand up.

2 *Sayeda:* I can't do lattice.

3 *Wahida:* OK. We'll do one together. OK? We'll do 24 times four. First we draw a box . . . Then we do two lines that way, the diagonal way. Yes . . . well done.

. . .

4 *Wahida:* The first sum is 30 times five equals . . . If you want to do lattice you can. Or you can do your own way, or you can do in your mind, but I would love to see some working out.

Spelling

5 *Wahida:* Now we're going to do spelling test. Are you ready Sayeda?

6 *Sayeda:* Yes, Miss.

7 *Wahida:* I'm going to give you at least 20 seconds for each of them, OK? The first one is tricycle. Tricycle. Tricycle has three wheels. Tricycle. The next one is commandment. Commandment. I *command* you to do as quickly as you can, Sayeda. Otherwise you're going to get in *big* trouble. Commandment . . . Don't look at each other's work, Sayeda especially. Now you're going to mark it yourselves.

Homophones

8 *Wahida:* Now we're going to do homophones. Who knows what homophone is? No one? OK. I'll tell you one and then you're going to do some by yourselves. Like watch. One watch is your time watch, like 'What's the time?' watch; and another watch is 'I'm watching you. I can see you . . .' So, Sayeda, you wrote some in your book haven't you? Can you tell me some, please? Can you only give me three, please.

9 *Sayeda:* Oh, I wanted to give you five.

10 *Wahida:* No Sayeda, we haven't got enough time. We've only got five minutes to assembly.

11 *Sayeda:* Son is the opposite of daughter . . .

12 *Sayeda:* And sun is . . . It shines on the sky so bright.

13 *Wahida:* Well done! That's one correct one! And the next one is?

This school session is very different from the teasing, erratic, co-constructed text of Lee and Cathy. In this script, Wahida is unequivocally director of the play while Sayeda takes the role of obedient pupil. 'Miss' Kadija is firmly relegated to teaching assistant, directed to take children to assembly, give out equipment and deal with the guinea pig:

Wahida: Miss Kadija, could you put it back please now, the dear little thing.

Wahida as older sister clearly sees her role as preparing Sayeda for the both social and cognitive demands of 'big school'. She is painstaking in her rehearsal of the procedural rules of the English classroom.[4] She begins each session with 'Good morning, class . . .'; praises Sayeda's good behaviour, 'Good girl for putting your hand up', 'Well done!' and later promises 'I'm going to give you a sticker . . . a headteacher's sticker . . .' She reminds Sayeda of school rituals and time-tables: 'Did you remember to write the date first?' 'We've only got another five minutes until assembly'. She instructs her sister in the marking routines: 'Put a tick [check] near it if you got it right, put a cross if you got it wrong'. 'Now you're going to mark it yourselves'. She reminds her pupil of the need to be polite, regularly using 'please': 'Can you tell me some, please? Can you only give me three, please?'

Her teaching style is explicit and methodical. She introduces each new topic and gives clear instructions: 'We've done your reading. Now we're going to do maths; I'm going to give you some sums. And then we'll do English'. 'Now we're going to do spelling test. Are you ready?', 'I'm going to give you at least 20 seconds for each of them', 'OK, Sayeda, I want your results now, please'. She follows a detailed lesson plan, carefully limiting the tasks to what she knows the younger child is capable of with a little help. We see her working in the zone of proximal development, carefully scaffolding Sayeda's learning by:

- providing examples and models
- using direct instruction to check up on past learning
- giving alternatives if the younger child is in difficulty.
- giving her sister confidence by using encouraging phrases such as 'Well done!', 'Good girl'.

For both sisters this is a learning experience. Sayeda is acquiring far more than socialization in what it means to be a pupil, however. The literacy learning here is not 'assembled from informal bits at hand' (Roskos and Carroll 2001: 8) nor is it unstructured and loosely assembled. On the contrary, this is conscious teaching of school literacy, the transmission of valuable 'cultural capital', the benefits of which will be evident to Sayeda when she reaches the relevant stage in the National Curriculum.[5] For Wahida too, this is a learning experience. She can be seen 'creating her own scaffold' (Roskos and Carroll 2001: 4), stretching herself beyond what would be expected in the real classroom, exercising her memory, her knowledge of English and her skills in literacy. Her knowledge of the National Curriculum English syllabus is detailed and accurate. Her grasp of 'teacher language' is impressive, given that her first language is Sylheti. It is perhaps not surprising, however, when we remember that, living as she does in a self-contained community and attending a school where 100 percent of the children are Sylheti speakers, her English school teacher is her only model for English.

The question arises as to why Wahida's playing school should differ so fundamentally from that of Lee and his sisters? As a British-born child of Bangladeshi parents, Wahida is a product of two cultures. Like any 10-year-old Londoner, she enjoys playing school: she takes her pupils on school trips, looks after the school guinea pig and has birthday parties. In the Bangladeshi community, as in many migrant communities, however, learning is a serious business and Wahida spends much of her after-school time in formal community classes learning Standard Bengali and reading the Qur'an. If she is to be successful in the United Kingdom, she knows she must become proficient in English and as the sole fluent English speaker in her household she is responsible for transmitting those skills to her younger siblings. In Wahida and Sayeda's playing school session then, we see the children syncretizing elements of both cultures, combining the fun and spontaneity of 'English school' with the seriousness and attention to detail of their Bengali heritage.

Conclusion

We have examined two playing school sessions, both executed with great verve and enthusiasm. Although they differ at the micro level, particularly in their interpretation of the teacher's role, they have many common elements. Importantly, both scripts incorporate macro-level factors currently shaping children's education in the United Kingdom. We noted how innovations in the curriculum such as the literacy hour and learning objectives are incorporated into play schemata.

Such unsupervised play scripts can also provide insights into how such societal changes affect school life. Lee's exhortations to 'be quick' throughout the text, and Wahida's request for only three examples as 'we haven't got enough time', may mirror teachers' real anxieties about the rigid and heavily prescribed nature of the current UK National Curriculum, which leaves little time for sustained writing, quiet reading or imaginative play. Wahida's detailed and carefully structured lessons clearly reflect the analytical approach to English embodied in the new literacy syllabus. Her emphasis on marking and correct answers is possibly attributable to the prominence now given to the standard assessment tasks (SATs), the standardized national tests and their much publicized results. Finally, we noted that neither group included imaginative play in their playing school timetable. Although sociodramatic play provides valuable contexts for learning, as our children's texts have clearly shown, the heavy emphasis on formal teaching and testing in the National Curriculum means that even at primary level, there is now no time to play.

Notes

1   The literacy hour is a strictly prescribed hour of literacy consisting of 30 minutes' whole class work, 20 minutes' group work and 10 minutes' plenary session.
2   'Siblings as mediators of literacy in two East London communities' ESRC funded project (R000222487) 1998–9. Principal applicant: Eve Gregory. Researchers: Ali Asghar and Ann Williams.
3   Busy Lizzies are pot plants that grow easily and quickly.
4   See Street and Street 1995 for an example of how procedural rules work in one US primary school context.
5   A National Curriculum was introduced in the United Kingdom in 1989.

Chapter 5

Buzz Lightyear in the nursery

Intergenerational literacy learning in a multimedia age

Clare Kelly

It is a bright summer morning in Livingstone nursery (preschool) in the East End of London. Jamie has reluctantly said goodbye to his mother as usual (all names of participants are pseudonyms). After looking a little lost, he makes straight for me to talk about his radio:

Jamie: Yeh, it used to go round me neck but it's broken now . . . It's in the bin [wastebasket]. [laughs]
Clare: Oh that's a shame. Have you got . . .
Jamie: Mind you, mummy . . . mummy does throw broken toys in the bin.
Clare: Well that's probably the best place for them.
Jamie: Yeh . . . you have to don't you because you can't play with 'em.
Clare: No. You've got lots of videos as well haven't you?
Jamie: Yeh. Bob the Builder, Buzz Lightyear . . . that's all Michael ever watches . . . Buzz.
Clare: Michael's your brother?
Jamie: Yeh. That's all he ever watches . . . Buzz.
Clare: What's your favourite one?
Jamie: Thank God!
Clare: Which one do you like best?
Jamie: Eh. Tots TV.
Clare: You told me you watched Bob the Builder last night didn't you?
Jamie: Yeh. I still watch . . . and . . . and I say [turns, putting hands on hips] 'No I'm not watching Buzz everyday' [laughs] I think to meself . . . I think to meself . . . Watch a different film or somefing. Watch . . . watch Bob or somefing . . . or Tweenies.

This short conversation with Jamie, who at the time was 4 years 6 months, reveals a wealth of information about his strengths and interests as a literacy learner. In common with all children in the nursery, Jamie's involvement with his home world is of prime importance; it is a constant reference point. He gives us a strong indication of his deep interest in media technology, in this example, radio and video, and reveals how knowledgeable he is about children's TV and films. The discussion of differences between his preferences and those of his brother reveal the social nature of his experiences and make it clear that favourite videos are replayed and watched repeatedly.

We can also speculate from the structure and content of this conversation that Jamie is confident when talking to familiar adults and has drawn directly on language from his own speech community to communicate with clarity. In relaying this short anecdote, Jamie uses storytelling techniques, including speaking in the first person, changing the pitch and tone of his voice and presenting an episode as a piece of performance inviting amusement from the listener.

Yet within minutes of this conversation, when another child brings a book for us to look at together, a very different Jamie is revealed.

Jamie: I don't know how to read. I can't read.
Clare: Could you tell me about the story?
Jamie: No, can't read . . . I can't do nuffink. [laughs]
Clare: Of course you can.
Jamie: Can't do nuffink. [laughs]
Clare: Yes you can. I know you can. I've seen the picture you drew of yourself. Julie showed it to me.
Jamie: I can't do nuffink . . . I'm shy . . . I'm shy.

What can account for this swift change? Where has Jamie's confidence and fluency gone? To answer these questions we need to consider what counts as literacy learning at home and at school and examine the extent to which young children can encounter a congruence between their experiences and knowledge in both contexts.

The social construction of literacy

An analysis of Jamie's experience is framed by a theory of language learning as socially constructed knowledge and understanding that develops through inter-actions with more experienced members of the community (Rogoff 1990). Young children develop implicit and explicit understandings of the nature, uses and possibilities of reading and writing through observing and participating in literacy practices which are culturally situated (Teale and Sulzby 1986).

Children come to school with different experiences of how to act and interact during literacy events and may hold different values and beliefs about the nature of literacy. For some children, these experiences and understandings will match those sanctioned by the school, for others there will be significant differences.

Research into the relationship between early literacy learning and later success in reading at school has identified particular practices (Wells 1985), resources (Wade and Moore 1996) and knowledge (Bryant and Bradley 1985; Tizard 1993) as advantageous. Taken at face value these links may seem 'natural' and 'normal', yet if we look beyond such culturally bound discourse, it is clear that success is interpreted within a paradigm that embodies one model of literacy learning, a model that is promoted and legitimized by the school.

Advice to families of young children in Britain gives the impression that literacy learning involves an ideal set of practices leading to the transmission of a universal set of skills and suggests a single interpretation of literacy:

> Children who are read to regularly, hear stories, learn nursery rhymes, look at books, visit libraries and so on are much more likely to learn to read easily.
>
> (DfEE/QCA 1997: 32)

It is sometimes assumed that low income or minority families provide inappropriate environments for fostering or modelling literacy or valuing literacy development.

Literacy problems are linked to family inadequacies, such as perceived intergenerational illiteracy which is passed on in an almost pathological manner. Family literacy programmes make reference to 'breaking the intergenerational cycle of reading failure' (Adult Literacy and Basic Skills Unit (ALBSU) 1993: 8) and have been introduced extensively across the United Kingdom to strengthen the links between home and school and steer families closer to a schooled view of literacy learning.

Many studies discredit the notion that minority families do not value or support literacy development. Barton and Hamilton (1998) identified the wide range of literacy activities engaged in by parents who may have difficulties with reading and writing. Heath (1983) highlighted the different ways in which literacy was perceived by families who did not use print in ways that were shared by the school. Taylor and Dorsey-Gaines (1988) identified the variety of contexts for literacy learning that challenged the notion of an autonomous instructional activity as the prevalent mode. Rogoff (1990), Gregory (1998) and Gregory and Williams (2000) recognized that parents may not be the most influential mediators of literacy for children and have highlighted the role played by children and other adults in informal settings.

These studies have begun to question important assumptions underpinning official policies and show that we still know very little about practices and beliefs about literacy held by families of very young children.

Jamie's route to literacy

Jamie was one of a group of children who took part in a larger ethnographic study designed to enable a greater understanding of the knowledge, expectations and assumptions about print and literacy learning that are integral to the different cultural worlds of home and school. The children attended the same nursery school and the data collected for each child included semi-structured interviews with family members and nursery staff, audio-recorded interactions in the home, diaries kept by family members and weekly participant observations in the nursery over a period of eighteen months.

It has been possible to begin to document the complexity of these young children's experiences of literacy and the distinctive norms, genres and participants (Hymes 1974) in each setting and use these as a framework for interpreting the children's experiences. In this chapter we see more clearly the influence of one important mediator in Jamie's life.

One of the key observations to emerge from this study was that family members other than parents were prime movers or 'guiding lights' (Padmore 1994) in mediating culturally specific ways of understanding and participating in literacy events. In Jamie's case his grandparents, with whom he lived since birth, were influential in introducing him to and negotiating his understanding of texts and the uses of literacy within the family and community.

Studies are beginning to track the influence of grandparents in transmitting literacy practices and values by providing materials (Gregory *et al.* 1996), offering support and encouragement (Padmore 1994) and modelling ways of sharing texts and taking meaning from them (Whitehead 2002). This work draws on Rogoff's (1990) proposal to widen the concept of 'guided participation' to include the 'flexible webs of relationships' (p. 97) that children are involved in with companions and caregivers as they focus on shared cultural activities. With the increasing divorce rate and rising numbers of single parent families, grandparents are more likely to be called on as a childcare resource and become involved with family learning.

The community

The nursery that Jamie attends is situated in the middle of a large, densely populated local authority housing estate (housing project) in East London. In common with similar inner city areas, there are high levels of unemployment, overcrowding and disadvantage. The school serves a culturally and linguistically diverse community.

The nursery building stands in sharp contrast to the gleaming structures of Canary Wharf, which tower above it. Canary Wharf is an opulent development that has grown since the early 1990s to accommodate the overflow of merchant banks and other financial institutions from the City of London. It includes up-market shops, restaurants and other services for business people who work in the expanding number of high-rise buildings. It is also visited by the affluent owners of luxury apartments built on the riverside, who have chosen to live in this prestigious part of London.

Since the Middle Ages, the area surrounding the nursery has been home to a range of people from mainland Europe who escaped from war and famine. In the 1960s, many people from the area of Pakistan later to become Bangladesh, settled in this part of the East End, often living in houses previously inhabited by Jews who had come to England to escape from the pogroms of Eastern Europe.

The signs on the shops, which have changed from Hebrew to Bengali, are testimony to this shift in population. More recently, refugees and asylum seekers have been temporarily housed on the estate after fleeing from war and persecution as so many others have done before them. So the area has a historic tradition of housing a shifting cosmopolitan population with a diversity of traditions and customs, who serve the City of London, but often live in poverty.

Today, inhabitants of the estate where Jamie lives range on a continuum from those whose families have lived in this part of the East End for generations, many of whom have ancestors who arrived in the nineteenth century, to others who have come to live in the area relatively recently and may not have their extended families nearby for support.

Jamie and his family

Jamie is the first child in a family that has lived in this part of the East End of London for four generations. His mother Michelle and her sisters were born in the same hospital as Jamie and attended the same primary school that he will go to when he is 5. Michelle left school at 15 and started work as a shop assistant. Jamie, his mother and younger brother Michael live with his maternal grandmother, Margaret, with whom he shares a bedroom.

Michelle tells of her mum's involvement in helping her and her sisters prepare to go to school.

> She showed us how to count using our fingers and toes, And she read us Peter and Jane whenever she had the time and she taught us how to write our name.

When Jamie was a baby he was cared for by his grandfather, who has since died.

> When he was born my dad looked after him. Mum worked and so did I. They did physical things. He showed him how to use bottle lids, building stuff. He got him plastic tools, hammers and saws. He passed away when Jamie was two and a half. He still asks where he is. He knows he's up in the thunder and when it thunders he's talking to him.

Michelle says that her father was a great storyteller who entertained them with family stories.

> He used to tell stories about wartime, family stories about when he was evacuated and separated from his family. He used to tell stories about when he was a kid, what him and his brothers got up to. When we were having dinner or in the living room we'd say 'tell us about it then'.

She says that Jamie 'listens to everything and everything is a story for him'. She comments on his interest in technology.

> He loves videos, my mum buys them for him – and computer games – he watches them over and over again. He walks round with them under his arm.

His computer games often draw on his interest in film. Singing along with the soundtrack of children's songs, he can adeptly navigate his way through the PlayStation game of *Aladdin* or the *Reading Rabbit* that invite him to click the mouse to identify letters of the alphabet, numbers and shapes hidden in the picture and reward him with stickers and pictures to be coloured in on the screen. These games involve Jamie in quite sophisticated manoeuvres as he makes predictions, hypotheses and interprets different symbolic systems, while engaged in reading both visual images and print. But his experiences playing these interactive games, which are essentially story-based, are also informing him about narrative.

If we are to interpret literacy as culturally situated, this will involve examining the different configurations or sets of literacy practices, including use of media, that apply in different contexts. Jamie's interest in technology and popular culture is encouraged by his mother and grandmother, who buy him videos, and computer games. His grandmother sits with him while he watches videos allowing favourite sequences to be replayed, singing along and talking back to the screen, supporting Jamie and Peter's attempts to re-enact the story alongside the screen, suggesting props they could use, laughing at their antics. Perhaps parallels can be drawn with the warmth, pleasure and security that can be experienced by young children when sharing books with adults (Whitehead 1997).

There are also similarities to be found between children watching a video repeatedly and exclusively for days or weeks as Jamie has done and wanting the same book read repeatedly at bedtime. Jamie and his brother are adept at using the remote control, they fast forward, replay and pause to suit their own purposes. Naima Browne (1999) suggests how this self-regulated behaviour supports children's literacy learning by giving them knowledge of the story and a clearer understanding of narrative features, as well as enabling them to explore the particular narrative and characters in more depth. She also remarks on the significance of film and video as catalysts for children's dramatic play and storytelling.

Michelle and Margaret devote time and energy to helping Jamie become familiar with the experiences he will have in school. Michelle doesn't remember learning to read but her mother, Margaret, says that the teachers were strict:

> You stood one on each side of her and read a page or two of your book, If you got it wrong you were for it. I don't know how she heard half the time, because she was often doing something else as well. Going to read to the teacher or the headmistress was always a big thing – you had to get it right.

They buy Jamie books from the local shops and his favourites are Disney books, which Michele says 'he likes to colour rather than read'. He plays board games with Margaret and they do number puzzles. When they read *Spot the Dog*, which

Jamie has brought from nursery, she reads it through, lifting the flaps to show him the pictures underneath. Jamie 'listens with a serious look on his face and enjoys the pictures'. When Margaret has finished, he looks at them again, turning the pages for himself. He is also learning the alphabet, Michelle says, 'We kept on singing it to him but we didn't think he was paying attention but then he came out with it.'

Michelle and Margaret choose books and comics that feature favourite characters and stories from TV and films because they know these will interest Jamie. Such experience of intertexuality is likely to enable Jamie to become familiar with different versions and emphases and the transfer of narrative from one medium to another.

Jamie at nursery

The nursery aims are laid out clearly in a booklet for parents and are divided into aims for children and principles for teaching and learning. Aims for children include the development of confidence, independence, self-esteem and a sense of respect and responsibility. Guiding principles include the centrality of learning through play, the belief in parents as partners, respect for social and cultural experience, belief in the value of talk, first-hand experience and a positive approach to learning. There is also an antiracist statement which reiterates the school's commitment to:

> Reflect our positive respect for the differences in culture, race and religion and language of all ethnic groups represented in the school.

The language policy, also available to families, is divided into sections that cover speaking and listening, reading and writing and in each case specifies aims, principles of planning and examples of a range of activities that are likely to take place with groups and individuals in the nursery. There is a strong emphasis throughout on the place of story as a unifying mechanism and a vehicle for developing all language modes. Nursery staff identified consistency of approach and shared principles as a reason for choosing to work in the school.

At nursery Buzz Lightyear, a space ranger from *Toy Story*, is currently the subject of Jamie's drawing and model-making and much discussion with any adult who may be nearby. He is particularly interested in Buzz's main forms of transport, rockets and planes. Jamie engages in dramatic play on his own or with other children. This too, often involves Buzz Lightyear and other popular heroes from television and video.

> Jamie is deftly folding paper to make an aeroplane, he tells me his nanny showed him how. 'They have lights. Buzz is . . . Buzz is driving . . . 321 blast off . . . oh no, its wings has come off . . . it's died.'

It is likely that Jamie's understanding of and familiarity with narrative is developing from his experience of hearing family stories, sharing books and comics, but also from TV and film (Robinson 1997) and computer games (Marsh and Millard 2000). As Jamie watches and re-enacts scenes from his favourite videos at home, he is learning about the structures and conventional features of narrative and can use this information to inform his own storying as he borrows from his store of knowledge and creates new meanings through his play. Robinson suggests that there is a commonality between print and televisual narratives which allows children to learn about the genre and is more significant in their understanding of literacy than learning to read print and images on or off the screen. Jamie has a wealth of material in his cultural repertoire on which to draw in his play and creation of imaginary worlds.

Jamie, Georgie, Haroun and Katie are outside in the nursery play area, running between two wooden playhouses. They are rolling on the ground:

Jamie:	He's eating us he is [runs to house 1]. Gate's open, gate's closed. [Haroun presses an imaginary 'button']
Jamie:	Can't hear it can we? Go on then. Put your seat belt on. You've got to weigh yourself.
Haroun:	You're bigger.
Jamie:	Your turn to weigh Katie. Weigh yourself [Jamie sits on a shelf]. A rocket. Hurry up to the space rocket. Hurry in the space rocket.
Haroun:	Open it up [presses 'button']. Yah-yah- yah
Jamie:	You can get dead Katie.
Katie:	No, I'm in the space rocket [runs back to house 2].
Jamie:	It's going to go dead isn't it? Quick, close the gate. He can't get in now. Don't go out there will you, a monster will get yer. [Katie goes out and lies on the floor. Jamie approaches her]
Jamie:	All right? [She gets up and they run back to house 1]
Jamie:	Come on Georgie, it's a shark.
Haroun:	Shark.
Jamie:	It's a space rocket.
Katie:	I want to get out.
Jamie:	Shark, shark.
Haroun:	Shark.
Jamie:	We're better off in this one [moves to house 2].

In this sequence, the children have entered the realms of fantasy to pursue a theme of good and evil, with a focus on escaping from danger, to which they all implicitly concur. They are key players in situations that draw on several of Jamie's favourite videos with swift action that is linked with computer games. Jamie is a prime mover and has an authority and command that is not manifested in out-of-play situations where he tends to be more solitary. He also shows his knowledge of the world of space where astronauts wear seat belts and are weighed before they go onboard.

The children, led by Jamie, are enacting events through play which are helping to develop the skill of storytelling, so important for their language and literacy development (Meek *et al.* 1977; Whitehead 1997). Marsh (1999) found that children who were considered by their teachers to be uninterested or unconfident in literacy activities were more inclined to move from role play fixed on characters from popular culture to reading and writing activities that were attached to the role.

The nursery staff believe that literacy learning should emerge naturally through play and in situations that have meaning for the children. Jamie is in Orange class where the team plan many opportunities for children to see and hear written language and each week there is a story focus from which different activities emerge. For example, a focus on the traditional tale of the *Three Little Pigs* gives opportunities for children to re-enact the story using props and puppets they have made, listen to a tape of the story read by Nick (the nursery teacher) in English and Mohammed, a father of one of the children, in Sylheti, contribute pictures and captions to a wall collage and browse through the picture books on display that present different versions of the story. There are also many opportunities for learning about contextualized print through displays with captions written by children and staff, name cards, labels on resources, lists to sign, for example, to use the computer and the older childen take it in turns to ask the adults who wants tea or coffee and mark it in the staff book.

'Storytime' is the main context created by the staff for a joint focus on reading, normally the text is a picture book. It is consistently planned for each morning and afternoon, over the course of a week, given importance through clear labelling and accompanied by a specific set of signals and behaviours.

Adult: Can you remember what you do at storytime? Do you need to be touching someone else now?
Samia: No.
Adult: No, because they don't like it.
Harvey: Touch your own body.
Adult: Touch your own body – yes! Look with your eyes.

This deliberate routine with explicit expectations, demonstrates to the children that there are particular ways of interacting around texts; ways of sitting, concentrating, paying visual and aural attention and particular verbal interactions around books that are encouraged and rewarded. The pattern of interaction is dialogic in nature, questions are asked and answered and children are encouraged to turn-take. Reading the story is a collaborative venture, a social experience and a negotiation between the adult and children who are invited to participate (Cochran-Smith 1984). Storytime is the occasion when staff introduce and reinforce culturally specific norms, attitudes and values and although they may well reflect ways of reading storybooks in some homes, they will be unfamiliar in others. Studies have shown that social interaction around a text is just one way of reading and not a universal practice (Heath 1983; Minns 1990; Gregory 1996). But children will need to accommodate what is, to some, the unfamiliar world of school literacy if they are to realize the success in school that their families want for them.

Jamie joins in with songs and accompanying hand actions before the story begins and he sits gazing intently at the illustrations in the books, but does not join in the dialogue and joint sense-making that is encouraged by the adult, nor does he volunteer any comment or information as many of the other children do.

As we have seen, Jamie's main experience of texts are oral retellings of family stories, compelling viewing of TV and video and participation in computer games, all supported by his grandmother, who spends so much time with him. He is often to be found at the computer, particularly when digital recordings of class stories, songs or outings are replayed.

Jamie's interest in technology and its links with storying are evident in the following observation. The nursery team have recognized the importance of technology for many children and Nick (the nursery teacher) has made a film of a train journey he made from London to the seaside town of Weymouth, which he has edited and added a musical soundtrack to. *A Day Trip to Weymouth – starring the children of Orange Class* is written on the screen. The film starts in the nursery as Nick ostensibly leaves the children to catch the train. The film is on a continuous loop and chairs are set up in front of the TV like seats in a train, with a driver's seat and hat at the front. There is a ticket office next to the chairs, with paper, handmade books, pens, scissors, a hole punch, stapler, photocopied tickets and a telephone. Jamie sits on his own in the driver's seat in front of the TV, wearing the hat and staring intently at the screen, which shows the train journey along the coast. He is singing along to the soundtrack. He turns to Yasmin who has come to sit on one of the seats and says 'I never been to the seaside'. He continues to watch the screen and then turns to her again and says 'My nanny can't do *PlayStation*'. He watches the film through almost three times then he takes off the train driver's hat and moves to the ticket office to make some tickets.

Jamie's interest in the visual nature of the narrative is evidenced by the fact that he watches it three times. The connection in his mind between different forms of technology is obvious from his comment to Yasmin and this was his way into mark-making in a playful situation that had meaning for him. The nursery team had planned to exploit children's interest in media through the provision of a video film that had their class as its starting point and an internal narrative which encouraged role play. Jamie was the driver and seats were set up like a train. It also gave children an opportunity to extend their knowledge of literacy and explore functions in everyday life giving them a greater understanding of it uses. In this case, this was one of the few occasions that Jamie was observed moving spontaneously to mark-making. This mirrors the ways of learning referred to by Leichter (1984) where children's knowledge about literacy is not the result of direct teaching, but is picked up effortlessly in daily routines and participation in familiar events.

Conclusion

Jamie's entry to reading and writing is likely to be through his absorbing interest in technology, which is perhaps less visible in a busy nursery than his apparent nonchalant attitude towards the less interactive medium of books. He has come to the nursery with a set of expectations about texts and rules for participating in literacy events which have arisen from his experiences at home which are in turn shaped by the experiences and assumptions of the two women who care for him.

As we have seen, Jamie's literacy learning is a complex activity that is taking place at the heart of his lived experience, supported by the mesh of social relationships that are open to him at home and at school. If children whose experiences do not form part of the dominant discourse are to be empowered as literacy learners, their teachers will need a sensitivity to their interests and preoccupations and a commitment to recognize and help them use their 'funds of knowledge' (Moll *et al.* 1992) so that new experiences at school develop from those at home, not negate them.

Let us finally turn to Jamie and his grandmother, whose shared cultural knowledge has its basis in an oral tradition that has been transmitted over generations:

> As I leave the nursery to get into my car, Jamie and his grandmother Margaret are going home too. Margaret lights a cigarette and they walk up the road hand in hand. After a few metres, they stop and turn to face each other, Jamie is recounting an incident from his day and Margaret listens intently, facing him, still holding his hand. After several minutes have passed they turn and carry on up the road.

Acknowledgements

I would like to thank Jamie and his family for their generosity in sharing their private world with me and the nursery staff for enabling me to observe their knowledge and skill at first hand.

Chapter 6

Storytelling and Latino elders
What can children learn?

Irma M. Olmedo

Many advocates of urban school reform call for educators to find ways to actively involve the community in the educational process. Educators write about the importance of involving parents as partners in schools and developing thematic units that integrate knowledge and skills from various disciplines to provide a more holistic view of the curriculum. These goals of school reform and curriculum renewal have rarely become an integral part of many urban classrooms, however. It is easier to 'talk the talk' than 'walk the walk' when it comes to making community members true partners in the educational process and developing integrated interdisciplinary multicultural curricula. Occasionally schools will hold an ethnic festival or celebrate a holiday and invite parents to participate, whether to cook a meal, teach a dance, or share something of their ethnic culture. Rarely do schools develop ongoing projects in which students interact with community people, and even more rarely do they use these experiences as content and context for curriculum building and literacy development.

This chapter analyses storytelling activities of a group of elderly Latinas, grandmothers or *abuelitas*, as they interacted with fourth graders from a dual language school in Chicago. The research is based on an intergenerational project called Project Generations, between the children, mostly 9 year olds, and residents of a senior citizen centre. The argument presented here is that schools should explore ways to engage children in learning about the community through actual community-based activities across generations. Some activities, if well planned, can be meaningful learning opportunities for children and can open up possibilities for enhancing curriculum content and literacy development. Moreover, given the important role that elderly people have traditionally played in some communities of colour, there may be other lessons to be learned when young children are exposed to their wisdom.

An important component of Project Generations was to also examine the value of community-based projects for teacher education. Teacher educators argue that teachers should be sensitized to the benefits of providing a multicultural dimension to their curriculum. Nevertheless, much of what passes for multicultural curriculum has been criticized by educational theorists as superficial, inaccurate or subject to stereotyping the other. In addition, given that many teachers come from ethnic, racial and class backgrounds different from those of their students, it is difficult for these teachers to understand aspects of the community culture that can be used for curriculum development. Moreover, without actual experiences with community members, a static view of culture may be conceptualized, one which may stereotype members of communities that contain within them a great deal of diversity.

Theoretical background

The literature and research on multicultural education, which is quite extensive, addresses the need for teachers to find ways to affirm cultural diversity in the development of curriculum and implementation of instruction (Giroux 1992; Sleeter and Grant 1993; Nieto 1996; Valdés 1996; Banks and Banks 1997). Some of the multicultural curriculum models highlight the need for teachers to broaden their understanding of the cultures of their students and families so that the concepts children are exposed to are authentic portrayals of the characteristics of these populations. Moreover, the literature highlights the importance of integrating this knowledge into all the content areas, rather than as isolated information for special holidays and occasions. Banks' model for the integration of ethnic content into the curriculum provides a challenge for educators to move beyond the heroes and holidays approaches to culture, the most common way that ethnic cultures are portrayed in the curriculum (Banks and Banks 1997). Moreover, by highlighting the knowledge construction process, the model provides a rationale for teachers to engage students in enquiry-based projects whereby the students themselves construct the knowledge, rather than depend on a 'banking model' where concepts are prepackaged for them. Critical theory, by focusing on structural inequalities in society, provides a challenge to educators to engage students in learning activities through which they can understand the perspectives of the other, such as racial and ethnic minorities (Giroux 1992; Kincheloe and Steinberg 1997).

One component of Project Generations was to explore the funds of knowledge of Latino senior citizens. The 'funds of knowledge' concept presents a theoretical framework for challenging the deficit models of Latino communities that have characterized a great deal of educational theorizing (Moll and Greenberg 1990; Moll *et al.* 1992; Vélez-Ibáñez and Greenberg 1992; González *et al.* 1995). It recognizes that community members have intellectual and vocational resources, skills and knowledge, wisdom that is generally not acknowledged as relevant to the educational process of the schools.

Senior citizens have a wealth of knowledge of many areas in their culture. This knowledge is often lost because younger generations do not display interest in or may not be provided with opportunities to dialogue with elders about what they know. This is therefore a double loss, to the elder who feels unappreciated and to the younger generation member who could benefit from the funds of knowledge of the ancestors. Loss of this knowledge is especially critical in communities of colour whose histories and traditions may not be a part of the public record because they are poor, immigrant or non-English-speaking.

Another body of research literature relevant to Project Generations was the literature on oral history and reminiscence (Sitton *et al.* 1983; Allen 1987; Berger-Gluck and Patai 1991; Seixas 1993; Olmedo 1997). Oral history approaches can serve to include the experiences of underrepresented groups in school curricula and provide children with opportunities for inquiry learning. The body of research on the use of reminiscence in working with elderly people also provided guidance for this project (Baum 1980; Molinari and Reichlin 1984; Olmedo 2001). This research attests to the potential of oral history, reminiscence activities, life history and autobiography with elderly people in affirming their life experiences and improving their quality of life in institutional settings.

The literature on narrative highlights its value for providing affirmation and self-understanding for the narrators, especially elderly people and others who have been silenced in our society (Benmayor *et al.* 1987; Myerhoff 1992; Hatch and Wisniewski 1995; Olmedo 1999). Teachers who seek to engage students in listening to the life stories of elderly people can discover that narrative comprehension and production are important features of literacy development (Schieffelin and Gilmore 1986; Johnson 2000).

Project Generations

The women engaged in Project Generations were residents of a senior citizen centre in the northside of Chicago, a diverse community with a heavy concentration of Latinos, both citizens and immigrants. Over the three years that this research was carried out, 22 women between the ages of 68 and 92, predominantly Spanish-speaking, participated in the project. (Three native English-speaking women participated in the group but their stories were not analyzed for this chapter.) The majority of the residents of the centre were Puerto Rican, but there was also a Guatemalan, a Panamanian and a Mexican in the group of women who chose to participate in the project. For the most part the women had had minimal schooling, less than four grades in their countries.

The children engaged in the project were fourth graders, mostly 9 year olds, who came from a Spanish-English dual language public school in Chicago. The dual language school aimed to foster Spanish-English bilingualism among all the children in the school. The school was racially, ethnically and linguistically diverse, with about 70 percent of students from Spanish language home backgrounds and some African American and Euro-American children of various ethnicities. The project was cross-cultural because of this ethnic and racial mixture. It fostered bilingualism because the children had to interact with the *abuelitas* in the appropriate language. In addition, the teacher would generally pair up a Spanish-speaking child with a native English speaker so that the more fluent Spanish-speaking children could serve as language mediators for their less bilingual peers.

The entire class of 22 children would visit the senior centre once a month for approximately two hours. The children would meet in pairs with an *abuelita* for their activities and discussions in a large community room in the centre. Each month the teacher had a series of activities and themes that formed the topic of discussion at the centre, topics that were related to themes in the fourth grade curriculum. For example, one curricular theme was learning about the Rainforest. In this theme the teacher integrated geography, maths, science, aspects of ecology and environmental studies into the activities. Language and literacy development were always part of the curriculum objectives and therefore reading, writing and listening to stories were also included into the unit.

During the visits the children interviewed the *abuelitas* about their life stories and engaged them in a variety of activities, such as storytelling, maths games, arts and crafts. Sessions between the children and the women, as well as classroom lessons related to the activities, were videotaped and/or audiotaped, field notes were taken and participants were interviewed for their impressions of the activities. One level of analysis for this chapter examined how the *abuelitas* engaged in storytelling and the potential connections of the stories to the curriculum.

As the project researcher, I would generally meet with the *abuelitas* the day before the children's visit. In these sessions we discussed the topics or activities planned by the teacher. The purpose of these sessions was to have the women share experiences and stories with their peers and have them consider how to share these with the children. These sessions were also videotaped for analysis. Often at these meetings the women would start out claiming that they did not know much about the topic. The initial belief of the women was that there was nothing they could contribute to topics taught in school curricula because they themselves had had so little schooling. They did not appear to recognize how much they knew about many of these topics merely from their life experiences.

One aspect of the project involved the children writing a book that included their versions of the stories told by the *abuelitas*. This was a strategy for promoting language and literacy and enhancing the children's writing skills. These books were presented to the *abuelitas* at the end of the year in a school ceremony held in their honour. The process of writing, editing and publishing these stories ensured that Project Generations was not conceived as only a nice field trip for the children or a service activity for the elderly women but as a legitimate educational activity linked to the academic curriculum of the school.

Abuelitas' narratives and the curriculum

The stories analyzed here were all told in Spanish, the language used by most of the *abuelitas*. In this chapter I analyze three narratives and discuss them in relation to five features that characterized their storytelling approaches. First, the stories and narratives were generally linked to the women's personal experiences. Even in situations where they could have told a story without linking themselves to it or inserting themselves in it, they rarely appeared to do so. This personalizing of stories may have increased the attentiveness of the children who demonstrated much curiosity about these women's lives and especially about their youth. Second, the stories or narratives frequently contained moral lessons or *consejos* that the women tried to transmit to the children. Delgado-Gaitan (1994a) describes the prevalence of these types of narratives in the conversations of Latino adults as a way that parents transmit their values to their children. A third characteristic of the storytelling was the informational detail that was contained in some of the narratives and which could be used to expand curricular concepts. A fourth aspect was the performative quality of the storytelling episodes, the ways that the women employed to dramatize the telling. A fifth feature was the strategies the women employed to enhance the children's comprehension. The analysis of these narratives will also point to the kinds of skills that students were able to learn from listening to the stories and subsequently using them as a basis for writing their own versions.

As the children pursued the thematic unit on the Rainforest, there were a lot of conversations about animals, insects, plants, weather, products from the rain forest, geography, environmental issues and endangered species. The children brought books with them with pictures of some of the animals that could be found in the rain forest. The pictures served as a stimulus to some of the conversations and the basis for some planned activities, such as a true/false game about animals in the rain forest. The teacher also encouraged the children to elicit stories about a happy, sad, or frightening moment in the women's lives as a stimulus to story sharing.

The first story analyzed here was told by doña Myrna, a soft-spoken Puerto Rican woman in her seventies who attended the Generations sessions fairly regularly. (All names are pseudonyms.) After the children in her group had spoken about the animals in the rain forest, including insects, she told the story of the *dengue* mosquito in Puerto Rico, a mosquito that had caused an epidemic of fevers in the 1970s on the island and which had in part been responsible for her migration to Chicago.

> *Doña Myrna:* También se corre el peligro de picarte por el mosquito del dengue. También se puede dar ahí en la selva, en los tanques; en las aguas claras también crecen. Cuando hay agua clara, empozada, si no está tapada ahí se cría el mosquito, el mosquito del dengue. Luego se va al fondo y cuando tiene alitas que crece entonces sale de ahí y va y pica la persona. Y esa picada si tú no te atiendes se te vuelve en dengue. Hay tres clases de dengue. Uno le dicen, tiene fiebre, le dicen el flu. El dengue hemorrágico que es el más malo, porque cuando pica a uno que tiene la enfermedad del dengue y entonces te pica a ti, te transmite la enfermedad porque ya llevaba la sangre de ese paciente que estaba enfermo. Entonces ese dengue a ti te baja la defensa del cuerpo. Tú te quedas sin fuerza, con fiebre; si no te mandan ligero al hospital puedes morir. Cuando yo me vine de Puerto Rico habían 30 muertos

porque había dengue allá. Eso fue unas de las cosas que me hizo venir porque yo padezco de alergias.

You also run the risk of being bitten by the dengue mosquito. It can also be found there in the jungle, in tanks; in clear waters they also grow. When there is clear 'welled' water, if it isn't covered, the mosquito can grow there, the dengue mosquito. Later it sinks to the bottom and when it develops wings and grows then it leaves there and goes bites someone. And that bite, if you don't take care of it, can become dengue. There are three types of dengue. One is called, it gives a fever, they call it the flu. The 'hemorrhagic' dengue is the worst because when it bites someone who has the dengue and then it bites you, it transmits the disease because it was already carrying the blood of the patient that was sick. Then the dengue lowers your body defences. You'll be left weak, with fever; if they don't send you to the hospital right away you can die. When I came here from Puerto Rico there were already 30 deaths because of the dengue there. That's one of the reasons that I came here because I'm very allergic.

Several features of this story can be highlighted. Doña Myrna communicated a great deal of information related to science concepts such as the life cycle of the mosquito, the transmission of disease and their symptoms. Though not quoted in this passage, she proceeded to describe other insects, including a range of different types of mosquitoes that were common to Caribbean islands and their characteristics. None of this knowledge was a result of formal academic science study in school but rather from her lived experience with mosquitoes in Puerto Rico and the dengue epidemic. Whereas the children may have thought of mosquitoes as one insect, in the conversation with her they learned that even in the insect world of the mosquito there was extensive diversity. She used a personal experience as a strategy to connect herself to the story, how the dengue fever influenced her migration to Chicago.

The second story analyzed here was told by doña Gloria. She was a self-confident Panamanian woman in her seventies who had married one of the residents in order to have legal status in the US. The centre had celebrated the wedding between them with music and dancing. Doña Gloria was a very social woman who loved to tell jokes, to cook and to dance. In one of the Generations sessions, she decided to talk about Panama, where she grew up, and she brought down a small souvenir of a little hut, an example of the kinds of houses that were typical of the interior of the country. She pointed to each part of the hut as she described it.

Doña Gloria: Esto se llama paja. Paja. ¿Por qué paja? Porque ellos eran muy pobres para hacer material de cemento de así. Porque no tenían dinero. ¿Verdad? Mi país se llama Panamá y esta estructura es del interior de Panamá. Se llama interior porque está afuera de Panama . . . un countryside . . . ¿ No? Entonces esta parte de ahí se llama Caballete. Caballete. Y esto es para que no se les moje en la casa y cuando el agua cae aquí. El agua puede correr por toda la paja y se escurre. Entonces ellos no se mojan. Entonces, se me olvidaba, esto donde está montada la casa se llama base. Una base. Como aquí cuando hacen la base de cemento y montan una estructura ahí. Entonces esto es una estructura de madera. Porque todavía no tienen dinero para hacer la base de mampostería, de cemento.

This is called straw. Straw. Why straw? Because they were too poor to use cement. Because they didn't have money. Right? My country is called Panama and this structure [house] is from the interior. It's called interior because it's outside of Panama . . . the countryside . . . No? Well, this part over there is called the ridge. *Caballete* [As she points to the top of the house]. This is so they won't get wet and when the water falls over here, the water can run down the straw and drain. Then they don't get wet. Then, I was forgetting, this where the house is mounted is called a base. A base. Just like here when they make a cement base and they build a structure there. So this is a wooden structure. Because they still don't have money to make the base out of masonry, of cement.

This narrative conformed most closely to the didactic mode found in classrooms. One feature to consider were the strategies that doña Gloria used to make her narrative comprehensible to the children. Krashen (1982) addresses the importance of comprehensible input in teaching concepts to English language learners and ways to shelter instruction to maximize comprehension. Doña Gloria's description of the house was rather complex and she tried to ensure that the children understood. She pointed to each of the sections of the hut as she explained each part, highlighting the new vocabulary by repetition. She spoke slowly and articulated carefully as was evident in the videotape. She repeated her explanations and rephrased several sections: i.e., they were very poor – they didn't have money; so they won't get wet – so the water can run down the straw; the selection of the word cement as an explanation for the more difficult word *mampostería*. At one point she even code-switched to English, using the word 'countryside', to distinguish the interior from the capital city, perhaps realizing that her explanation of 'interior' may not have been that clear.

Though the entire narrative is not quoted here, in this and other narratives doña Gloria managed to address issues of the geography of Panama and Central America, the effect of geography and economic factors on home construction and the kinds of animals that could be found in the country. She even told a story about large turtles that she used to cook in Panama, describing how she would cook them, how good they would taste and explaining that they were becoming extinct. This led to a discussion of features of the rain forest which were being destroyed because of development, another theme that was pursued as part of the fourth grade science curriculum, the environmental impact of development policies on the environment. Though the children could have read about these themes in a social studies textbook, it is not likely that they would have shown as much interest in the reading as they displayed to her as she told her stories.

The third story was told by doña Zaida, a Guatemalan woman, an active member of a fundamentalist Christian church whose religious beliefs would sometimes be an indirect theme in her narratives. She had grandchildren living in Guatemala whom she missed a great deal. Interacting with the children in Project Generations appeared to fill a void for her. She would often tell stories that included her grandchildren as characters. In one of the sessions related to activities of the rain forest, she decided to tell a story about Guatemalan ants to her group.

Doña Zaida: Les voy a decir de unas hormigas. Yo visitaba a mi hija. Mi hija. El esposo de mi hija es ingeniero agrónomo, él se dedica a la agricultura pero solo la del café. Una vez que yo fui a visitarlos fuimos a una reunión. Cuando regresamos toda la casa estaba llena de hormigas. Pero no había ni un pedacito sin hormigas. Entonces yo le dije a mi nieto Cristian, 'Cristian trae una escoba para matar todas estas hormigas'. Mi nieto contestó, 'Abuelita, a esos animales no se les mata porque estos animales vienen a traer comida y se las llevan. Ellas están buscando qué comer. Y vas a ver abuelita que en un ratito no van a haber'. 'Pues yo no voy a poder dormir con esos animales ahí', le digo. '¿Verdad? ¿Cómo vas a poder dormir con todo lleno de hormigas?'

David: ¿En tu cama?

Doña Zaida: Hasta en la cama había. Mi nieto sacudió, 'Acuéstate abuelita'. Yo me acosté. Al otro día me desperté a las 6 de la mañana. No había ni una hormiga. Todas se habían ido. Son las hormigas proveedoras. Ellas consiguen qué comer y lo almacenan para cuando ellas ya no pueden salir por el frío. Así hacen en mi país. Eso yo no lo sabía porque no vivía ahí pero mi nieto sí. Estaba como de tu edad, pero ahora tiene como 13 años.

Doña Zaida: I'll tell you about some ants. I was visiting my daughter. My daughter. My daughter's husband is an agricultural engineer. He works in agriculture but only in coffee production. Once when I went to visit them we went to a meeting. When we returned the whole house was filled with ants. There wasn't even a small spot without ants. So I told my grandson Christian, 'Christian, bring a broom so we can kill all these ants'. My grandson answered, 'Grandma, one shouldn't kill those little animals because they come to bring food and then take it back. They're looking for something to eat. And you'll see grandma that in a little while there won't be any'. 'Well, I won't be able to sleep with all those insects there', I told him. 'Isn't that true? How would you be able to sleep with everything full of ants?'

David: In your bed?

Doña Zaida: Even in the bed there were some. My grandson shook [the sheet].

'Lie down, grandma'. And I lay down. The following day I awoke at 6 in the morning. There was not even one ant, all of them had gone. These are the provider ants. They find things to eat and they store it for the time when they can't go out because of the cold. That's what they do in my country. I didn't know that because I didn't live there, but my grandson did. He was about your age but now he's about 13.

The two children who were listening to the stories were quite engrossed as they listened. She dramatized the story by using dialogue and changing voices to imitate the speech of her grandson. She used voice intonation and repetition to dramatize the large number of ants in the house. She made herself a character in the story and also tried to connect David to the story by comparing his age to that of her grandson's. Her religious orientation was evident in the comments that she attributed to her grandson that the ants were not to be killed and that they also had to try to survive. In other stories she articulated positions about the sacredness of God's creatures more directly.

Myerhoff (1992) addresses the performative quality of the group sharing of stories from her own research. During the telling of her story, doña Zaida became a performer before the children, dramatizing some aspect of the story, taking on the role of the interlocutors in the original story, shuddering as she recounted the frightening aspect of the story and generally engaging the children in her performance. She seemed to want the children to share in her feelings about the ants and those of her grandson.

Children's literacy extensions

Project Generations fulfilled a variety of objectives in the classroom curriculum. A critical part of that curriculum was the development and extension of language, literacy and writing skills. These skills were especially important given the dual language orientation of the school and the commitment to develop and enhance the children's bilingualism. One classroom activity connected to the project was the writing of stories and books based on the narratives told by the women. Students were encouraged to write the stories in the language spoken by the *abuelitas* so that the books could be presented to them as a culminating activity at the year-end ceremony. Some also wrote the books in both English and Spanish, receiving help in the translation from classmates and the teacher. The children used the computer lab to write drafts based on the questions or themes that they had discussed with the *abuelitas*. These drafts were subsequently revised to provide more details and information or to correct language errors. Eventually they produced a finished product that could be bound as part of a book.

Following is the text of the story written by David as part of his book and based on the previous story told by doña Zaida. As many of the children had learned to do, he referred to doña Zaida as *mi abuelita*, a sign of respect for elderly people.

Mi abuelita me contó que una vez cuando ella se fue a la casa de su hija o su nieto vio muchas hormigas en la casa. Y la casa estaba llena de hormigas. En la casa no había un espacio sin hormigas. Mi abuelita dijo a su nieto que traiga una escoba para matar las hormigas, pero su nieto dijo que estos insectos no se matan y las hormigas traen comida y cuando está muy frío agarran comida. Entonces el nieto dijo a su abuelita que se duerma en su cama y se durmió. Cuando se despertó ya no había ninguna hormiga.

My grandmother told me that once when she went to her daughter's or grandson's house she saw many ants in the house. And the house was full of ants. In the house there wasn't even one spot without ants. My grandmother told her grandson to bring a broom to kill the ants, but her grandson said that one shouldn't kill those insects, that the ants bring food and when it's very cold they grab [obtain] food. Then the grandson told his grandma that she should sleep in her bed and she fell asleep. When she awoke there were no longer any ants.

David's story exemplifies the process of knowledge construction at work. His written reconstruction of the story shows that he understood that stories have a beginning, a middle and an end and that the writer must select the important details for the writing. He did not merely repeat the story the same way it was told to him. For example, he did not use the direct quotes that doña Zaida had used in her story. He omitted information that was peripheral to the essence of the story, such as the son-in-law's profession or the meeting that doña Zaida was attending before returning to the house. One feature of the story that he emphasized was the large number of ants present in the house. He was able to recapture the drama of the story through the repetition of certain phrases, just as doña Zaida had done. He started by saying that there were many ants, then he emphasized that detail by saying the house was full of ants and then again he dramatized it when he said there was not even one spot without ants. These were also aspects of the storytelling style of doña Zaida.

Conclusion

The examples included in this chapter show that the *abuelitas* engaged in this project did have funds of knowledge that they were able to share and that connections could be made between this knowledge and curriculum content. The women initially claimed that they could not teach anything to the children since they themselves had had so little formal schooling. However, they came to appreciate how much they knew about a whole range of issues, knowledge that came predominantly from their lived experiences. When one member of the group volunteered an experience or story, it would stimulate the memories of others who would then join in to share their own stories. The group sharing of stories took on a performative quality as the women became actresses and audience for each other, trying to dramatize features of the experiences they wanted to share. Because of the performative skills that the *abuelitas* exhibited during the story-telling episodes, they were able to actively engage the children as an audience. The adjustments that the *abuelitas* made in their language use meant that the stories were made more comprehensible for the children who were developing their Spanish skills.

In Project Generations the children were able to engage in enquiry learning. In preparation for the visits the children discussed what elderly people could do. Their responses highlighted what 'old people' could not do, they could not run or do anything fast and they did not know very much because they would start to forget things as they got older. The children discussed the kinds of questions they would want to ask the *abuelitas*. Though as a class they developed sample questions for the sessions, in actual interaction they were able to raise their own questions to get clarification, satisfy their curiosity, or get more details. Moreover, through the related activities, such as rewriting of the stories, they made judgements about what features of the stories were important and what ways of retelling would capture the style used by the *abuelitas*. The children were developing their literacy skills, sometimes in two languages.

When the children were interviewed and asked about any surprises they experienced as a result of the activities with the *abuelitas*, one child responded, 'They know a lot of stuff!' The fact that the women were able to share detailed stories about issues that the children were studying in school was a surprise to many of them. This surprise challenged misconceptions about elderly people, especially those with little formal schooling.

Analysis of these stories showed that they contained information and concepts that could be connected to the elementary school curriculum. These included issues such as geography, science concepts about animals, plants and the insect world, effects of economics on people's ways of living, including home construction, diet, mobility and causes and effects of migration to the United States. Though the school project may not have been consciously developed with critical theory in mind, by engaging the children in meaningful activities with a population of poor elderly Latinas, some of them non-English-speaking migrants, children were exposed to people who ordinarily have no voice in this society. The children are learning that these people have important things to say and share and that their stories have academic legitimacy.

If urban schools are to find ways to involve the community in the educational process, teachers have to believe that community members have something to offer that is relevant to what is taught. They can believe this only if they have ongoing opportunities to interact with community members in the context of planned activities with their students. If multicultural education is to become more than a code-word, classroom lessons have to be based on authentic infor-mation about people, enhanced through appreciation for community funds of knowledge. Teachers have to explore ways to infuse this cultural knowledge into all areas of the curriculum and not merely as colourful add-ons for the celebration of holidays or ethnic festivals. A critical aspect of this infusion is the ways that literacy skills can be enhanced when children have opportunities to go beyond the traditional classroom and textbook lessons and engage in enquiry with elders of a community. Project Generations provided an opportunity to research how inter-generational, cross-cultural learning experiences can contribute to accomplishing these goals.

Part II

Friends as teachers

Introduction to Part II

Children's peers participate in the web of learning relationships. The chapters in this part analyze peer teaching and learning with special attention to the classroom and broader sociohistorical contexts in which such interactions occur and to cognitive and social aspects of these interactions. The importance of children's first language is clearly illustrated. Together, these chapters expand our understanding of the supportive interactions that generate learning and the potential power of peers as mediators of language and literacy learning when their knowledge and skills are recognized and put to use.

In Chapter 7, Susi Long, Donna Bell and Jim Brown focus on three 5-year-old Mexican American children in Bell's kindergarten and the strategies used by the children and their Spanish- and English-speaking peers to scaffold each other's literacy and language learning. Emphasizing the power of peer interactions, the authors describe the expertise of both peer teachers and learners, particularly in informal and play interactions. They illustrate the many ways the children took control of their own learning as well as Bell's role in creating a classroom community in which the Mexican American children, their language and their abilities were visible and valued.

Charmian Kenner, in Chapter 8, describes a peer teaching project. Four 6-year-old children, one Syrian, one Palestinian and two Chinese, who were learning Arabic and Chinese in schools organized by their communities, were asked to teach these scripts to four peers in their regular school classroom. Kenner provides a close analysis of the children's reinterpretation of the socially constructed sign systems they were learning in their community schools and of their appropriation of related literacy practices. She describes the positive outcomes for all the children: for the bilingual ones whose biliterate expertise was appreciated by their peers and teacher and for their monolingual peers whose interest in other cultures and language was stimulated.

Within the context of British policy on English for immigrants, Yuangguang Chen and Eve Gregory, in Chapter 9, provide a finely tuned analysis of bilingual exchange teaching in the interactions of two Chinese girls, the 9-year-old one newly arrived from Hong Kong, the 8-year-old girl born in Britain and fluent in Chinese and English. Though the older one knew little English, she took control of the lesson as the younger child helped her understand her school work. Based on this investigation of the social and reciprocal nature of bilingual literacy and problem solving, the authors argue that the concept of *synergy* be used instead of *scaffolding* or *guided participation* to characterize the girls' joint activity.

Chapter 10, by Manjula Datta, provides an analysis of friendship as a pathway to literacy, using excerpts from interactions between three 7-year-old boys in an inner London primary school – one Turkish, one Anglo-British, one Algerian French – and two 9-year-old boys of Greek origin in a Greek community school. Datta illustrates the children's sharing of linguistic expertise and cultural knowledge as the developing bilinguals as well as the native English speakers took on the role of expert. Given the opportunity to interact freely in friendship groups and the provision of culturally relevant texts, the boys together constructed personal, meaningful connections to the texts they were reading.

In Chapter 11, Rebecca Rogers and Melissa Mosley analyze a community of practice among White working-class 7 year olds in Mosley's second grade classroom. The context consists of a unit on African American history taught from a critical literacy perspective as well as the children's community where they lived and where their parents worked. Arguing that the *goals* of a community of practice were their central concern, they describe the construction of a critical stance by the peer group as the children developed a sense of their own agency and an interest in taking action for social justice through their discussions, questioning, negotiations and role play.

Chapter 7

Making a place for peer interaction

Mexican American kindergarteners learning language and literacy

Susi Long with Donna Bell and Jim Brown

> Nobody is ever going to teach me. I will not remember. When I play [with my friends], I understand but if [teachers] teach me, they just tell me, 'OK, say this' and I say it and I never remember it.
>
> (Kelli, age 8)

These words capture a key finding from a nine-month study of cross-cultural learning (Long 1998a, 1998b). My 8-year-old American daughter was learning to get along in home, community and school worlds in Iceland. In contrast to teacher-led lessons in school, her informal interactions with peers provided the primary contexts for language and literacy learning. Moving back to the United States, this finding motivated my interest in understanding more about how second language learners and their native-speaking peers support one another and about the opportunities they might or might not have for meaningful interaction in classrooms.

The move back to the US took me to South Carolina in the southeastern region of the country. The state has a limited history with new language learners and is just beginning to explore related issues. Since the early 1990s, however, the Latino population – largely Mexican American – has tripled in South Carolina. In 2000, that population composed 2.4 percent of the state's population. Settling in to my new job as a university faculty member in a college of education, I was immediately involved with children and teachers in local schools. Through my work in one school in particular, I became aware of the growing Mexican American population in the state. It is significant that I had not already learned about that population through media, community events, or even through academic activity at the university. Searching for information, I found newspaper articles that revealed a strong assimilationist attitude: 'Assimilating the Hispanic population into the American cultural mainstream . . . will be a long process in South Carolina' (West 2001). Although admirable attempts are being made to embrace the Mexican American population,[1] it is clear that Mexican Americans are barely acknowledged in most parts of the state and rarely embraced for the rich contributions they can make to life in South Carolina.

Interested in understanding more about marginalization in the state, I interviewed a key figure in the State Department of Education about the realities of growing up Mexican American. Her parents immigrated to the US from Mexico and she was raised in Texas before moving to South Carolina. In the course of our conversation, I asked what she thought about the terms *Hispanic* and *Latino* (commonly used as labels to refer to Spanish-speaking groups in the US). She said:

> My personal preference now is to be referred to as Mexican American [rather than Hispanic or Latino]. This wasn't always the case. Growing up in Texas in the late 1940s and 1950s was no fun at all. Being of Mexican heritage was not a good thing. Just to give you an example, while touring in the southwest as a member of [a university's] chapel choir – I was one of their soloists – we stopped at a restaurant to eat lunch. There, prominently placed on the front door, was a large sign that read, 'Mexicans and dogs to the back'. Today, of course, I am very proud of who I am, thus my preference to be referred to as Mexican American.

She continued by explaining, 'I am just now at a place where I feel safe identifying myself first as Mexican American'. When I thanked her for sharing her experiences, she further illuminated the feeling of marginalization saying, 'No one ever asked me to talk about my heritage before'. I asked what she thought the situation was like for Mexican American children in South Carolina today and she said, 'I expect that they experience a lot of the same experiences and feelings that I faced as a young child . . . they are dark enough to be different and their double whammy is they speak a different language'.

As I grew in my awareness of the fact that the Mexican American population in South Carolina was large and growing but severely marginalized, I also began to realize that many local teachers were not equipped with knowledge or experiences that allowed them to understand, appreciate and thereby embrace second language learners in ways that would enrich the lives of all students. Grounded in the earlier study of my daughter's experiences in Iceland, I wondered about the opportunities that developing bilinguals and their English-only peers had (or did not have) to learn with and from one another. I wondered if, given the opportunity, these children might use the same kinds of strategies that my daughter and her friends used to scaffold language and literacy learning. What other kinds of strategies would they use? How might peer interactions positively impact on the learning of the native-speaker as well as that of the new language learner? What kinds of environments supported such interactions? Finally, how might teachers develop and use deepened understandings of culture and interaction to create contexts that would enrich the learning and perspectives of native-English speakers while supporting second language learners learning to get along in English contexts? These questions led to the initiation of a six-month study of six second language learners (5 year olds) in an American kindergarten. I wanted to know whether or not these children and their native-English-speaking peers were strategic in their support for one another and, if so, what kinds of strategies they used. In this chapter, I focus on three Mexican American kindergarteners from that study: Marcial, Martita and Juan.[2]

Looking at contexts and getting started

Marcial, Martita and Juan attended kindergarten in a school that drew from predominantly low socioeconomic communities (86 percent of the families qualified for free or reduced lunch meaning that parents' income was below that which required them to pay for breakfast or lunch at school). The student population in the school was 78 percent African American English-only speakers, 12 percent bilingual or developing bilinguals (children whose first language was other than English) and 10 percent White monolingual English speakers. All of the 5 year olds in the school district who were learners of English as a second language were bused to attend kindergarten in this school. In Marcial, Martita and Juan's class of 23 children, there were 16 non-native English speakers representing four different language backgrounds: Spanish, Romanian, French and Mandarin.

Using field notes, videotape and audiotape, Donna (the kindergarten teacher) and Jim (a graduate assistant and supervisor of student teachers in Donna's classroom) collected data from September to the end of March during formal and informal school rituals and routines including: whole class lessons, free choice activity times, independent reading and writing periods, one-on-one teacher–child interactions, transitions from the classroom to other classes (art, music, physical education), lunchtime and recess. School data also included representative samples of children's writing and drawing and interviews with the children to seek further understandings about their perspectives on language and literacy learning.

Donna, Ms. Alvarez (Donna's teaching assistant and a native-Spanish speaker) and I made home visits to interview parents of the three children who are the focus of this chapter. The purpose of these interviews was to learn about the parents' background (reasons for coming to the US, logistics of the move), their personal language and literacy histories, how literacy was used in the homes and perspectives about literacy learning.

Donna, Jim and I collaboratively analyzed data during multiple analysis sessions in which transcribed and documental data were scrutinized for emergent patterns. Those patterns were named and coded as categories and considered in terms of frequency, quality and significance of evidence. Each of us further examined data sets related to specific categories. Interpretations were shared across the research team as a form of triangulation through which individual interpretations were confirmed or unconfirmed.

Big ideas that guide the work

The work described in this chapter is grounded in a sociocultural perspective of learning and a commitment to looking critically at language and literacy practices for the purpose of addressing issues of social justice by affecting change in classrooms. Because traditional understandings of language and literacy learning are grounded in a deficit perspective that looks first at gaps in children's knowledge (what they do not know), their social and cultural histories are too often ignored and they enter school viewed as blank slates. Thus, this work was initiated based in the beliefs that

- there are valid and sophisticated language and literacy systems in every home
- by devaluing what they already know and hold dear, we limit the learning potential for all children
- we learn through interactions with other learners in meaningful contexts
- learning is based on opportunities to connect what we know with what we are coming to know.

The works of Lev Vygotsky, Barbara Rogoff, Gordon Wells and Judith Lindfors have greatly influenced the development of the conceptual frame that underlies this study. Vygotsky's (1978) view of learning as a social process came to life as data were collected through interactions with participants and observations of their interactions with one another. This perspective guided not only method but also analysis as we looked at strategies used among peers to support participation and growth. Rogoff's (1990) notion that learners guide one another's participation as they move seamlessly in and out of expert and novice roles became a key expansion of Vygotsky's theory for us as we considered the children's interactions. Analysis of data was further influenced as we examined Wells' (1999) explanation that, as we learn with one another, there is no designated teacher, that the more knowledgeable other need not be present but that we draw on all that we have experienced to create new contexts for learning. Finally, Lindfors' (1999) interpretation of Vygotsky's zone of proximal development as the place where we engage one another in 'going beyond' (Lindfors 1999: 14) provided a lens through which we considered children's learning as they interacted with adults and with one another.

In the field of language acquisition, the works of Michael Halliday, Roger Brown and Brian Cambourne were also influential. The notion that we learn language as we use it purposefully, form following function (Brown 1970; Halliday 1975) was key to understanding the importance of children taking control of their learning in meaningful contexts. Our work was also guided by the understanding that learners are supported when they receive authentic demonstrations and when they are comfortable enough to risk approximations while receiving feedback that nudges them in new directions (Cambourne 1988).

Focusing on the importance of valuing what children already know, the works of Heath (1983), Taylor and Dorsey-Gaines (1988) and Moll *et al.* (1992) served as a foundation that urged us to look for validity in language and literacy learning beyond the walls of the school. From them and from Ladson-Billings (1995),

Purcell-Gates (1995), Nieto (1999) and Delpit and Dowdy (2002), we better understood the need to make visible the worlds of children whose homes and families have long been ignored in terms of the richness they have to offer all learners.

Operationalizing these ideas to consider how they might be used to affect change, the work of Freire (1973) and later Shor and Pari (1999) brought an important critical component to the notion of learning as social. These perspectives supported our commitment to bring unheard voices to the forefront and to use findings to think differently about teaching and learning. Finally, the concept of syncretism as applied to learning in and out of school helped us further interpret 'creative process[es] in which people transform culture as they draw on diverse resources, both familiar and new' (Long and Volk, 2004).

Getting to know Marcial, Martita, Juan: beliefs and practices at home

At the beginning of the school year, when asked if they could read, Martita, Marcial and Juan each explained that they could read only in Spanish. As Juan said, 'Puedo leer in español porque sé el español, y mucho español, pero no inglés' (I can read in Spanish because I know Spanish and a lot of Spanish but not English). The children seemed to see school as the place where literacy learning would take place. Even before they learned much English, they seemed confident that they would learn to read at school. During the second month of school, Juan said, 'Ahora estoy en la escuela, inglés es fácil' (Now I am in school, English is easy). The children also believed that once they learned to read and write at school, they would be able to help their mothers communicate in the English-speaking society. Juan explained, 'Si voy a la escuela, entonces enseñaré a mi mamá a comó aprender a leer' (If I go to school, then I will teach my mother how to learn to read). During parent interviews, all three mothers, monolingual speakers of Spanish, talked about the ways that their children helped them in the English-speaking community by translating at local shops and making phone calls. Even though their mothers could read in Spanish – 'Mi mamá sabe el español. Ella puede leer en español' (My mother knows Spanish. She can read in Spanish) (Marcial) – the children seemed to view reading in English as an important goal. The children viewed their fathers as readers in English – 'Mi papá sabe más inglés que mi mamá y mi mamá sabe apenas un poquito'. (My father knows more English than my mom and my mom just knows a little bit) (Martita). Learning to read was a standard that was highly valued in each home; the children were told that it was important for them to learn to read.

When asked about the reading and writing that was done at home by the children or by the parents, their mothers explained that they did little or no reading and writing at home. At the same time, a wide range of literacy artifacts was in evidence in each home – wall plaques with biblical verses, videotapes, English-language audio and videotapes, Spanish-language magazines and letters from Mexico. Their parents communicated the attitude that learning English was essential to success, praised the children's school work, asked their children for help with English and studied English themselves.

Juan, Martita and Marcial at school: syncretizing knowledge strategically

Peer interaction during informal engagements at school provided key scaffolds for language and literacy learning as Juan, Marcial, Martita and their peers used specific strategies and artifacts together. Their interactions were syncretic as they used aspects of their own cultural and linguistic backgrounds to help them make sense of new experiences. In the following paragraphs, data excerpts illustrate how the children strategically used language and cultural understandings from home and school to create opportunities for the successful participation and learning.

Engaging peers in side-by-side reading

A strong pattern that emerged across the data was the children's support of one another as they engaged in side-by-side reading. This typically happened as the children were coming in the classroom at the beginning of the day and during the free activity times each morning and afternoon. In various configurations, they would sit side-by-side and informally share a storybook together. In the process, they used specific strategies to support their interaction and merged their varied schema to create a new kind of reading experience that promoted success for all parties. For example:

> During free activity time early in the school year, Marcial walked to the bookcase and selected an English picture book. He sat on the floor and began to read the pictures (a reading strategy that had been demonstrated by the classroom teacher) aloud in Spanish. A few feet away Kiesha, an English-only kindergartener, sat on the floor reading the book, *Jack Be Nimble*. She used the pictures to read the story aloud in English. Kiesha finished the book, closed it and looked at Juan. He looked at her, she moved closer to him and she opened her book again, holding it so that he could see the pages. Then, Kiesha began rereading her book in English, this time reading directly *to* Juan. Martita moved closer so that she could also see the pages. Both Martita and Juan looked at the pictures in the book as Kiesha turned the pages and read the book aloud to them. Later, Martita and Juan sat with one another and picture-read using the same behaviours that had been demonstrated by Kiesha.

In this way, Kiesha subtly implemented a practice that supported Martita and Juan's participation in an English language and literacy event. As the Mexican

American children watched and listened to her read, they blended their own previous experiences with her demonstrations of reading in English and reading with a partner to create new understandings. Marcial, who, prior to this episode, had not been observed reading with a peer, moved from reading solitarily to reading with a friend. Through their interactions they used and learned the following strategies to be able to participate successfully:

- reading with a peer
- holding the book so that both children could see the pages
- turning the pages one at a time
- telling the story to one another by reading the pictures.

Translating and clarifying

Early in the year, the bilingual Spanish/English-speaking children provided support for Juan, Martita and Marcial by translating from English to Spanish and by clarifying adults' meanings and intentions. One example occurred in late September when Ms. Alvarez, the teaching assistant, was reading an English picture book to a small group of native-Spanish-speaking children including Marcial, who was just beginning to learn a few English words, and Maya, a Spanish/English bilingual. At one point, the teaching assistant stopped reading and asked the children, in English, to describe an illustration:

Ms. Alvarez:	Tell me what you see here.
Marcial:	[Looks closely at the illustration]
Ms. Alvarez:	What do you see here?
Marcial:	[Looks confused]
Maya:	¿Qué ve usted aquí? What do you see? [Maya translates Ms. Alvarez' question into Spanish and then she says it again in English]
Ms. Alvarez:	Tell me about the picture.
Maya:	He is looking.
Ms. Alvarez:	Marcial, what do you see here?
Marcial:	Hay un chico y un perro. [There's a boy and a dog]
Maya:	He sees a boy and a dog.

In this episode, Maya provided support for both Marcial and Ms. Alvarez by clarifying and translating. For Marcial, she translated the teaching assistant's English question, 'What do you see here?' into Spanish and then provided the English translation. Although Maya knew that the teaching assistant spoke both English and Spanish, she made the decision to translate for Marcial. When Marcial did not respond immediately, Maya seemed to know that he needed time to study the picture and to formulate a response. She then clarified his behaviour for the teaching assistant by explaining, 'He is looking'. Maya became the mediator who understood and was able to respond in ways that were supportive using strategies that the teaching assistant did not use. In a true syncretization of culture and language, by translating and clarifying, Maya created a situation in which Marcial could comprehend and participate with success. She drew from both cultures as she

- translated the adult's words into Spanish for Marcial and repeated the phrase in English
- understood Marcial's need for time to look and think
- interpreted Marcial's silence for the adult
- translated Marcial's response for the adult.

Providing demonstrations of appropriate behaviour

Often unintentionally, the bilingual or English-only children provided demonstrations of appropriate classroom behaviour that were observed and adopted by Martita, Juan and Marcial. By observing and mimicking behaviour, they learned what to do and say in the classroom, in the lunchroom and on the playground. This occurred consistently during the first months of the school year when they paid particularly close attention to the bilingual Spanish/English-speaking children and copied their behaviours. For instance, during a music lesson one day in early September:

> The music teacher stood in front of the class and the children sat in chairs arranged in a semicircle. The class was singing a song that required them to repeat lines after the teacher. While the other children were singing, Juan looked around the room, waved to the researcher and played with his chair but did not participate in the lesson. When Rocio, a bilingual Spanish/ English speaker, began to participate by singing and mimicking the teacher's movements, Juan looked at Rocio and began to sing and move.

In the beginning of the year, Marcial, Juan and Martita typically looked to their bilingual Spanish/English-speaking peers for guidance through demonstration – they watched and followed what the Spanish-speaking children said and did. As the year progressed, however, they began to include the monolingual English-speaking children as experts from whom they could learn. This is an example of an interesting shift in their ability to use understandings from other children's experiences. At first Martita, Juan and Marcial seemed more comfortable patterning their behaviour after children who were from their Mexican American neighbourhood and later, they more confidently took the lead from the native English-speaking children in the room. Strategically, the children:

- observed
- mimicked behaviours and movements
- took the lead from children who spoke their native language
- later took the lead from other children.

Enacting cultural roles through sociodramatic play

During free activity time, many of the children in the classroom often enacted the roles of adults in their cultural worlds. A popular form of sociodramatic play was *playing school*. The following illustration provides an example of the way the children involved themselves in the enactment of cultural roles through play. This school-play episode took place late in the year (March) after Martita, Juan and Marcial had developed some competence with English. Martita, in the role of teacher, led a reading lesson for a small group of children. Each child held a copy of the same book. In this example, Martita emulated the teacher's prior demonstrations of specific literacy strategies. Martita began by giving teacherly advice as she helped the children read the sentence, 'This tiger lives at the zig zag zoo':

Martita:	OK, like this [points to the words in the book as she reads]. This tiger.
Other children:	[Reading with Martita] This tiger [they stop at the word 'lives', because they don't recognize it].
Martita:	Something. Say 'something'. Skip it. [She is using the 'skip it and go on' strategy that the teacher has taught them; using the word 'something' as a place marker, Martita skips the word and leads her group to continue reading.] This tiger *something* at the zig zag.
Martita and Juan:	Zig zag.
Children:	Zig zag zoo.
Martita:	This tiger l-l-l-l-l- [beginning to sound out 'lives']

Martita enacted the role of teacher by using precisely the same reading strategies that the teacher demonstrated daily in whole class shared reading experiences. Given the opportunity to play teacher, Martita was able to practice the cultural roles of teacher as well as student. At the same time, she was able to support the others by acting as expert. Syncretically, she merged prior knowledge with the opportunity to play sociodramatically and supported peer participation strategically as she:

- pointed to the words as she read them
- stopped at a new word and suggested that they skip it and read on
- used the generic word, something, as a place marker while she read on for clues to the unknown words
- demonstrated/led the group in sounding out the initial consonant.

Celebrating the use of both Spanish and English

Celebrating one another's ability to use multiple languages was a striking and important aspect of the children's support for one another in this classroom.

Over and over, they applauded their peers' ability to speak languages other than English. They honoured bilingualness. The following data excerpt illustrates one such celebration. In this instance, the teacher led the class in reading the Morning Message (a message that she had written to the class on the board). She asked for volunteers to come to the board and circle words they recognized:

Teacher: Juan, what word do you know?
Juan: [Walks to the board; points to the word, 'October'] October.
Teacher: That's a big word.
Juan: [Circles the word 'October' with a marker]
Rocio: He is learning a lot of English.
Teacher: He is. He is learning a lot of English.
Rocio: He knows a lot of Spanish too.
Teacher: Yes!

In this episode, Rocio used specific strategies to support Juan. He:

*   publicly congratulated Juan for his progress in learning and using English
*   publicly congratulated Juan for his ability to speak Spanish as well as English.

Appropriating strategies demonstrated by the teacher

As evidenced in many of these examples, the strategies used by the children were often appropriated from the teacher's demonstrations. Syncretically, the children took what they learned from the teacher and merged those strategies with their own methods of supporting one another. In two further examples, specifically tied to teacher demonstrations, this phenomenon is evidenced as the children experienced Donna's use of specific strategies and later emulated them in their own interactions.

In the first example, an important quality in Donna's teaching was revealed as she interacted with the children. Ever-conscious of the need for Martita, Juan and Marcial to be seen as and to see themselves in the role of expert, she regularly solicited their help as she used their language. One day in October, for instance, she was reading an English book to the class about a scarecrow. She tried to say some of the words in Spanish but she did not know the word for *scarecrow*. She pointed to the picture of the scarecrow and looked at the children. Juan offered, *Espantapájaros* (scarecrow) and the teacher repeated the Spanish word. Juan corrected her pronunciation and Donna thanked him. This kind of interaction occurred frequently in the children's interactions with one another. Typically, an English-only child, building on the model established by the teacher, would ask Martita or Juan or Marcial, 'How do you say that in Spanish?'

Donna also used repetitive texts, illustrations and objects to support all of the children as emergent readers. During the early weeks of school, the repetitive nature of songs and stories and the use of illustrations and props were particularly supportive for Martita, Juan and Marcial allowing them to participate with their peers. The children were often observed using these texts, illustrations and props when they were engaged in independent activities. For example, one day in January, Marcial chose to play with a storyboard set up at the side of the room. On the board there were cut-out pictures of characters and objects from *The Three Bears*, a story that Donna had read to the class. Taking control of his own engagement, Marcial used the repetitive nature of the story and the opportunity to manipulate cut-out pictures to engage successfully. He pointed to each cut-out picture and counted them aloud in English:

One two three	(as he pointed to each of three bowls)
One two three	(as he pointed to each of three chairs)
One two three	(as he pointed to each of three beds)
One two three	(as he pointed to each of three bears)

Conclusion

Marcial, Martita, Juan and their peers used these and many other strategies as they interacted with one another in Donna's kindergarten class. Syncretizing language and experience, the children promoted participation while broadening and deepening the learning potential for everyone. Using strategies too often overlooked or dismissed as interesting but unimportant by teachers and parents, the children became important mediators of one another's learning. In contexts initially created by the teacher but extended and enhanced by the students, they moved fluidly in and out of the roles of expert and novice (Rogoff 1990) as they engaged one another in going beyond (Lindfors 1999).

At first glance, the strategies used by these children may not seem to present anything new. They are certainly not unfamiliar to those who have worked with second language learners. However, rarely do we see children's ability to strategically support one another presented in terms of what we can learn from *them* as skillful mediators of learning. It is not merely interesting that the children were experts in strategically helping one another nor merely fascinating that they drew from varied cultural experiences to co-create new possibilities for successful participation. It is highly significant that, given supportive contexts, the children took risks to draw on all that they knew to take control of their learning in important ways.

What does this mean for teachers? In this study, it seems clear that the children's ability to be strategic was supported by an environment in which materials, time and an atmosphere that honoured differences made the children feel free to risk the interactions that would result in their participation and growth. In this classroom the children had opportunities to interact meaningfully and on their own terms, they received important demonstrations from the teacher about how their varied experiences could enrich the lives of everyone, they were expected to develop proficiency as English-language speakers but not at the cost of losing home and community culture, their ability to code switch was held in high esteem, and they were valued for what they knew. To create such contexts, it is essential that teachers get to know homes, families and communities; look for what children know rather than what they do not know; value home and community knowledge and bilingual capabilities; notice and learn from the ways that children skillfully support one another; and provide opportunities for children to interact comfortably and purposefully.

Early in this chapter, I shared comments from an interview with a key figure in the South Carolina State Department of Education. In that interview, she also shared how, as a first grade teacher in predominantly English-only schools in South Carolina, she worked to help children appreciate the richness of her own cultural heritage. While parents of some of her students initially displayed negative bias with regard to her use of Spanish as she taught the children songs and phrases, the children quickly came to understand that being Mexican was a rich and wonderful thing to be. As she said, 'A teacher can make the difference about how children feel about other children'. A teacher can also make a difference by constructing environments in which children can use their expertise to co-create learning opportunities through which everyone can contribute and grow.

Acknowledgements

To Donna Bell and Jim Brown, I extend my thanks. Their devotion to careful collection of data made this study rich in illustrations of children living and learning together during the moments that often go unnoticed. They looked and listened with care and insight.

Notes

1   In March 2003 the University of South Carolina sent a group of key figures from the state government to Mexico to learn firsthand about politics, culture and relocation issues so that 'South Carolina leaders can be more responsive to Mexican citizens who relocate in the state' (West 2001).
2   Pseudonyms have been used in this chapter for the children and for the teaching assistant.

Chapter 8

Community school pupils reinterpret their knowledge of Chinese and Arabic for primary school peers

Charmian Kenner

6-year-old Ming is showing his primary school classmate Amina how to write in Chinese. For Amina, this is a new experience. Ming is drawing on his knowledge from Chinese Saturday school, which he attends each week. Ming writes the strokes needed to produce the Chinese character for 'seven'. Amina says 'That's not seven!' but she attempts to write it. Ming corrects her by pointing out that sometimes her writing looks like the English number '4' and sometimes like the English letter 't'. He shows her again and is vigilant about his own production of the Chinese character, commenting at one point 'That's too lumpy' and deciding to do a circle round the offending example 'cos that's what my Chinese teacher does when I get it wrong'.

In becoming literate, children learn to interpret the graphic sign systems used by the society in which they live. These sign systems are socially constructed and taught to children through particular sociocultural practices. Children make meaning by reinterpreting the concepts and practices presented to them. If they then have the opportunity to teach their peers, they will re-present the meanings they have made, giving us insights into their learning. In the response of the peer pupils, we also see how young children approach the enterprise of learning to write and read. Peer teaching involves a negotiated exchange of knowledge between child instructor and pupil which is enriching for both and teachers may wish to foster such interactions in the classroom.

This particular peer teaching project was part of a research study about bilingual 6 year olds learning to write in more than one language: either Chinese, Arabic or Spanish as well as English. The aim of the study was to investigate how young children interpret the links between form and meaning in their different writing systems. Over a period of one year, we observed six children growing up in London, learning to read and write in their family language at community-run Saturday schools while simultaneously encountering English literacy at primary school. To gain further insight into children's understandings, we set up peer teaching sessions in which each child taught primary school classmates how to write in Chinese, Arabic or Spanish.

In this chapter, I shall focus on peer teaching sessions conducted by the children learning Chinese and Arabic. Selina and Ming, whose families came from Hong Kong, were learning Chinese, and Tala and Yazan, whose families came from Palestine and Syria respectively, were learning Arabic. These children were all in their second year of community language school at the age of 6 and continued throughout this year. They had a sustained opportunity to experience the teaching input and pedagogic practices of their respective Saturday schools. Sadhana and Brian, whose families came from Ecuador and Colombia respectively, were learning Spanish, but attended Saturday school for a shorter time. While they did make use of their experiences in peer teaching, their approach was less clearly formulated. The value of consistent attendance at community language school in building children's knowledge and self-confidence in their other literacy is therefore emphasized by the findings of the research.

Enabling children to demonstrate their knowledge

The peer teaching sessions had an open-ended format. The bilingual children brought their community language work with them, often in a small backpack which most of them used for transporting these materials between home and Saturday school. As the researcher, I brought some additional materials from homes or community language schools. With regard to Chinese, for example, these included Chinese New Year banners, storybooks and the particular type of exercise book used in Chinese schools (with squared grids on each page for the writing of characters). Plain and lined paper and a variety of pens, pencils and erasers were also provided. With these materials as a resource, the children were encouraged to show their 'pupils' how to write in Chinese, Arabic or Spanish. Sometimes I asked them to explain a particular point, if this had not arisen spontaneously.

The activity took place at primary school with the cooperation of the children's class teachers, twice a term for 45 minutes to an hour on each occasion. The session was located in another room rather than the classroom itself, in order to aid concentration. Sometimes a whiteboard and coloured pens were available and the children enjoyed making use of these.

One or two 'pupils' for each session were chosen either by the children themselves or by their teachers. The criterion for choice was that the pupil was not familiar with the writing system to be taught, so that the bilingual child would need to explain the system to them. All the children also taught their entire primary school class at some point during the year, for periods ranging from ten minutes to an hour and a half.

A social semiotic approach to analysis

Our research was conceived within a social semiotic framework, which sees writing as a sign system developed and taught through social interaction (Kress 1997,

2000; Kenner 2000a, 2003). The features identified as significant by young children depend partly on what is presented to them as important by teachers and family members. However, children transform this input through their 'interest' as sign-users, which stems from their location as individuals in particular sociocultural contexts (Kress 1997: 11).

Through their learning, children build up an understanding of symbolic meanings. Our findings from this project showed that the participant children were concerned with several aspects of meaning: what graphic symbols stand for, how symbols are written and how the writing system is taught. In other words, they paid attention both to curriculum and to pedagogy.

In peer teaching, we saw the child instructors attempting to convey these different kinds of meaning to their pupils. Meanwhile, the pupils attempted to grasp the key features of the new curriculum and new pedagogy. To achieve these goals involved negotiation on both sides, a process which developed the learning of instructor as well as pupil.

The peer teaching relationship

According to Foot *et al.* (1990: 6), peer teaching is subtly different from peer collaboration in that the child teacher is assigned a formal role with a particular status. Within this asymmetrical relationship, one child provides instruction and guidance to another, based on their greater knowledge. Such a teacher–learner relationship can stimulate cognitive growth, as argued by Vygotsky (1978), because children are introduced to new ideas through social interaction, which can then become internalized as individual learning. In peer teaching, both the teacher and the learner child can clarify their thinking through dialogue and negotiation, as shown by Gregory (2001) in a study of the 'synergy' which is produced when older siblings teach younger ones at home.

In our study, we found that the bilingual children chose particular graphic symbols to teach and showed their pupils how to produce these accurately. In doing so, they demonstrated an awareness of key features of representation in the writing system concerned. Their pupils' responses revealed that they were aiming to identify the characteristics of Chinese or Arabic writing. As the bilingual children taught, they emphasized the need to practise writing in order to learn it and offered certain pedagogic formats and strategies to guide their pupils' work. The pupil children showed that they were looking out for these guidelines and making use of them. Through presenting their ideas and answering questions, Selina, Ming, Tala and Yazan took their own learning further.

I shall now give examples of these processes taking place in peer teaching interactions and then consider the potential benefits of peer teaching for the child instructors, pupils and classroom teachers involved in the project.

Teaching Chinese: Ming with Amina

When teaching Amina, Ming showed his awareness of the curriculum and pedagogy of his Saturday school. Meanwhile, she quickly realized that the content of this writing system and the ground rules of learning Chinese were very different from her experiences in primary school English lessons.

The form of the character

Chinese writing consists of thousands of characters, each of which represents a different meaning. The characters are built up from a repertoire of basic stroke types and stroke patterns. At Chinese school, Ming learned to write each stroke with precision in a particular sequence, to produce a correctly rendered character which could not be confused with any similar-looking one. Considerable importance was also placed on the aesthetic value of the final product. In the first-year class, there was plenty of discussion between teacher and children about the length and angle of each stroke and its balance with respect to other strokes.

As Ming taught Amina, he put these principles into operation. He demonstrated the character for 'seven' and Amina tried to follow his model (see Figure 8.1). At times her version began to look like the English numeral '4'. Ming realized that Amina was likely to interpret Chinese writing from an English point of view; a few moments earlier she had written one of the curved Chinese strokes as if it was the English numeral '2' and he had commented 'No, not 2, do it in Chinese'. In this case he told her 'That's a 4 – that's wrong'. At another point Amina's writing resembled the English letter 't' and again Ming noticed this: 'That's wrong – that's a T'. When showing her for the second time, he made an aesthetic evaluation of his own work, saying 'That's too lumpy'.

Amina's response was to make more effort to write the character for 'seven' according to the model provided by her 'teacher'. When she went on to learn the character for 'three', she showed that she was beginning to self-critique the details of her Chinese writing. This character consists of three horizontal strokes, of slightly different lengths. Children at Chinese school are encouraged to get the relative lengths just right and Ming pointed out to Amina that one of her strokes was too short: 'Make it even more bigger'. He also knew that each of her characters should be centrally placed within the squares of the grid used by learners. Amina had heard Ming comment about one of her earlier attempts at the character for 'three': 'She did this one wrong – not in the middle' and she went on to correct herself with regard to a later attempt 'Oh – I did it wrong . . . I didn't do it in the middle'.

Practising the character

As well as paying attention to the precise form of Chinese characters, Ming had also noted the pedagogic activities used in Chinese school. One such activity is

Figure 8.1 Amina practising the Chinese character meaning 'seven', based on Ming's instructions

that children practise each character many times to help them remember it and to ensure that it looks harmoniously balanced, writing in pencil and rubbing out their efforts until they and their teachers are satisfied. Ming required Amina to do the same. She was using an exercise book from Saturday school and Ming showed her how to set out the pages in order to practise the characters. He wrote the first symbol that he wanted her to learn in the square at the top right-hand corner of the page and said 'Keep carrying on to do it in lines till you get to that one' (indicating that she should practise it in vertical columns moving across the page until she reached the bottom left-hand corner).

Correction and evaluation

Ming employed the correction techniques of his Chinese teacher, doing a circle round one of his own characters for 'seven' (which he considered substandard) 'cos that's what my Chinese teacher does when I get it wrong'. He pointed out the need for Amina to practise a character again, using a new model provided by the teacher: 'If she gets that wrong the teacher writes it and you have to write it all down there' (indicating a whole column).

During lessons at Chinese school, the teacher would give marks out of 100 for work done so far. Ming's evaluation of Amina's work involved the amount of work she had done unaided: he wrote '60' on the page where she had practised 'seven' because 'she needed help'. At the beginning of the lesson, he had predicted that she would require help because she would not be used to such rigorous writing practice: 'If her hand gets tired, I'll do it' and he was proved right. Amina asked when writing 'seven': 'Can you finish it for me please?' When writing 'three', she began to shake her wrist and Ming commented 'Is your hand tired?' He began writing instead of Amina but warned her 'You're going to get 50'.

This led to an exchange between the two children, conducted with humour but with an underlying serious intent. When Ming teased Amina 'You're going to get 10 – because you let the teacher do it', she grabbed the pen with renewed resolve. He encouraged her: 'Do some more then you get 90'. Later she stated with determination: 'I want to get 100'. Amina had recognized the reward system used in Chinese school and was prepared to make the efforts required for high achievement.

Revision and testing

After demonstrating each character and asking children to practise it, Ming's Chinese teacher would revise all the characters learnt in each lesson and tell children to continue revising at home in preparation for their next test. Ming had understood this entire pedagogic sequence and ensured that Amina underwent the same sequence within his lesson. Early in the session he said 'When she finishes she's going to have to do a test – if you get 100 it's perfect, 90 is excellent'.

Having showed Amina how to write several characters, Ming stated 'Then you have to revise – I've got lots of words to revise – *so* much!' He then proceeded to give Amina a test, dictating Chinese words to her and marking her work afterwards. His conclusion was 'You have to practise', commenting to me 'She got 0'.

Aiding both children's learning

In the course of Ming's peer teaching session with Amina, exchanges took place which showed that both children were thinking about the underlying principles of the Chinese and English writing systems. Such principles are not always explicitly discussed in children's school experiences, but peer teaching can encourage them to articulate their ideas.

Amina began to interpret Chinese writing by using the English system she already knew, suggesting that one of the Chinese strokes which Ming showed her could be the letter 'C' or 'U'. She was surprised when Ming pointed to a Chinese character and said that it meant 'seven', or that another one meant 'people', and resisted this information at first, saying 'No!' However, she then started to realize that characters might have a visual interpretation; when she saw a square divided into four smaller squares, she said 'window'. Later, she said 'I know how to do "mouth"' and drew an oval shape.

Amina was partly correct in formulating this idea, because many Chinese characters were originally derived from visual symbolism (the character she thought was 'window' was in fact 'field', and 'mouth' is represented by a rectangular shape which is a stylized version of Amina's oval). However, in most cases the system no longer operates on a simple visual connection between character and concept. Ming was clear that Chinese is not a straightforwardly pictorial system. When Amina guessed 'window' he laughed and when she drew an oval to represent 'mouth', he dismissed this by saying 'That's wrong, she has to write in Chinese, not draw pictures!'

Amina continued to explore the visual possibilities of Chinese when given her 'test' by Ming at the end of the session. Undaunted by his inclusion of words he had not yet taught her, she used a different shape to represent each one, starting with the symbols he had shown her for 'ten' (which looks like a cross) and 'mouth' (a rectangle) and continuing with a triangle, a half-moon shape and so on. Although Ming awarded her '0' for the test, because 'she did pictures', her strategy showed that she had moved quite rapidly from challenging the existence of a different writing system to looking for the concepts on which this new system might be based.

The sounds of Chinese words were also of interest to Amina and she began to grasp some of their characteristics. She heard Ming saying the Chinese numbers from 'ten' upwards, which are built up by combining 'ten' ('sap') with the numbers 'one', 'two' and so on (so 'eleven' is 'sap yat': 'ten one'; 'twelve' is 'sap yee': 'ten two'). Amina echoed Ming, hearing 'sap' as 'sat' and producing combinations such as 'sat mee' and 'sat gau', picking up the 'sing-song' sound of the different tones used in Cantonese. She then invented further combinations of 'sat' with one-syllable sounds, saying 'sat ma' and 'sat ka'.

As Amina did this, she tried to follow the way she had seen Ming writing the numbers, with the 'cross' symbol which represents 'ten' followed by the symbol for the other relevant number, 'one' for example. Amina's version was to produce a cross followed by a square for her invented number 'sat ma' and a cross followed by a triangle for 'sat ka'. Again Ming challenged her – 'You can't do that' – but Amina was taking a logical approach to recognizing and representing the elements involved in these numbers. She made a direct reference to her own thought processes (both present and future) by saying '"sat ma" – cos I'm doing Chinese numbers – I know I'm doing "sat ma" – when I'm learning Chinese I think in my bed'.

At the end of the session, Ming read out his name ('Lai Sei Ming') from the cover of his Chinese school exercise book and said 'My Chinese name'. When I asked if it was different from English, he replied 'Yes, that one's got three words and the English one's got four'. It turned out that Ming was referring to the three characters used for 'Lai Sei Ming' in Chinese, compared to the four letters used to write 'Ming' in English. He added with regard to the English version ('Ming Lai' in its entirety): 'I got some different ones . . . Ming is four, seven if it's together'. Ming's position as teacher seemed to stimulate his expression of this key difference between the logographic system of Chinese and the alphabetic system of English.

Teaching Chinese: Selina with Ruby

A similarly detailed analysis of Selina's work in peer teaching sessions showed that, like Ming, she was putting across the basic principles of character-writing as taught in her class at Chinese school. Selina was in a more advanced class and received extra tuition from her mother at home. As a result, she laid an even greater emphasis on the accuracy of her pupil's strokes and her friend Ruby responded to this by monitoring her own work with comments such as 'That bit was too long'.

Selina also insisted, as Ming did with Amina, that Ruby practised each character for several columns. Ruby quickly picked up this idea and also noticed the custom of leaving a blank column before starting to practise a new character. She explained these pedagogic principles to a fellow pupil in a later peer teaching session, by running her finger down two blank columns, then jumping one column and pointing to the next, saying 'Do it there' for the next character to be practised.

As with Ming and Amina, exchanges between Selina and Ruby highlighted concepts about Chinese writing. For example, many Chinese characters consist of two graphic units, one on the left-hand side and the other on the right-hand side. The character 'read' is an example. When Selina wrote this character, Ruby asked 'Is that one word?', pointing to each of the two components. Selina answered 'It's half a word'. To clarify the situation Ruby continued: 'Is that [pointing to the left-hand component] half of that one?' (pointing to the right-hand component). Selina replied 'No', putting the palms of her hands parallel to each other and moving them together, thus indicating that the two components combined to make a word. Still unsure, Ruby asked 'Are they the same word, or different ones?' to which Selina responded with irritation 'Yes, same words!' and Ruby acquiesced with 'OK'. Her friend's persistent questioning required Selina to define her own thinking about this concept in several different ways.

Teaching Arabic: Tala with Emily

Arabic, like English, is an alphabetic system but with a different script and directionality. In addition, the script is always written in cursive and children have to know how to join letters to each other. Six of the alphabet letters cannot be joined to the next one and a small gap must then be left before continuing with the word. Here I shall look briefly at some of Tala's exchanges with one pupil,

Emily, as she showed how to write her brother's name 'Khalid' in Arabic. This word is written in two parts, 'Kha-' and '-lid', because according to the rules of Arabic writing, the letter 'alif' which represents the 'a' sound cannot join to any following letter.

Tala was faced with the challenge of helping Emily to write a word in an unfamiliar script. So while writing her own example of 'Khalid', she gave detailed verbal instructions to Emily: 'Do that – it's like a triangle, but it's got a line like here . . . go "wheeee" like this' (as she finished with an upward stroke). Emily tried to follow this lead, saying as she wrote 'It looks like an "L" . . . it looks like steps'. As Amina had done with Chinese, Emily was interpreting an unfamiliar script from the basis of English and of visual images. However, Tala realized that Emily had over-interpreted her instructions, with the result being too stylized and she commented 'It's not exactly like that – she's done steps'. Indeed, Emily's version looked like steps in a staircase, rather than the fluid curves typical of Arabic writing. This difficulty continued during the lesson and to help her friend produce more appropriate writing, Tala resorted to a technique used by her own Arabic teacher. She provided a 'join-the-dots' version of the words required.

The pedagogy in Arabic Saturday school also involved practising each word and Tala asked Emily to do this with 'Khalid'. She pointed to her own model and said 'You copy it all the way down to here' – putting a horizontal line further down the page – 'and when you think you've done it right'. Emily began writing, but as she did so, the two parts of 'Khalid' gradually diverged from each other until they became separated by a large space. Tala knew the importance of keeping the two parts of the word together and asked Emily to do the task again, stating 'They need to be close to each other'.

Tala was also vigilant about writing each word with right–left directionality. When Emily decided to write 'Khalid' from left to right, Tala rubbed it out and emphasized her mistake, saying 'Don't you even know how to do anything yet, Emily?' When teaching the next word, Tala provided an arrow on the right-hand side (another device she had seen used in Arabic teaching), saying 'Start from this way'. However, Emily forgot again and Tala pointed out 'Wrong way! I give you the arrow again'. This time, Emily remembered.

As seen in the Chinese children's peer teaching, Tala was concerned with the form of her pupil's writing and with the pedagogy which helped with the production and practising of that form. Peer teaching also prompted her to express her thoughts about how Arabic writing worked. When teaching her primary school class, she explained that 'Khalid' had to be written in two parts. She said 'Can I tell you something? You know this and this [indicating the two components], they're not actually together. They have to be split up. This says "Khal" and this says "lid" [circling each part]'. Although Tala had made a slight error in joining the /l/ sound to 'Kha', she showed her understanding of the principle involved.

Teaching Arabic: Yazan with Imrul

When teaching Imrul how to write in Arabic, Yazan had to deal with similar issues to those encountered by Tala with Emily and found his own solutions. He showed his friend how to write 'Yazan' in Arabic and Imrul interpreted the first part of the word as the English numeral '3'. To Imrul's comment 'You writed a 3, didn't you?', Yazan replied 'No', because he was clear that Arabic was a different script from English.

Faced with the task of writing 'Yazan', Imrul was somewhat daunted, saying 'Oh it's too hard, isn't it'. Yazan encouraged him by offering the reward used by teachers in Arabic Saturday school: 'You have to try to do it – I give him a sticker'. However, he added 'But not now, when we finish all the way from here', gesturing down the length of the page. Imrul would have to practise the word a number of times before the sticker was forthcoming, just as Yazan was expected to do in his Arabic class.

As Imrul hesitated, Yazan gave him some help regarding directionality. He said 'Write this first', pointing to the right-hand side of the word. Like Emily, Imrul found this idea difficult, saying 'No I can't, I'm writing this first, yeah, shall I?' and proceeding to start on the left-hand side. Yazan displayed less concern about this than Tala would have done, but wanted to make sure that Imrul remembered the dot which was part of one of the letters in 'Yazan'. He reminded Imrul about it twice and pointed out exactly where it should be placed. Dots are a significant feature in Arabic writing because they can distinguish otherwise similar-looking letters from each other. Yazan and Tala's teachers would remind children to add the dots when writing and I had observed that Yazan showed a particular focus on this issue at the time.

Yazan went on to show Imrul how to write numbers in Arabic and this led to a discussion in which the two boys explored the variety of meanings that a particular graphic symbol could have. First Yazan wrote the English sequence of numbers from 1 to 21, in a vertical column. Then he wrote Arabic numbers next to them in another vertical column, from 1 to 10 (see Figure 8.2). Having written the Arabic '7' (which looks like the English letter 'V') directly above the Arabic '8' (which looks like an upturned 'V') Yazan noticed that the combination of the two was reminiscent of an English alphabet letter. He commented 'Hey, this is look like a X'.

Imrul agreed: 'Yeah! It's an X' and proceeded to write an 'X' himself. He then said 'This is a number, isn't it?', thinking that 'X' must also represent a number in Arabic. Yazan replied 'No . . . seven, eight', pointing to what he knew to be the two individual Arabic numbers '7' and '8' which made up the apparent 'X'. As Imrul wrote his own version of Arabic numbers, in a third vertical column, he returned to the topic of the 'X', wondering whether he should write it. To clarify the issue, Yazan guided Imrul's hand to write the Arabic '7' (which looks like a 'V'). At this point Imrul said excitedly 'See that! It's a tick!' After a short pause, Yazan agreed that it looked like a tick, finishing the discussion

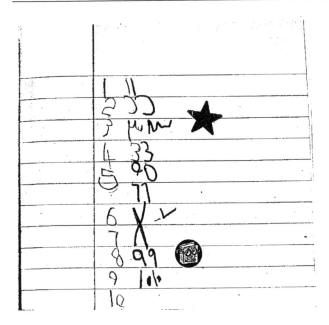

Figure 8.2 Yazan's writing of English numbers (left-hand column) and Arabic numbers
(middle column); Imrul's writing of Arabic numbers (right-hand column) with
a star and sticker awarded by Yazan

by stating 'But it's a seven'. Finally, Imrul was allowed to choose the long-awaited
sticker.

Peer teaching interactions as a tool for literacy learning

From the above examples, it can be seen that the teaching role stimulated the
bilingual children to display their knowledge of the literacy curriculum and
pedagogy of community language school. There were common features in the
concepts being taught by Ming and Selina and by Tala and Yazan, but each child
had their particular interests within this knowledge and their own way of presenting
it. Through a dynamic interaction with their peers, they consolidated and
developed their ideas. Meanwhile, the pupils were gaining new knowledge through
these encounters with their young teachers. They were challenged to think about
different ways in which graphic symbol systems might operate. Metalinguistic
awareness of this kind is a valuable resource and thus both sides gained from the
peer teaching experience.

The pupils were keen to participate in the sessions and to learn how to write in
different scripts. Some of Tala's friends did 'homework' between sessions and
Ruby brought her Chinese exercise book to each session, gradually filling it with

Chinese characters and seeing her work with Selina as part of an ongoing programme. As well as a fascination with the script itself, the children's interest involved the consolidation of friendships and a reaching out to other cultural experiences. Amina, as she sat back with a sigh of exhaustion after finishing her first page of Chinese writing, said 'I want to be Chiney'.

Peer teaching therefore has the potential to build on children's desire to make social, cultural and intellectual connections through multilingual literacy learning. Edwards (1998) gives many examples of activities in which bilingual children successfully presented concepts concerning their home languages and literacies, in classrooms around England, while D'Arcy (2002) describes how pupils from multicultural secondary schools in Birmingham taught their languages to student teachers. Children from ethnic minority backgrounds can also help each other to learn English, as evidenced by Datta's (2000) work on building up an 'intercultural literate community' in which children become models and partners in the process of learning to read.

In the peer teaching sessions in this study, the biliteracy experience of the child instructors was acknowledged by their primary school teachers and seen by their classmates as conferring authority. In a society which generally values monolingualism over bilingualism (Kenner 2000b), this was a reversal of the more usual power relationships experienced by bilingual children. As the research project continued, the primary teachers began to realize the extent of the biliteracy knowledge shown through peer teaching and this gave further status to the children concerned. Such teaching activities can thus enhance teacher–child relationships as well as peer relationships. With the opportunity for an increase in children's metalinguistic and cultural awareness and greater social integration, peer teaching offers significant benefits for learning in multilingual classrooms.

Acknowledgements

I would like to thank the other members of the research team: Gunther Kress, Hayat Al-Khatib, Gwen Kwok, Roy Kam and Kuan-Chun Tsai. Special thanks also go to the children who participated in the research and their schools: Lambeth Chinese Community School, the Arabic Community School in Hounslow, the Latin American Saturday School and Berkeley, Duncombe, Eveline Lowe, Richard Atkins and Wellington primary schools. This study was funded by the ESRC.

Chapter 9

'How do I read these words?'
Bilingual exchange teaching between Cantonese-speaking peers

Yuangguang Chen and Eve Gregory

Wington: *Ni di ji ding du?* [How do I read these words?]
Yuan: [reads] body . . . ribs . . . skeleton . . .
Wington: body . . . ribs . . . skeleton . . . *Cantonese ding gai?* [What are they in Cantonese?]
Yuan: *samti, paigua and guga*
Wington: *Nigo M tao de ji hai mieye?* [What is the word starting with M?]
Yuan: Muscle. *Cantonese hai 'jiyou'* [It's 'muscle' in Cantonese.]
Wington: *Niduo, niduo!* [Here, here!]
Yuan: Stomach, lung, liver, brain . . .
Wington: Stomach . . . lung . . . liver . . . brain . . .[1]

Wington (aged 9) is a newcomer to London from Hong Kong and is learning in a mainstream English classroom. Mostly, she sits alone and withdrawn, unable to participate in lessons. Yet today Wington and Yuan work intensely together on this text over the next hour. We begin to see that this is no ordinary collaboration between classmates. Yuan, one year younger, was born in Britain but also speaks fluent Cantonese. What starts as a human biology lesson becomes a complex exercise in language, literacy and translation. But who is teaching whom in the excerpt above? Paradoxically, although Yuan provides answers, it is Wington who takes a teacher's role, quizzing her and urgently pushing her into thinking about translations, pronunciations, explanations. Very few studies unpick episodes of mainstream classroom collaboration between bilingual friends, perhaps owing to the need to eavesdrop on their privacy as in the excerpt above. But such interactions have important lessons for researchers and teachers alike. This chapter investigates such teaching and learning and goes on to contribute new theoretical insights into the nature of scaffolding between bilingual peers.

Background

The second half of the twentieth century witnessed a number of different official reactions to the language needs of pupils speaking languages other than English in Britain. Between the Plowden Report in 1967 and the 1990s, educational provision for bilingual children passed through four stages: assimilation, specialism, integration and centralization. Children, aged between 8 and 10, especially those of recent arrivals, were the first to be affected by the changing policy.

In 1963 the Department of Education and Science (DES) report *English for Immigrants* signalled the start of the years noted for *assimilation*, which advocated an immediate need for special tuition for immigrant children and recommended the development of an intensive course in English language learning. In 1967 the Plowden Report recognized the linguistic and cultural differences between children, but emphasized the disadvantages suffered by many immigrant children. The focus was on teaching English as quickly as possible, with the minimum of disruption to the ongoing school routine. Thus a special term was coined for this kind of teaching or instruction, ESL (English as a second language). The Bullock Report (1975) marked a distinct shift from compensation and separation to a recognition of linguistic and cultural pluralism in schools and also stressed the importance of sustained and *specialist language assistance* for children well past the initial stages of learning and the importance for language specialists to work closely with the class teacher and for all teachers to become responsible for children's language learning.

Attitudes towards mother-tongue teaching were also largely optimistic during this time since the influence of a child's cultural identity and mother tongue were viewed as a source of cultural enrichment to all children in classrooms. One significant event was the Directive of the European Council in 1977 on *The Children of Migrant Workers* which acknowledged the right of children to tuition in their mother tongue especially until fluency in English was achieved. Influenced by this Directive, several small-scale projects arose promoting mother-tongue teaching. The Department of Education and Science set up two projects: the Mother Tongue and English Teaching Project in Bradford and the Linguistic Minorities Project. At the same time, Bedfordshire local education authority (LEA) assisted by European Community funds set up the Bedford Project to provide bilingual education for Italian speakers.

However, the optimism of the 1970s was short lived. The 1980s witnessed the sudden official move from focused English *and* mother-tongue teaching programmes to providing only English language support within the mainstream classroom. Mother-tongue teaching was to be provided separately by communities themselves outside mainstream schools. This change was due to increasing concern or complaints since the 1960s of poor performance by ethnic minority children within the educational system. In 1985 the Swann Report centred on the themes 'integration' and 'Education for All', calling for many changes under an antiracist strategy, whereby provision for bilingual children within a mainstream system became a main response to linguistic diversity. As a result, withdrawal [pull out] ESL lessons were removed; instead, language support teachers moved into mainstream classes to support teaching and learning across the whole curriculum. A shared view behind the change was the opinion voiced much earlier that in a mainstream class, 'immigrant infants [5 to 7 year olds] . . . will pick up the language just as a child picks up his native language from an early age' (Townsend 1971: 38). Many LEAs were in favour of this policy just because they had been reluctant to 'draw attention to the immigrant community' by making special provision, so it was then probably easier for schools to return to a tradition of ignoring diversity in language needs, rather than to begin exploring new teaching strategies (Bourne 1989: 5). However, 'being assimilated into an unchanged monolingual system is not what proponents of "mainstream provision" in the 1980s meant by the term'. Although they were firmly against separate provision (withdrawal) of all kinds they viewed language teaching as part and parcel of cultural knowledge and general curriculum knowledge by children, both of which were important for the success of newcomers to Britain.

Centralization has been the key feature of educational policy in Britain since the 1990s. Swann's (1985) incorporation of additional language provision into the mainstream has been justified and further developed through a much-centralized National Curriculum, which was implemented in 1989. The term 'equality of opportunity' was said to be the central theme of this centralization; issues such as 'ethnic minority achievement', 'individual needs of linguistic disadvantaged children', 'English as an additional language support' were strongly pursued though controversial. What is more, the centralized National Curriculum also created educational markets, based on parental 'choice' and new forms of funding. In response to market forces 'values of competition, individualism and separation have become important, social and racial justice and equity less so' (Tomlinson 2000: 22). Additionally, the pressure placed on individual teachers and schools to achieve well in the SATs (tests taken by children aged 7 and 11), which are published nationally, further problematizes the situation of newcomers like Wington. Schools are anxious to achieve well, meaning that the performance of the *majority* must be raised. Individual children such as Wington sit uneasily within these tensions and pressures upon teachers.

Insights into reciprocity and bilingual learning

Wington and Yuan's short dialogue opening this chapter spans interest across three main areas of research: bilingualism, literacy and the interactive nature of learning. We shall see that although existing studies partly account for what we see taking place between the girls, crucial questions remain unanswered.

From the mid-twentieth century, studies in the field of bilingualism from the US and western Europe have developed Vygotsky's thesis of 1935 that first and second language learning involve very different processes whereby 'the child assimilates his/her native language unconsciously and unintentionally but acquires a foreign language with conscious realization and intention' (Vygotsky 1962: 2–3). More recently, a number of research studies in both Britain and the USA have shown how bilinguals possess an enhanced metalinguistic, metacognitive and analytical awareness (Cummins 1984; John-Steiner 1985). Such awareness is particularly fostered when a child is able to transfer first language knowledge to the new learning task, a thesis termed the 'linguistic interdependence hypothesis' (Cummins 1984). These studies begin to explain Wington's acute awareness of individual letters and words. Her fluent literacy in her mother tongue means that she is very conscious of what she does not yet know in English; Yuan, likewise, is similarly aware of her responsibility as translator from one language to the other.

Studies on bilingualism during the latter half of the twentieth century have also moved towards a wider interpretation of 'bilinguality' (the psychological state of an individual) as being a multidimensional phenomenon involving not just a linguistic ability but social, psychological and cultural issues which can only be understood through a study of communication in intercultural contexts (summarized in Hamers and Blanc 1989). Successful communication, therefore, might depend upon 'similarity attraction' in terms of personal and cultural attributes, sometimes referred to as speech accommodation theory or on the child being treated as an 'important learner' (Schieffelin and Cochran-Smith 1984). Successful communication might also relate to a shared interpretation by participants of what constitutes 'work' and 'play' (Gregory 1994b). These perspectives explain why Wington works enthusiastically with her friend in her first language, as well as her eye for detail and accuracy, essential aspects to literacy learning in Mandarin (Kenner 2003). However, aspects of Wington's learning still remain unexplained. Why does she 'run before she can walk', trying to learn specialized English from a biology text rather than simple colloquial expressions from her friend? Why might individual words seem so important rather than learning one or two 'chunks' of language she could use appropriately in class?

Although a large number of studies detail various aspects of bilingualism and bilinguality, very few focus specifically on literacy learning in a new language. However, research into strategies used by young preliterate children learning to read in more than one language indicates that a lexical (word recognition) awareness is likely to be the most highly developed 'cue' or clue called upon by these pupils who usually have memories superior to those of monolingual children (Verhoeven 1987; Gregory 1996). The learning of important 'one-sight' words is seen as a key to children seeing themselves as 'readers' and gaining access to other clues (graphophonemic, syntactic, semantic and bibliographic). The method of translating words and texts in order to understand sufficiently their meaning is promoted by others interested in children already literate in their mother tongue (Williams and Snipper 1990). However, the interaction between these girls engaged in a literacy task is quite different from any lesson they know from their English classrooms. There is, of course, no bilingual literacy teaching in their school. Additionally, the method of repeating words and phrases is not one used by the teacher in her lessons.

During the 1980s and 1990s, literacy was included within a sociocultural paradigm, whereby literacy is seen in terms of a number of different cultural practices or 'literacies' which are shaped by the context i.e. the participants, the materials, methods and purpose for which they occur (Heath 1983; Street 1984;

Barton and Hamilton 1998; Gregory and Williams 2000). Each of these authors detail literacy practices taking place that contrast sharply with those of the mainstream school. Marsh (2003) extends the notion of 'literacy practices' to that of 'communicative practices' including visual or oral practices within which literacy might be embedded. Crucially, home and community communicative practices are inherently purposeful, are group oriented and are learned through an apprenticeship with more experienced members of the group who mediate appropriate behaviour (Baynham 1995). By comparison, mainstream school literacy practices tend to be without specific purpose beyond completing the task itself, individual oriented and transmitted by direct teaching.

What we see taking place between the two girls in this study is a complex syncretism of community and school practices. Paradoxically, what might appear to be a purposeless task of repetition gives Wington access to the subject-specific vocabulary needed for the lesson. The repetition would be a familiar method to her from early literacy learning in Hong Kong; the meanings of words are certainly being mediated through translation. Yet who is actually mediating what and to whom? Although Yuan 'teaches' Wington the words, it is Wington who tells Yuan *how* to teach her and Yuan, it seems, who obeys.

The interactive and social nature of learning has long been recognized across academic disciplines. In the early 1950s (translated into English only in 1978), Vygotsky argued that social interaction with a more competent member of society is the means by which cultural knowledge is acquired and that all learning takes place first on an *interpersonal* level between participants before it is internalized on an *intrapersonal* level within the individual self. Different researchers illustrate the nature of interpersonal learning through a range of metaphors. During the 1970s researchers detailed ways in which caregivers provide finely tuned tuition to young children as they complete cognitive and linguistic takes, referring to this as 'scaffolding' (Wood *et al.* 1976) whereby adults provide a 'loan of conscious-ness' (Bruner 1986) to the child. Like a scaffold, pieces are gradually removed as the child gains confidence and competence. This metaphor, although still widely used as a generic term has been criticized for implying a passivity on the part of the child (Stone 1993). Since the 1990s, the metaphor of 'guided participation' coined by Rogoff in 1990 has focused more upon *the child as co-constructing meaning* with an adult.

Work and play between peers and siblings, however, has revealed a much more equal relationship in teaching and learning. The metaphor of 'synergy' (Gregory 2001) has been used to show that both younger and older siblings learn from each other, particularly when children are bilingual. The older child learns as much through explaining words in a new language as well as acting as a cognitive facilitator as the younger child who is being 'taught' through the medium of play. Peers who speak the same language also act as skilled facilitators of classroom learning as they participate together in 'collaborative learning' (Tharp and Gallimore 1988; Chang-Wells and Wells 1993). Mother-tongue speakers can also play a crucial role in initiating children into a new language. Susi Long

(1997) shows how a group of Icelandic girls carefully structure the learning of an English-speaking novice, revealing skills well beyond those of adults and the classroom teacher.

The value of cooperative classroom learning, in which peers work together on academic tasks and provide one another with motivation, guidance and feedback (Damon 1984; Slavin 1987), also suggests that in circumstances in which children have practice in interaction, they may be very helpful to one another. Peers can serve as guides in academic activities in the classroom, especially if such interaction is encouraged in the classroom social structure, giving children experience as onlookers and in coordinated parallel activity, guidance and collaboration (Cooper *et al.* 1986). When teachers encourage and support peer interaction, children may develop skill in academically useful forms of interaction (Rogoff 1990).

However, Wington and Yuan's interaction does not fit any of the above metaphors describing guidance and support. A synergy is, indeed, taking place whereby both children teach and learn from each other. But, paradoxically, it is the child whose knowledge of the new language is very limited (Wington) who appears to control events. What, then, might be going on and what might be learned from this on both a practical and theoretical level?

Two Cantonese sisters and their mainstream class

Wington has recently arrived in London with her 10-year-old sister Kapo and their mother to join their father who, like the majority of the immigrants from Hong Kong early on, is working in the kitchen of a restaurant in Chinatown. Both children have attended school regularly in Hong Kong and are competent readers and writers in Chinese. The parents have had little education and are totally illiterate in English, but they want their children to be educated in English in order to improve their life chances. They believe that English-medium education will lead to social and economic advancement and they hoped for the high aspiration of English teachers for their children. Upon their arrival, Kapo and Wington were both sent to a primary school in the Soho area, where our study was based.

The school is accommodated in a four-story-high old Victorian building. The entrance is in the front yard, where children play games after class or have PE lessons. Nearly two hundred 5- to 11-year-old children are distributed in seven classes from Reception to Year 6. According to the headteacher, before Kapo and Wington joined, there were a few Cantonese children in the school but they were all born and brought up in London. Among them was Yuan, the little Cantonese girl (aged 7) who later become Wington's best friend. Although placed in the appropriate class for her age, Wington was sent to the Year 1 mainstream class for literacy lessons, because she was considered to need 'basic literacy tuition'. After a few months, Kapo moved on to a secondary school. Wington's class joined the class below and there she met Yuan, who became her mentor and friend.

The data discussed in this chapter form part of a much larger study into the schooling of young children who have recently arrived in Britain from Hong Kong and mainland China. Our work has mostly taken place in school settings including classrooms, libraries, dining halls and playgrounds. Participants include these two sisters and their friends alongside other older and younger children. Data have been collected mainly through participant observation and formal or informal interviews by video-recordings. The children are also keeping diaries (written in Mandarin) of their daily lives and their feelings during classroom lessons. A parallel group of older teenagers, now established in Britain and fluent in English, are talking and writing about their early memories of life in a new country. Access to the children's classrooms was obtained by offering to come and work as a voluntary helper to the children using both English and their mother tongue. We visited the school about twice a week for nearly a year, spending either a morning or afternoon in both classes and participating in most of their lessons and activities. In doing so, rapport and trust were established, which enabled us to take field notes, talk with children and teachers and even film and make audio-recordings. Analysis of data collected highlighted the crucial role of bilingual friends in both Wington and Kapo's learning. In this chapter, we focus on the younger children, Wington and Yuan and unpick their learning together. In the excerpts that follow, 8-year-old Yuan is helping 9-year-old Wington to read and understand a text on human biology, no easy task for a beginner in English. How do they go about this and to what extent do existing metaphors of the 'helping' process explain how they help each other?

Bilingual exchange teaching in one classroom

'Well, I help her just by telling her what to do and help her . . . er . . . that is . . .' (Yuan). In fact, the whole process is much more complex than this. Although Yuan indeed 'helps' her friend, we shall see that she does not, in any teacherly sense, actually tell her what to do. What we observe, therefore, is a complex interaction which we term 'bilingual exchange teaching' between the peers. We shall unpick three crucial features of this approach: translating, repeating and bilingual problem solving.

Translating and using the mother tongue

'Do you know the meaning?' 'No' said Wington. Then Yuan explained to her in Cantonese sentence by sentence, *Niguo xu hai gong yao yi guo dongmu, kyu hue hyudei cesuo genxi, kyu wun duo hao duo ye buo, kyu ng zongyi buo . . .* [This book is about an animal, when he went to his toilet, he found a lot of things he dislike . . .] Wington nodded.

On another occasion:

34	*Wington:*	*Come on, du nido la* [Come on, read here]	35 *Yuan:* constraint and relax.
36	*Wington:*	*Mieye yici?* [What is the meaning?]	37 *Yuan:* *xiushu tongmai fansong* [constraint and relax]
38	*Wington:*	*Xu nido yaomo gon guo* *luolai zuo mie yong?* [Does the text tell us what are these bones used for?]	39 *Yuan:* *yiding yao la, wo taitai.* [it should, let me have a look]
40	*Wington:*	*Hai ng hai nido ?*[Are they here?]	41 *Yuan: Hai* [yes]
42	*Chen:*	Did she manage to follow you?	
43	*Yuan:*	Um . . . yes.	

Translating is a complex skill, especially when vocabulary is specialized and difficult. Yuan gives literal Cantonese translations of 'constraint' and 'relax' which tax her own knowledge of Cantonese. Even more taxing is the task of explaining the function of such difficult words. As a competent Cantonese speaker, Wington almost takes over the role of teacher herself by directing Yuan to the text to find out answers. Yuan, herself, becomes more aware of her bilinguality through the process of translation. She realizes the double understanding of 'meaning' (literal translation and explanation) and has to think about all of this.

Repeating

(. . .) = written text in book

81	*Wington:*	You first.	
82	*Yuan:*	Meg was poor.	83 *Wington:* But a (family) farmer get (gave) her an egg.

[Yuan then could not turn the page quickly enough, Wington helped and said 'Niduo,ah' [here], Yuan then carried on]

84	*Yuan:*	'Soon I'll have a chicken' said Meg.	85 *Wington:* 'It will gran (grow) big and (lag some) en (eggs)'.
86	*Yuan:*	'Then I'll have more chickens'.	87 *Wington:* 'Then I'll have more chickens'.

[When Yuan noticed Wington was following her all the time, she paused and asked Wington to read on]

88   *Wington:* They will grow big and . . .

[but Wington could not manage to read by herself, then the follow-up pattern continued.]

89 *Yuan:* They will grow big and   90 *Wington:* They will grow big and lay
            lag some eggs.   some more eggs.
91 *Yuan:* I'll sell the eggs and . . .

[Wington this time got lost where to follow, Yuan pointed to the right line for her. After confirming in Cantonese, Wington went on.]

92 *Wington:* I'll soo (sell) the eggs
                and . . .

93 *Yuan:* buy a cow   94 *Wington:* buy a cow.
95 *Chen:* OK   96 *Wington:* It's your turn.
96 *Yuan:* Then I'll sell the cow's   97 *Wington:* Then I'll sell the cow's
            milk and . . .   milk and . . .
97 *Yuan:* buy a sheep   98 *Wington:* buy a sheep (repeated).
99 *Yuan:* Then I'll sell the sheep's   100 *Wington:* Then I'll sell the sheep's
            wool and . . .   wool.
101 *Yuan:* buy some clothes and . . .   102 *Wington:* buy some clothd (clothes)
                                                       and
103 *Yuan:* clothes (Yuan repeated   104 *Wington:* clothes
            the word)
105 *Yuan:* a house and . . .   106 *Wington:* a house and . . . (followed)
107 *Yuan:* But Meg didn't look   108 *Wington:* But Meg didn't look
            where she was going   where she *is* (was) going
109 *Yuan:* She fell down   110 *Wington:* She fell down
111 *Yuan:* The egg broke.   112 *Wington:* The egg broke
113 *Yuan:* Meg was still poor   114 *Wington:* Meg was still pull (poor)

Through the act of repetition, children take their first steps in learning to do things themselves. In the excerpt above, we see how Yuan provides a firm structure of support, whereby Wington takes over as much or as little as she can manage. She encourages Wington to continue the reading but allows her only to repeat when it is clear that independent reading is too difficult. In this way, Wington is able to pronounce and remember whole phrases of the new language – a task she could never manage on her own. Wington and Yuan's interaction has much in common with the support given by older, more competent Bangladeshi British siblings in East London (Gregory 1998) as well as the approach taken by adult Zinacantecan weavers initiating girls into the skill in Mexico (Childs and Greenfield 1982).

Shared problem-solving in two languages

Morning, Wednesday, December 11, in the literacy class of Wington and Yuan. We came as usual to join Wington's class. The teaching target today was to get children to understand and practise conjunctions like 'before', 'after', 'since', 'as', 'when', 'in case', 'athough', 'whenever' etc. The task was practised at two levels: at the first level, dozens of short sentences were given in a list and the children were supposed to make complex sentences (consisting of a main clause and subordinate clause) by matching up conjunction words and short sentences from the list. At the second level children were asked to make sentences of their own by using the given conjunction words. The first level task was easy and with little help from Yuan, Wington grasped the rule and finished matching up all of the words in the list even though she might not know exactly the sentence meaning. After that Wington went on to do the second level task. After struggling for a few minutes, she decided to organize the idea in Chinese and asked Yuan if she could work on these ideas with English equivalents. Yuan seemed very happy with this suggestion as she was struggling with what to write about. Wington then showed Yuan what she wrote in Chinese and read aloud to her because Yuan, like most of the British born Chinese, had only a very limited vocabulary, though fluent in speaking. With the help of Wington, Yuan quickly found the English equivalents for the Chinese expressions and also suggested some changes of different wordings and sentence patterns. The second level task ended with perfect sentences.

(Field notes from participant observation in Wington's literacy class)

A number of studies from both Piagetian and Vygotskian traditions focus on the sharing of decision-making or perspective as an important factor in effective peer interaction. Many of them confirm that the most productive interaction appears to result from arrangements in which peers' decision-making occurs jointly, with a balanced exploration of differences of perspective (Rogoff 1990). In bilingual peer interaction such as that between Wington and Yuan, shared problem-solving results from an exchange of ideas in the two languages as different codes reflect different perspectives through different labels of the concept. What the field notes of the observation demonstrate is that the bilingual interaction between Wington and Yuan has led to a level of understanding unavailable in solitary endeavour or even monolingual collaborative interaction. The data also support the notion that shared problem-solving underlies the cognitive benefits of peer interaction as the process would provide both children with motivation, feedback and a sense of their own contribution.

Conclusion

What is unique about bilingual exchange teaching between peers? This chapter shows ways in which friends speaking a common language give each other a confidence which would otherwise be impossible for children in the early stages of learning. Three aspects typify their interaction: trust, respect and reciprocity. First, Wington has the confidence to have a go and trusts Yuan, who allows her to do as much or as little as she is able to. In Wington's case, this means using word-for-word repetition, thus gradually being able to take on whole chunks of the language she is beginning to master. Second, there is the aspect of respect. During bilingual exchange teaching a special type of equality exists between the learners that is absent even between siblings. The older girl is respected for her overall knowledge of literacy generally, her knowledge of Cantonese and her experience of the world. The younger child acts as a mediator of the English language and literacy yet at the same time is almost like a pupil of Wington, the older child. Maybe this is because Wington is one year older and Yuan is very aware of her friend's superior knowledge of spoken Cantonese as well as the written Mandarin form. Third, there is the notion of reciprocity. As a competent speaker and reader of English, we might expect Yuan to take on the traditional role of the teacher, quizzing and testing her 'pupil' on her learning. Older Bangladeshi British siblings as 'experts' in East London certainly went about teaching in this way – reflecting the approach of both their mainstream and community class teachers (Gregory 2001). However, what we see here is the exact opposite. It is Wington, the novice in English, who is demanding individual words and meanings. In doing so, she almost takes over the role of the teacher herself, particularly when she quizzes Yuan on her knowledge of phonics: 'What is the word starting with "M"?'

What we have seen provides a new dimension to the debate on the nature of 'scaffolding'. The learning taking place between Wington and Yuan cannot be referred to as scaffolding or guided participation as outlined earlier, since the 'helping' is cognitively equally taxing on both sides. A synergy is occurring, which is similar to that described between siblings but with one crucial difference: the roles of the more experienced English speaker and the novice are reversed. Since the teaching and learning takes place bilingually, the younger child, Yuan, whose English is more proficient, has to translate and interpret for the older child. Wington, in turn, retains her status of age by her carefully focused questions and her overall control of the whole lesson.

Note

1 As many of our documented data and videotaped data, such as younger children's diaries, conversations with parents and observations of peers' interaction, are encoded in Chinese, translation is employed and viewed as a valuable skill in our data analysis. Transcription of audiotaped or videotaped data, particularly of conversation, needs to be related to methodology. It is carefully displayed in its original forms. Whenever taped data involved in two or three languages is to be turned into a written text,

we deliberately transcribe those alien sounds into Latin script followed by English translation so that people could understand the oral text and at the same time, could hear the actual foreign sounds as if they were personally on the scene. Besides a specific format is designed for certain purposes of data display, for instance, we displayed my transcription in a way that different languages used in my interview were catalogued into different columns, so that a broader picture of certain themes that we attempted to address could be better presented and well established for data analysis.

Y. Chen

Chapter 10

Friendship literacy

Young children as cultural and linguistic experts

Manjula Datta

As the title of this book suggests, there are many pathways to literacy. This chapter looks closely at friendship as a pathway to literacy within and beyond the classroom setting. For many developing bilinguals, reading becomes merely word-calling. Too often we see bilingual readers left with an advanced knowledge of grapheme–phoneme relationships, without being able to construct meaning from text or develop the motivation to read (Gregory 1996; Datta 2000). Excerpts from two small-scale case studies are presented here to illuminate the importance of providing appropriate social contexts in which bilinguals can play an active role. Significant to this is access to culturally relevant texts as well as opportunities for children to interact freely with one another as they transact with those texts, relating life meanings to text and text meanings to life (Cochran-Smith 1984).

In the first case study, 'Is that what you do in Turkey?' we see three friends engaged in a literacy discourse about their favourite books. In the second study, 'In Greek it will be "dendro-tria",' we are introduced to two children in a Greek community language school learning as they use shared linguistic and cultural resources. Common to both studies is the children's interest in the chosen text and their fluid interchange of cultural and linguistic knowledge, moving in and out of the roles of expert and novice (Rogoff 1990). In the process they construct literacy knowledge that is significant to them at a personal level and, through their interactions, they help to define the term, friendship literacy.

'Is that what you do in Turkey?'

Mehmet, Daniel and Sam are three 7-year-old boys who attend an inner London multicultural primary school, where the majority of the children speak English as a second language. Mehmet is Turkish, Daniel is a native-English speaker and Sam is of Algerian French origin. I first observed the boys when they were sitting on the carpet very close to each other listening intently to a story read by their teacher. Through an intimate and silent dialogue of facial expressions and gestures that expressed delight, surprise or astonishment they collectively affirmed their enjoyment and understanding. After the literacy session, I asked them, 'Would you like to share your favourite books with each other?' Their eyes lit up with anticipation and as Mehmet put it, 'Yeah, it'd be fun!' When asked to choose their books they walked to the bookshelf purposefully and had no hesitation in making their selection.

A study of their further interactions took place over two 60-minute sessions. My interest in observing the boys was manifold. Chief among those were peer or friendship learning and how collaborative interactions about books activated literacy exchanges. In particular, I wanted to see what literacy language, knowledge and skills they were developing and using to construct meaning. What role did the individual play in peer interaction? What possibilities were there for the boys to learn literacy from one another? Would this model of learning encourage them to take risks and to think creatively?

I recorded Mehmet, Daniel and Sam's interactions on audiocassette and made additional notes of their non-verbal communications. My only explicit guidance was 'What would you like to share with your friends about your books? You can ask questions if you like'. This open-ended question seemed to activate interactive talk at a personal level. Working in the privacy and quiet of the library enabled the boys to keep up the flow of talk without interruption. The data were then transcribed and analyzed closely against cultural and linguistic knowledge and children's learning. In the following section, two excerpts from the data are used to illustrate how the boys shared linguistic and cultural knowledge with one another as they moved in and out of expert and novice roles. The first excerpt is from a conversation that the three boys had as Mehmet shared a picture book called *Celebrations* (Kindersley and Kindersley 1997) which was about celebrations around the world:

Mehmet: [Showing the picture book, *Celebrations*] This is my best book. *Celebrations* is a book of all celebrations around the world . . . I mostly look at Turkish ones because I'm Turkish.
[Effortlessly opens the book to a page with pictures of children in colourful costumes and begins his interpretations] Children's Day is a big festival in Turkey.
This is the first President of Turkey [pointing to another picture in the book]. It's Ataturk and his strategy in war was very good.
[Commenting on the next picture] [When] children celebrate in Turkey, they kiss their family's hands and put them on their foreheads, they [the family] give them money.
Daniel: Is that what you do in *Turkey*? [emphasis on 'Turkey']
Mehmet: Well we do it in Turkey *and* England [emphasis on 'and']
Daniel: Oh that's good.
Mehmet: [Continues reading and commenting on the text] At Cocuk Bayrami – At Celebrations [translating Cocuk Bayrami for his friends] – we sing songs. My favourite song is about Ataturk . . . I watched the children's festival in Ankara on TV, I saw children from China dancing. I like seeing children from other countries . . . it makes me want to visit those places.

Daniel:	Do they give presents?
Mehmet:	Well some people give presents.
Manjula:	[Seeing Sam not asking any questions, I asked him quietly] Do you want to ask anything Sam?
Sam:	I'm thinking.
Daniel:	Do they give cards? Like with a piece of paper they fold and draw a card. Like Christmas cards with little reindeer and . . .
Mehmet:	Well no, they don't make cards but there is always . . . [Suddenly sees a picture of Simit, a twisted dough ring] That's my bestest bread. It's called Simit.
Sam:	[Speaking for the first time] Has it got chocolate on it?
Mehmet:	Well no. It has sesame seeds on it . . . I love it!
Mehmet:	[Turning his attention to a picture of a sports stadium] There's lots of sports in Ankara stadium.
Daniel:	What kind of sports?
Mehmet:	Like wrestling – even the children wrestle. Here's a Turkish man in wrestling uniform [pointing to a picture] – and running. On celebration day the Boy Scouts give flowers and an army man gives a round circle of flowers like this [he points to a picture of a wreath] [and lays it] on the place in Ankara where Ataturk died.
Daniel:	Do they put a stick up, with flowers on it? You have like in churches.
Mehmet:	[Does not respond to Daniel's question, he continues] Well [when] grandpa died . . . Do you know in mosques . . . when someone dies or when praying there's two places, one for ladies' prayer room upstairs, and downstairs men's prayer room. But children can sit anywhere! When I go to the mosque I just run up and down, up and down . . . and when grandpa died, in the mosque
Sam:	[Interrupting] He died? How? Did they bury him?
Mehmet:	I didn't see the burial but I saw his coffin and he was high up on steps. Maybe that's the steps to heaven.
Daniel:	Is it?
Mehmet:	Maybe, I don't know.
Daniel:	Oh, he might have rose up to heaven.
Mehmet:	Yeah.
Daniel:	In Eid do they dance around?
Mehmet:	In Eid yeah, they give cards . . .
Daniel:	Oh they give cards? [Daniel at last gets the confirmation that Turkish people also exchange cards]
Mehmet:	It says on the card, 'Eid Mubarak', and sometimes there's one in Arabic and one in Turkish.
Daniel:	Oh . . . [appears to be lost in thought]

Sharing cultural knowledge and children's learning

Through Mehmet, Daniel and Sam's interaction, we see multicultural literacy in action. Mehmet, a fluent speaker of Turkish, is able to display his expertise to his friends and maintain personal identity. 'I'm Turkish', he says proudly. His friends legitimize this by showing keen interest in what he has to say and by asking questions which elicit further interpretations.

In Mehmet's talk we see fluid knowledge of his heritage and culture as he skims, scans, translates and interprets parts of the text and responds to his friends' questions. Given the opportunity to talk freely about a book that he could relate to at a personal level, Mehmet is able to take on the role of expert. Daniel and Sam are his apprentices. Mehmet's knowledge about the Turkish heritage culture makes him the most empowered voice in the group, as he possesses the primary knowledge base. It would also appear that his careful selection of topics accompanied by a lively commentary on the cultural symbols and events grabbed his listeners' imagination. He shares his admiration for Ataturk, 'the first President of Turkey'. With pride, he tells his friends that '[Ataturk's] strategy in war was very good'. He informs how Ataturk is celebrated and respected in Turkish society when he says, '[We] sing songs . . . My favourite song is about Ataturk . . . [the] Boy Scouts give flowers . . . on the place in Ankara where Ataturk died'.

Talking about cultural and religious celebrations and social customs, he tells his friends, 'Children's Day is a big festival in Turkey [when children] kiss their family's hands and put them on their foreheads [and] they give them money'. Then, he explains how, at the Muslim festival of Eid, they dance and exchange cards with the greeting, 'Eid Mubarak', written in Turkish and Arabic. He also tells them that Simit is his 'bestest bread' and we see him sharing his knowledge and love of sports as he explains that Ankara stadium is the main venue for sports and that wrestling is very popular, 'even children wrestle'. We see Mehmet transforming his personal experience into an informative narrative for his friends as he describes events and traditions: 'in mosques . . . when praying there [are] two places, one for ladies' prayer room upstairs, and downstairs men's prayer room'. With great relish he tells his friends that children can sit anywhere: 'I just run up and down, up and down' and Daniel and Sam share a secret smile.

Clearly Mehmet draws on his cultural knowledge to make connections with the text and Daniel, and to some extent Sam, contributes to this multilayered talk, encouraging Mehmet to reflect and elaborate on his narrative. Looking closely we see that Daniel asks thoughtful and probing questions: 'Is that what you do in Turkey'? 'Do you give cards, like . . . ?' These questions help affirm Mehmet's identity as the expert while Daniel's questions suggest that he is looking for commonalities between cultures. It would seem that living and attending school in a very multicultural area has helped make him aware of similarities and differences between cultures. Through his school's celebrations of children's religious festivals of Eid, Diwali, Christmas, Chinese New Year and Hanuka, for example, Daniel has had access to looking at and sharing different celebrations, rituals and practices. It may therefore be inferred that on a bigger map, Daniel's line of questioning is informed by an awareness of multicultural literacy that can help avoid 'the impoverishment of uniformity in literacy' (Baker 2001: 330). His multicultural experiences have provided him with higher level 'mental contact' (Rogoff 1990: 181) as cultural meanings and symbols converged in some ways and diverged in others. Beyond this we see how Daniel's questions bridge two cultures. 'Like Christmas cards'? and 'Like in a church' would suggest that he tries to relate new cultural knowledge to personal knowledge. Daniel's expression, 'Oh that's good', indicates his affirmation of such cultural exchanges and his questions add different perspectives that allow Mehmet to enrich his narrative.

Sharing linguistic expertise and children's learning

In the data excerpt, we see Mehmet as a fluent language user. Not only does he show his literacy and linguistic skills in skimming, scanning and translating text, but also we see in him a true narrator. As Minami (2002: 48) writes, 'narratives enable individuals to make sense of their experiences in culturally satisfying ways'. Mehmet's use of narrative language is clear. He has a good sense of audience and uses narrative catchers such as 'Do you know?' and he inserts rhythmic speech and humour to hold his listeners' attention. He fluently transforms personal experience into information and weaves a story in the same utterance when he explains that in mosques there are two prayer rooms but when he goes to the mosque: 'I just run up and down, up and down'. Adding anecdotes of this kind embellish his narrative and produce the desirable effect as Daniel and Sam respond by smiling at each other. Narrative is central to children's learning, 'It is a way of ordering experience, answering both to emotional and cognitive aspects of social and cultural existence' (Bearne 1998:149). In the flow of his narrative, it seems that Mehmet invents his own myth when he tells that his grandfather's coffin was 'placed high up on the steps, maybe they're steps to heaven'. He expertly 'recruits the [listener's] imagination' (Bruner 1986: 26) and thereby strengthens his bond with his listeners (Egan 1992).

In Daniel, on the other hand, we see evidence of 'multiple perspectives . . . beholding the world not univocally but simultaneously' (Bruner 1986: 26). Mehmet's narrative activates his cultural knowledge and curiosity and adds to his personal knowledge energetically. Embedded in these interpersonal exchanges are most profound literacy developments – making fluent inferences, deductions, evaluating past knowledge to inform current thinking and asking questions (Britton 1972; Bearne 1998), necessary for school literacy development.

It may seem that Sam did not actively participate for much of the conversation. Algerian French, Sam was a developing bilingual. Although he understood most of what was said in English, he was still learning how to use a range of grammatical structures to communicate meanings clearly. Throughout the episode I observed him listening intently as he changed facial expressions and sometimes nodded in agreement. He seemed to be listening carefully so that he could make connections linguistically and cognitively. When I asked him if he wanted to ask anything, his response, 'I'm thinking', was germane. The collaborative network of friends allowed Sam space to look, listen and think; to make connections with emotions, thoughts and ideas; and to learn, from his peers, how to articulate those emotions, thoughts and ideas. When he felt ready to ask questions, they were matters of personal significance: 'Has it got chocolate on it?' 'He died? How?' 'Was he buried?'

In another episode, Sam was able to take the lead in the role of expert because of the opportunity to make choices and to talk freely as he shared a book with his friends. His choice of book, *Hairy Maclary from Donaldson's Dairy* (Dodd 1983), was well suited to his specific needs and developing linguistic strengths in English. The text's rhythmic grouping of sounds (Datta 2000: 235–46), alliteration and rhymes made it possible for Sam to read easily and led to choral chanting and linguistic fun. Sam read the book aloud with ease and vigour and Daniel and Mehmet listened to him attentively. He faltered in a few places, but the correct words were quickly given by his friends without disrupting the flow of his reading. Whenever he came to read the refrain, 'and Hairy Maclary from Donaldson's Dairy', they all joined in with a tone of finale. Their shared delight in the experience was obvious as they reached the climax of the book:

Sam: When suddenly [read in a big voice; his friends moved closer to him]

Everyone: [Reading in chorus] Out of the shadows they saw [tension building up in their voices] SCAREFACE CLAW, the toughest Tom in town [followed by a burst of hearty laughter].

A few things became clear to me from Sam's book-sharing episode. The animated choral reading of the last lines demonstrated how performing language can be an important aspect of the language learning process, helping bilinguals to connect with the sound and syntax of the new language emotionally. Their delight helps us understand how 'emotions are seen to be vital' (Johnstone 1993: 139) in the acquisition of a new language. As a developing bilingual Sam's choice of books with rhythm and patterned language seemed intuitive as the books provided linguistic experience of rhythm, rhyme and images that can be extremely supportive in the new language environment. Also, Sam's friendship with Mehmet and Daniel provided him with peer models, emotional support and the vision of taking small confident steps in learning the new language actively. All this was energizing for Sam (compare Vipul in Datta 2000: 171–2) and encouraged him to read beyond word calling. Daniel and Mehmet accepted Sam as a friend. There was no looking down upon his level of reading or choice of book. His sense of self seemed to develop strongly within the group.

It would seem that when given the opportunity to make choices and talk freely with friends in a stress-free environment (Dulay *et al.* 1982), the children were able to move in and out of roles to move the discourse forward. When given the opportunity to make personal choices, the developing bilinguals were able to step into the role of expert with relative ease and the native-English speakers seemed comfortable taking on the role of apprentice or novice. Moreover, through their social discourse, the participants' repertoire of literacy was activated and meaning was made at a very personal level. Comfort in moving in and out of expert–novice roles supported their fluid exchange of knowledge and broadened horizons of learning.

In Greek it will be 'dendro-tria'

Using data from the second case study, we look at how Antonios, an inspired student teacher, set up a model of 'friendship literacy' in his community language school and how this provided a context for 9-year-old friends, Nikos and Leonidas, to construct meaning together and to learn from one another. The boys went to the same mainstream school and spoke fluent Greek, which was their first language. Both were consecutive bilinguals (as opposed to simultaneous bilinguals), i.e. they learned the second language (English) on entering school and not simultaneously as they grew up learning Greek at home.

Antonios noted that despite the active support of parents, the children in the school did not seem to be motivated to learn, especially as they had to give up their Saturday play and television viewing. They also found it very difficult to keep their minds focused on what the teacher wanted them to learn. Antonios was looking for a teaching style that would engage the children's minds actively and decided to introduce a model of friendship literacy to encourage peer learning and peer teaching. Here is a brief account of how he proceeded:

- Antonios read the poem, 'The Navigator' aloud with tone, intonation and rhythm.
- The class collaboratively constructed the meaning of the word, navigator, discussing what it meant to them.
- In friendship pairs the children were asked to read the poem aloud.
- The children were then asked to read the poem in friendship pairs and talk about the significance of images in the poem and look at some literary features, e.g. use of rhymes.
- Finally the pairs were asked to evaluate this style of learning.

Antonios' selection of poetry as a context to activate literacy talk in Greek between the two friends is interesting. Poems contain specific linguistic features, rhythm, rhyme and alliteration, which are conducive to tuning into the phonology and syntax of a new language and are easily retained in memory. His choice of poem 'The Navigator' by the Greek poet, Rita Ploumi-Papa, was appropriate for this reason. Some lines from the poem are presented below in Greek with English transliteration (translating into English while keeping as close as possible to the way literary meanings are expressed in Greek, to give the reader a flavour of Greek ways of saying things). The navigator in the poem is a 10-year-old boy. The structure of repeated rhyming couplets is visible even to non-Greek readers:

Ο θαλασσοπόρος	*The Navigator*
Έχω ένα καράβι τόσο με πανιαά	I have a ship big with sails
θάλασσες αφήνει, θάλασσες περνά	That comes across the sea, travelling through the sea
. . .	. . .
Στην Ινδία, στο Βόλγα, στο Μισσισσιππή	To India, to Volga, to Mississippi
Τρέχει το καράβι μου, πάει σαν αστραπή	My ship runs, it goes like a flash
. . .	. . .
Προς τα πολυτρίχια λίγο παρά 'κει	Beside the brooms . . .
Το τιμόνι αν στρίψω να κι η Αφρική	If I turn the helm here it is Africa

Antonios observed, recorded and made field notes on the boys' literacy encounters and non-verbal expressions. Data were collected in a 90-minute session at the community language school, which Antonios translated freely in English, endeavouring to stay close to Greek expressions. I analyzed the data against the principles set out at the beginning of this chapter and throughout the process I was in close dialogue with Antonios to check for accuracy against his records. Antonios' observations showed that the boys were mixing languages to express and exchange thoughts and ideas. It is a normal linguistic characteristic of bilinguals to make switches to keep up the flow of conversation. The following excerpts from his English text offer examples of literacy encounters between Nikos and Leonidas around the poem, 'The Navigator'.

Nikos and Leonidas began by reading the poem taking turns. At the end of the poem Nikos made the first comment:

Nikos: This is good. It's not like the poems that we learn in English school. It is talking about . . . a 10-year-old boy who imagines that he is a captain in a boat and he travels in many beautiful places such as cities, rivers and countries Ινδία, στο Βόλγα, στο Μισσισσιππή, China, Suez, Constantinople and Panama . . . I think that his dream is to become a captain and meet a lot of people when he grows up. Have you read anything

Leonidas: [Interrupting] I really liked the poem because there are so many descriptions so you can imagine how is the place where this boy is dreaming . . . When it says that 'I have a ship such big with sails' or

'Sitting close to a flowerpot of mint' you can see these pictures in your mind and feel like the hero of the poem. It has fun . . . See, it says, 'Beside the broom a beat away from them; if I turn the helm, here it is Africa'. It is sure that the boy has a big imagination as he thinks that he is going to find Africa beside the brooms! I have never thought to search for a country near the brooms! [Leonidas laughs]

Nikos: It is not his fault! [Nikos switches to English as he is upset at Leonidas making a joke about the young Navigator's use of metaphor] You said that there aren't countries beside the brooms! We all know that, but this [is a poem to] show how much the boy wants to visit places, that 'if he turns the "broom" he can see Africa'.

Leonidas: OK, Nikos. Don't be angry. I didn't say that. [My dream is] to learn Italian, it's one of my best countries and I imagine I'll talk to my [Greek] grandmother for many hours. But she doesn't speak a word of Italian.

Nikos: [Nikos again switches completely into English as he responds still in anger] It's your dream but there's no way to learn [teach] your grandmother Italian! [Nikos switches back to Greek in a familial tone] Why your grandmother Leonidas?

Leonidas: Because I love her so much and we discuss lots of things. I live with her a lot of time because my parents work till late.

Nikos: [Nods in sympathy. Traditionally it is a norm for Greek grandmothers to look after children.] The poem also tells us about China. China is opposite Japan. It's bigger than Japan and has lots of people. They wear different long clothes and have bicycles to go to their work. [I like the poem because] it is easy to understand and it is about a boy like us . . . I think that we have some commons with him . . . The best part for me is when his mother calls him to eat and he forgets all his dreams! It is very funny and I like it because I like food! What was your best part in the poem?

Leonidas: Where it says that he wants to go to Volga and Mississippi. I want to see all these rivers standing in a boat. Do you know how many times I went on the Thames River cruise? A lot.

Sharing cultural knowledge and children's learning

The excerpt shows the children's ability to switch between languages and expert–novice roles as they engage in a wide-ranging literacy discussion. As they talk, they use many aspects of literacy discourse. They visualize settings, identify implicit meanings and take a critical stance as they give reasons for their personal views. Importantly, we see the boys making personal links with many aspects of the poem. It seems that the theme of the poem and their emotional relationship with a shared heritage culture supports their use of these valuable literacy skills.

Antonios noted that Nikos and Leonidas appeared to be excited and proud to be reading a poem by a Greek poet. Nikos' comments demonstrate this, 'This is good. It's not like the poems that we learn in English school'. We also note their empathy for the protagonist of the poem. 'You can see these pictures in your mind and feel like the hero of the poem', reflects Nikos' familiarity with the cultural artifacts that the poet uses – images of sight and smell. For example, 'I have a ship such big with sail' conjures up images of sailing ships that he sees while playing by the sea in Cyprus on family holidays. Or 'Sitting close to a flowerpot of mint . . . ' reminds him of the familiar smell of home cooking. Nikos' comment that 'we have some commons with him' echoes this as well. Further, he adds that, 'it is about a boy like us' and talks about commonalities such as his adventure and his love for food. Continuing with the theme Leonidas relates to the navigator's 'big imagination', which moves him to construct a very personal image eloquently, 'I want to see all these rivers standing in a boat'. We also see the boys sharing the implicit humour in the poet's style, 'It's very funny when his mother calls him to eat and he forgets all his dreams', says Nikos, which is matched with Leonidas' comment, 'I have never thought to search for a country near the broom'. Leonidas finds the literal meaning of the metaphor (broom) very funny. All this contributes to a rich tapestry of meanings co-created by the young readers.

Sharing linguistic expertise and children's learning

As a part of teacher guidance, the children were asked to identify and talk about the use of rhymes in the poem. This gave rise to a very interesting and high level linguistic discussion on how original rhymes are lost in translations. Leonidas started reading the poem again in Greek and English. When he came to the third couplet, he exclaimed:

Leonidas: Look Nikos! [Leonidas switches into English completely in excitement] In [the] Greek [text] the rhyming words make sense but when you read them in English [looking at the translated version] there is no rhyme!
Nikos: What do you mean?
Leonidas: [Reads some of the rhyming words again to emphasize his point that the words rhyme in Greek but not in English]
thalassomahos/monahos (sea-fighter/alone)
kavi/karavi (capes/ship)
Mississippi/astrapi (Mississippi/flash)
[He continues to emphasize this by citing a couplet from the poem]
Στην Ινδία, στο Βόλγα, στο Μισσισσιππή (Mississippi)
Τρέχει το καράβι μου, πάει σαν αστραπή (flash)

Leonidas explains the contrast between the Greek and its English translation saying that in Greek, Μισσισσιππή and αστραπή (Mississippi-astrapi) rhyme, but that in the English translation, 'Mississippi' and 'flash' (astrapi) do not rhyme:

Leonidas: They are heard totally different. The rhyme does not exist.

Nikos: You are right, maybe because Greek words are different from English words. Let's make up some rhyming words in English.

Leonidas: I can think of two rhyming words in English *tree* and *three*, but in Greek it will be *dendro-tria* (tree-three) [Both laugh]

Nikos: What's the Greek word for rhyme?

Leonidas: I don't know so much Greek.

Nikos: Yes, neither do I, but we can find it from the vocabulary!

The boys find a vocabulary (dictionary) and find that in Greek, the word 'rhyme' is *rima*:

Leonidas: It sounds like rhyme.

Nikos: Yes, I think that this is a Greek word.

Leonidas: Interesting!

Antonios noted that throughout their talk the children demonstrate the bilingual characteristic of code-switching, 'the use of more than one language in the course of a single speech act' (Gumperz 1982: 59). These switches are influenced by many factors: to express familiarity or solidarity, to show shared interest in topics of conversation or to show emotions. In this excerpt, we see that Nikos switched to English when he was upset and angry with Leonidas' joke around the metaphorical use of 'broom' in the poem. Because the poem was written in Greek, he seemed to feel that Leonidas was mocking the language. Later, Leonidas' sudden switch to English was triggered by his excitement at discovering the disappearance of rhyme in the English text. These switches between languages show the boys' expertise in using multiple sources of information – language referents – to communicate ideas about culture and language and to make deeper and personal meaning of the poem. At a metalinguistic level we see fluid interchange of roles and linguistic expertise. Leonidas' discovery of the loss of rhymes in the translated text poses a problem and Nikos offers a possible explanation 'because Greek words are different from English words'. We also come across some unique expressions in their text, which result from mixing expressions from both languages such as, 'we have some commons' and 'big imagination'.

The children made some significant points about friendship learning style in their evaluation as their conversation around the poem continued:

Nikos: [Looking at his watch] Do you know that we are discussing the poem for a long time?

Leonidas: Yes, and the strange thing is I enjoyed it because we could say whatever we wanted and there isn't a teacher to tell us that this is wrong, try again, think more and all these things!

Nikos: Yes. It was like a talk.

Leonidas: And it is better than reading it by myself . . . This [reading together] has more interest!

Nikos: But, if there isn't a teacher you can't get 'congratulations' or something like that.

Leonidas: Yes, [and] we could laugh and say things . . . But the teacher who knows more things he thinks that everything is easy.

Evaluating their learning experience, the boys expressed their desire to use the same model of learning – friendship literacy – in their English school. Their comments highlight the importance of a stress-free environment and opportunities for social interaction, both important conditions for and benefits of friendship literacy. Their comments sum up those conditions and benefits as they said, 'we could say whatever we wanted', 'it is better than reading it by myself' and 'we could laugh'.

Conclusion

Mehmet, Daniel and Sam, Nikos and Leonidas supported one another's language and literacy learning through their friendship, thus the term, friendship literacy. Their friendship allowed them to talk freely around selected texts and allowed fluid interchange of expert–novice roles, enjoying the experience of sharing, appreciating and supporting one another. Friendship and acceptance within the group energized and motivated a shared culture of learning, 'a joint culture creating' (Bruner 1986: 127). Individuals in the group were able to construct themselves strongly as readers. They exchanged thoughts and ideas fluently without the fear of being wrong and made personal connections with new meanings through free interactions. Together, they co-created knowledge, understanding and new perspectives and created a connected discourse between home and school. This was clearly supported by the security and fun that friendship literacy offered. Comments like, 'I want to do this again in my Greek school and English school' indicate emotional and motivational involvement with the process. It is clear that, for these children, language was not a neutral means of communication or representation; it was primarily 'a means of cultural construction in which our very selves and sense are constituted' (Chambers 1994: 22). Shared meaningful contexts and personal construction of texts empowered the learners in both the studies to move fluidly between different levels of reading skills – literal, inferential, deductive and evaluative – for deeper understanding and enjoyment of text. They easily transferred these skills from one language to another (Cummins 1991).

Through their interactions, we see literacy as a social construct. Expert and apprentice roles were fluidly acted, interchanged and reversed in different contexts of the same discourse. Knowledge is seen to be jointly constructed and contributed to by all the participants as they built integrally on each other's contributions to the conversation (Rogoff 1990). In the process, the children's transactions with texts went far beyond mere word calling. Their conversations reveal a depth of comprehension and connection to text that might not have been possible in settings where they had no access to culturally appropriate resources and in which there were no opportunities to allow conversations to emerge freely. This is particularly significant for bilingual students, since research evidence suggests that bilinguals' underachievement in schools 'is not caused primarily by lack of fluency in English [but is] the result of particular kinds of interactions in school that lead culturally diverse students to mentally withdraw from academic effort' (Cummins 1996: 65). Friendship literacy can help cross barriers in multicultural classrooms and engage students positively and energetically in the pursuit of learning. As Leonidas said, 'the strange thing is I enjoyed it'.

Chapter 11

Learning to be just

Interactions of White working-class peers

Rebecca Rogers and Melissa Mosley

In 2001, a major manufacturing plant located in Crossroads announced plans to close the assembly plant that would result in 2,600 people being out of work.[1] The workers of the assembly plant decided that if the company was going to shut its doors, then they would have to shut down the most efficient plant in the country. Led by the local trade union, they developed a five-year plan for boosting productivity. The efforts have been successful. The newspaper reports, 'local workers have shown marked improvements in the most recent audit . . . if they stay on track, the workers have been told that they might be able to garner the prize of being the automaker's best plant'. A worker stated, '[w]e need to keep making improvements daily and show [the company] we mean business as far as being the best of the best' (Cancelada 2001). The workers remain optimistic they can change their own fate despite the fact that after a year of increased productivity, company executives have announced that their cost-cutting plan, which includes the plant closure, remains on track.

Rather than walk out on their jobs or protest the flight of many American-based companies to areas of cheaper labour, the workers of Crossroads accepted the challenge to *work together* to *work harder*. It is a story of collective action that emerged from a community of practice that ultimately benefits the interests of management until it shuts down. These contradictions, hard work and the changing face of the world of work, make up the threads of life in Crossroads.

This plant is one of the places where the parents of the White and working-class children who participated in this study work. Other children in this study are sons and daughters of electricians, waitresses, cement pourers, teachers and assembly line workers. The nature of work in Crossroads involves adjusting to layoffs and downsizing in manufacturing plants and an aerospace corporation, both major sources of employment. At the same time that the worker response to the shutdown was announced in the newspaper, the 7- and 8-year-old students in Melissa Mosley's second grade classroom were engaged in a six week unit on African American history,[2] focused specifically on civil rights and the abolition of slavery. The unit was situated within a critical/accelerative literacy framework.[3]

In this framework, we set out to study peer interactions charged by the Littleton's (2002: 248) challenge of 'careful analyses of discourse which focuses on the continual, subtle processes of negotiation and renegotiation of meaning. There is also a pressing need for analyses which consider the particular historical, institutional and cultural contexts of collaborative activity'. To foreshadow our conclusions, there were many different types of peer interactions between the White, working-class students in this classroom. Arguably, the social nature of learning and the peer interactions would prepare the children for the new world of work that includes communities of practice and peer interactions. However, we shall demonstrate that within a critical literacy curriculum, it is not the existence of a community of practice that is important but the issue of 'community of practice toward what ends'. Specifically, our research question was: in what way does a socially just framework emerge from a community of practice within a White, working-class classroom? In this chapter we focus on peer interactions within a unit on African American history and the problem-posing and solving that led to the investigation of a current day problem, one of relevance for the children and their families. We demonstrate how, through peer interactions, the children learned to question each other, question the authority of the text and question social practices.

The changing working class

The world of work is changing. The 'fast capitalist' society characterized by communities of practice, a global economy and dramatic shifts in the workforce are replacing the factory-model of work (e.g. Gee 2000; Wenger et al. 2001; Florida 2002). In the changing world of work, there is a flattened hierarchy and workers think creatively and flexibly and are responsible for not only consuming and synthesizing information but for producing knowledge. Many constructivist classrooms mimic the type of community of practice that will prepare children for the new workforce. There has been, however, a 'back to the basics' backlash in federal policies and state mandates. Gee (2000) points out the contradiction in a workforce that insists on communities of practice and a 'back to the basics' model of school that is reminiscent of a factory model of education.

Peer learning and communities of practice

Wenger (1998) defines a community of practice as a unit where people share mutual engagement, a joint enterprise and a shared repertoire (of actions, stories and artifacts). Wenger (1998: 7) writes: 'communities of practice are an integral part of our daily lives. They are so informal and so pervasive that they rarely come into explicit focus, but for the same reasons they are also quite familiar'. Every *community of practice* consists of an ideologically laden set of beliefs, actions and assumptions. When students or workers jointly problem-solve they are always doing so in someone's interests. This set of practices can serve just or unjust ends. Most communities of practice, however, are discussed as politically neutral and as children or adults talking and working together towards an objective 'joint enterprise'.

Peer interactions are central within a 'communities of practice' framework. Ellis and Whalen (1990) offer three reasons why peer learning is more effective than learning alone. First, to learn, children need the opportunity to talk and think about what they are doing. As they talk, they hear what they do and do not understand. Second, in collaborative groups children are focused on completing the problem-solving goal. Third, the group situation forces children to engage in higher order thinking skills such as analysis and synthesis. Much of this has been repeated in the literature on socio-constructivist perspectives on teaching and learning (e.g. Tudge 1990; Jennings and Di 1996; Almasi and Gambrell 1997; McCormack 1997; McMahon 1997; see Joiner *et al.* 2000 for a careful critique of the literature on collaboration). Sawyer (2002) offers a new perspective to the literature on collaboration with the concept of emergence. He argues that the goals of the group interactions emerge from the group, rather than being the property of any one individual. Crook (2000) asserts that peer learning has too seldom been situated in a sociocultural-economic framework in which its real problems and solutions arise.

Methodology and context

Woods Elementary School, the site of the research, lies within a closely packed group of small tract houses in the city of St. Francis. The school lies in the large suburban school district of Crossroads. The school's report card reflects its high achievement. Parent–teacher involvement is high. About 15 percent of the students receive a free or reduced meal at Woods Elementary School. Melissa's classroom consists of fourteen White students, six African American students and one Asian American student. The large population of White students reflects the population in St. Francis, where 85 percent of the residents are White and 11 percent are African American.

Situating ourselves, the intervention, data collection and analysis

Our intention, within the action research framework (Allen 1999; Cochran-Smith and Lytle 1999; Wells 2001), was to improve our own teaching and our students' literacy, especially with socially just forms of literacy instruction. The first researcher is a European American woman university professor from a working-class family. The second researcher is a European American woman from a working-class family in a suburban Midwestern city. We each took the role of teacher and researcher in the project. We focused our data collection and analysis on two groups of five case study students. We used children's literature (e.g. read alouds, listening centres and guided reading books) to learn about injustices, to critique textual authority and as a tool of social action.

We collected data every morning during the two-hour language arts block for a total of six weeks. The language arts block was comprised of guided reading using levelled texts, independent reading, word work, read alouds and shared reading, peer writing and writer's workshop and peer discussions after listening to books on tapes. During this time, we focused our data collection on formal and informal peer interactions. We recorded peer interaction episodes in field notes and on video and audiotape. We also collected documents and conducted interviews with the students (Spradley 1980; Emerson *et al.* 1995).

We focused our analysis on the language arts episodes where peer interactions occurred. We used Hennessey and Murphy's (1999) definition of peer collaboration – 'children actively communicating and working together, talking and sharing their cognitive resources to establish joint goals and referents, to make joint decisions, to solve emerging problems, to generate and modify solutions and to evaluate outcomes of dialogue and action' – to guide our analysis. At the end of each data collection session we discussed things that surprised us and changes we would make.

Analysis of the data was qualitative, ongoing and informed by the literature. We first analyzed the data chronologically. We developed codes that indexed the type and function of peer interactions (e.g. teacher initiated/teacher led, challenging the text; student initiated/teacher led, maintaining the status quo; student initiated/ student led, challenging social practices). Our second analysis was a discourse analysis. We analyzed the field notes and transcripts by idea units (Gee 1999) and focused on the content of the peer learning. Our third analytic technique focused on the process of peer learning (e.g. how the children collaborated as they constructed understandings). At this stage in the analysis, we recontextualized our analysis within and across the unit at the local, institutional and societal domains.

Questioning each other: making meaning of Whiteness

Melissa started the unit on African American history with read alouds and instructional level literature that the children could read that related either to the civil rights movement or to the abolition of slavery. In discussions that occurred early in the unit, the students agreed that unequal treatment of African Americans was unfair but their discussion was about 'them'. They failed to include themselves, as White students, as a group of people implicated into the actions of slavery and civil rights. They had a number of misunderstandings that were sorted out through peer interactions. For example, they collectively did not understand what 'the big deal was' that Rosa Parks and other African Americans had to sit on the back of the bus because, 'at least they weren't walking'.

Many of the misunderstandings were rooted in the historical lack of attention paid to the role of Whites and associated privilege in texts, in the curriculum and in the children's lives. On this issue Stuart-Wells and Crain (1997) write:

> [Whites] disassociate themselves from racial inequality, as if the colour line had been drawn without their involvement . . . The turning point in the

civil rights movement occurred when Whites began to believe that there were no more vestiges of discrimination, a misunderstanding that led to frustration in black communities and eventually to rioting . . . because they [Whites] never clearly understood the subtle and not-so-subtle ways they created segregation, Whites conveniently ignore the relation between White privilege and black deprivation.

(Stuart-Wells and Crain 1997: 84)

As students explored the literature and other texts in the classroom more in depth with their peers, we heard them making sense of their Whiteness, a line of inquiry that is necessary for an antiracist curriculum (McIntyre 1997; Ladson-Billings 2001).

In an interaction around the book *The Underground Railroad* (Johns 2000), Paul took a historical perspective, an important aspect of critical literacy. In this discussion he took the perspective of the White slave owner who would be angry if someone took his property away. He realized the emphasis put on personal property in our society and made sense of how that ideology comes into play in a historical event. Instead of accepting Paul's assumption, with prompting from the teacher, Curt disagreed with him. He asked Paul *why* he would feel bad and asked him to consider a different perspective:

RR:[4]   Maybe. How do you think it would have felt to be on the Underground Railroad?
Curt: I think it would feel like very happy because you are going to freedom.
RR: What if you were a conductor?
Curt: I would feel so happy because I am leading the people to freedom.
Paul: I would feel kind of bad because I would be taking away from the owner and I didn't get the owner's permission.
RR: What do you mean the owner?
Paul: Like the owner of the slaves. Taking the slaves without the owner's permission.
RR: Can someone respond to Paul?
Curt: Why would you feel bad? Because you should be happy because you are running away from slavery.

Curt felt comfortable, within the context of the guided reading group, to challenge his peer's feelings and intentions about helping a slave escape to freedom. In addition, he reinforced his position when it came into question with Paul's argument. Questioning beliefs and intentions is at the heart of critical literacy.

This was the first time that a student identified themselves as a White person in the discussions. This may be because most texts that focus on slavery illustrate White people as oppressors. Within this framework, there is little incentive for White children to relate to the actions, motives and intentions of their ancestors.

They seem to be in the precarious position of locating themselves in discussions about race but not wanting to identify with what it meant to be White in history. Children's literature often does not give many examples of people of European descent taking roles side by side in the struggle for equity – who Stuart-Wells and Crain (1997) refer to as 'visionary Whites'. Indeed, when we asked the children how they would feel if they were at Martin Luther King Jr.'s speech (after they listened to the speech), Sam responded, 'If I was there and I was White, which I am, I wouldn't feel very good but I would apologize' (guided reading lesson). Melissa knew it would be difficult for the children to step into action, to interrupt social injustices, if they could not see themselves as working for justice within the context of literature and in the social world (informal interview, 27/1/03).

Questioning the text: making meaning of history

The comfort of asking and answering questions of their peers generalized to their joint critique of the authority of the text. The next interaction occurred during a guided reading lesson (23/1/03) in the book *The Bus Ride* (Miller 1998). The book is a narrative of a young girl, constructed after Rosa Parks, who refused to give her seat up on the bus. The girl is brought to jail and the text states that the girl's mom thinks the police are 'wasting their time' and should be catching 'real criminals'. Melissa asked the children if they agreed with the text:

Sarah: In this picture, there might be some crime and they're just wasting their time watching her, making sure she's not going to escape and there is probably crime out in the city.

Larry: But Sarah, back then that was a crime, because it was against the law back then.

Sam: Yeah because back then, like Martin Luther King Jr., like Larry said.

MM: What do you think Katrina?

Katrina: Yeah because there could be other Blacks or African Americans doing it too.

MM: Doing the same thing Sara did?

Katrina: Yeah because they thought it was brave.

Sam: [I have a question . . .

MM: Because they thought it was brave?

Sam: Miss Mosley, I have a question.

MM: Yes?

Sam: Why is this guy, a policeman, Black? That guy's Black and that guy's White. So why can't she sit on the bus? I don't get it, there's a Black . . .

Sarah: [Hey maybe, different places, like if there is two places in a police station, like this one's the White room and this one's the black room. What about that? So what if he's just walking to his room?

Sarah began by stating that the police were wasting their time because there were other crimes in the city to take care of. Larry used his historical understanding of segregation laws to disagree with Sarah and stated, 'back then that was a crime, because it was against the law back then'. The safe forum of the peer interactions where the students are encouraged to ask and answer big questions provided the context for the children to challenge each other's assertions. A few interactions later, Sam directed a question to the teacher, rather than to his peers. Sam had been intently examining the illustrations in the book. He noticed that there was an African American policeman in the illustration and wondered why, if there were African American policemen, why African American people could not sit anywhere they wanted to sit on the bus. This marks a departure from his earlier response that sitting in the back of the bus was better than walking. It also marks his critical interrogation of the text. Sarah indicated she believed the police headquarters was segregated and he was just walking through the White section of the police headquarters. In the same discussion, Sarah raised a question about the gap she saw between the illustration and the text. She stated, 'I don't get it. It says many White people and black people came up to shake her hand but I don't get it. I see black people but I don't see White people. Except for that one'. The children began asking questions of each other, of the text and of the historical conditions of racism.[5]

Melissa decided that the window was passing for her students to get involved in a project that could affect a local issue. That is, they were problem-posing with their peers at the textual level but not at the social level. Melissa called students into a whole group meeting, with two intentions. The first was to reinforce that Martin Luther King Jr. was concerned with all human rights. The second intention was to discuss the children's rights and help them to identify any places where their human rights were denied. Students identified things at school that were unfair, but the conversation ignited when the issue of neighbourhood vandalism arose:

Katrina: People throw stuff in our yard.
MM: What kind of stuff?
Katrina: Like trash.
Student: They put it in my yard too.
MM: How many people does that happen to? [Half the class raise their hand, the conversation continues to other neighbourhood vandalism examples]
Student: People throw rocks at our window.

The conversation continued with examples from students about people putting things in mailboxes, knocking over mailboxes, throwing eggs, toilet paper and other acts of vandalism. The students began to rally. Some students related the vandals to teenagers in the neighbourhood:

Brad:	My brother is a teenager and he doesn't do something like that.
MM:	Good for him. OK, so this might be something we can actually do something about. What do you think?
Student:	Speech!
Katrina:	Signs?
Class:	PROTEST!
Student:	What about call the police?
Sam:	Boycott.
Andrew:	I think you should get one of your friends and go door to door and see if they got TPed and if they did, you can have a sign.[6]
Paul:	Make posters.
Larry:	Put it in the newspaper, like with garage sales.
Student:	A website.
Student:	A letter.
Sam:	Another thing you could do is get some flyers.

Students began to use prior knowledge of non-violent resistance to apply to what could be done about the vandalism in their neighbourhoods. Most of the ideas presented (e.g. speeches, protests, signs) were from the discussions of civil rights and the abolition of slavery. The students moved from personal issues of unfairness (e.g. who is captain in kickball during recess) to a problem they were concerned about in their community. They drew on their prior knowledge of social justice to create a framework for social change. Their collective engagement in this discussion was an indicator that this was an issue that students would be passionate in exploring. The feeling of oppression had been ignited within the children in an issue that was, literally, close to home.

Questioning social practices and social action: two examples

Working for equity

We were impressed with the students' sense of caring, the critical questions they asked of each other, the texts they were reading and that they had found an issue that was important enough to move them towards action. Melissa wanted to push a little further and asked them to generalize the conditions of inequity to their own working class lives. These were inequities that remained invisible to them. In a capitalist society, working-class and race issues are often kept separated and thus they continue to feed into social inequities through their invisibility (Roediger 1991). Working-class issues and values were brought into the classroom through the children's comments about their parents' jobs and their attitudes towards authority (Willis 1977; Foley 1990; Weis 1990; Finn 1999; Hicks 2002). Indeed, their issue of vandalism was a working-class issue in its concern for the maintenance of property and order. To avoid the unproblematic reproduction of class inequalities, as was demonstrated in the opening vignette, Melissa wanted her students to work together to solve social problems that benefited their interests and the interests of others. She decided to use a text from their community – the same text that started this chapter.

With all of the children gathered together in the read aloud corner, Melissa held up the newspaper article that reported on the workers' response to the closing of the plant. 'This is happening at the plant', Melissa told her students. Larry responded, 'Oh yeah, I heard they are going to take it down but a few people will lose their jobs and some people don't want it to go down'. Melissa read the newspaper article about the plant closing to her students:

Curt: If they close it there won't be any cars for [us]!
Paul: Not about that! They are nervous about being shut down and about being fired and they are not doing their best.
MM: Actually, they are doing their best, they are working harder. Why are they working harder?
Andrew: Um, my dad, don't think it's going to close, because they have been saying they are going to close for a long time, they are working their hardest because they have done it before.

Paul questioned Curt's misunderstanding about the consequences of the plant closing, and instead asserted that the workers are facing injustice, rather than the consumers. Melissa brought the conversation back to the issue of the workers' strategy for maintaining jobs. Sensitive to the issue that many of the children in the classroom had parents who were laid off, had been laid off, or were looking for work, we decided to simulate discussions through role playing where the students had to step into the role of the workers, the community and management to explore the issue of social justice for workers.

[Workers]
Curt: We could make our own Plant!
Student: We could make our own business
All: Yeah
Paul: We would have to go to the
Curt: [management
Paul: No we'd have to go to the video, to the television stations and put it on a commercial,
Curt: They know everywhere is [the cars] and that means if they see a car, that means . . .
Pam: What if they see a new [name of car]
Paul: What if it doesn't have a [name of car] sign on it?
Curt: How are we goin to build it, we don't know how to build it
Pam: OK, hold on, shhh, don't talk

Andrew: But it takes like 2 million dollars just to build a Plant.
Student: Yeah!
Andrew: Because you need a place to get your checks at, and a place where you get hired and a place for them to get cars stocked up.

Andrew used his knowledge of the plant to scaffold his group's understanding of the problems with the idea of building the plant. Pam recognized his authority and quieted the group to hear his contribution. Paul, Curt and Andrew posed problems in this interaction that are responded to by the others to construct an alternate ending of the story. The students showed their understanding of the nature of protests and offered opposing viewpoints. Pam said, 'We shouldn't be doing anything, we shouldn't get mad'. Curt responded, 'Protest to keep the thing open'. The students recognized the need for social action and also referenced the news and community as sources of support for their cause. They drew up a petition to sign to keep the plant open and quickly received signatures of the students in the groups of management and community. The narrative they jointly constructed had a different ending than simply working together to work harder.

Re-enacting history

The teacher set a framework for social justice when combining the issue of playwriting as a genre to communicate a message to a group of people with the concerns that formed from the discussions around neighbourhood vandalism. Students collaboratively wrote scenes from a play that included people from history and from the local community. The scenes were a culmination of the unit on African American history as the students transferred what they knew about the intentions of change agents. The plays were also an avenue for the students to explore their roles as agents of social change and join the ranks of those who had rallied and protested for the rights of human beings in a democratic society. The playwriting was a representation of the same conviction and sensitivity that the workers of the automobile plant showed in their protest strategies. The final scene of the play was written by a group of three students and demonstrated peaceful protest, collective action and human rights. We end with the following scene constructed entirely by a group of peers:

Setting: Martin Luther King Jr.'s house, in the past
Characters: Martin Luther King, Jr., Coretta Scott King, Rosa Parks, teenagers
[Stage directions: all are in Martin Luther King Jr.'s house making signs.]
MLK: I want my sign to say no ding dong ditching
Coretta: I want my sign to say no TPing.
Rosa: I want my sign to say no littering.
Teen 1: We used to do that stuff, now we are helping to fight against it.
Teen 2: Yeah, we are helping to protest against vandalism and for equal rights.
        [They make signs, then take them outside and march]

Coretta: We want equal rights.

Teen 2:   No more fighting. Non-violence and no vandalism!

Rosa: We're still fighting for equal rights even if the police stop us. We're still fighting.

MLK: The laws don't make sense.

Coretta: It's not fair that we can't get along.

MLK.:   I have a dream that one day that freedom will ring. I have a dream that one day the nation will not be judged by the colour of their skin. I have a dream today.

Conclusion

The students in Melissa's classroom are preparing for a more just work order as they engage in communities of practice that have an explicit function aimed at social justice. The problem with an uncritical transition between school and work is the reproduction of work in the interest of the capitalist economy rather than in the interests of the social good. What is missing, advocates of the New Literacy Studies offer, is 'critical framing', what Gee (1999: 52) refers to as thinking 'critiquely'. Without critical framing, we have workers who problem-solve with peers, who are dedicated to the companies they work for, think creatively and flexibly but do not think about whose interest their work is serving.

In Melissa's classroom, the community of practice evolved as peers became critically literate and challenged each other, textual practices and social practices. The collective problem-posing and solving emerged when individuals collaborated in a series of creative activities, activities that are not the property of any one individual but emerge from the collaboration. The children collaborated to pose and solve problems at the textual and the social level.

The peer interaction was on a continuum from teacher supported to independent. The amount of teacher support gradually decreased over the course of the unit as the students posed problems that were of interest and concern to them. By the end of the unit, the students had constructed a problem (vandalism) and a solution with their peers. We would argue that the presence of the teacher in peer discussions is less important than the type of role the teacher takes up within these discussions. When we analyzed the role of the teacher in the guided reading groups, in the read alouds and in the peer discussions, the teacher's role had been that of facilitator, rather than that of transmitter of information. Within a democratic classroom, the teacher can enter the conversation as an active participant. An interesting aspect of the analysis that has come up but that we have not addressed in this chapter is the division between the level of understanding of racism and socially just practices in *discussions* and their level of understanding in *practice*. This points to the importance of a zone of proximal development in a critical literacy framework.

We have situated the discourse of collaboration within the larger sociocultural context of the working-class communities in which these children live. Many times we could see the enactment of the town's traditional patterns of working-class life that includes racist (and classist, sexist) ideologies. At other times, the students were charting a new course. We intend for the tale to capture the complexity of the tumultuous times the children and their families face and demonstrate how the peer interactions embedded within this critical/accelerative literacy framework are hard at work, resisting social inequalities.

Acknowledgements

This research was supported by the Sociological Initiatives Foundation. We would like to thank Lisa Gordon and Melissa Kniepkamp for their help in collecting data. A special thank you to the Literacy for Social Justice Teacher Research Group for providing feedback and encouragement on this research.

Notes

1   All names in this research are pseudonyms to protect the confidentiality of the students, the school and the district. Melissa Mosley's name (the teacher and co-researcher in this study) has not been changed.
2   Throughout this chapter we use the term African American to reference the historical, cultural and political roots of people in the US who are descendants of Africa. We have not edited the transcripts where the children refer to African American people as 'black people'.
3   By critical approaches we refer to approaches whose emphasis is on helping children develop a sense of agency with and within literacy practices so they are able to accomplish ends that are in their own and others' self-interest, while at the same time resist the coercive nature of language and literacy. Lewison et al. (2002) define four components of critical literacy that we draw from in this chapter: interrogating multiple perspectives, disrupting the common place, developing multiple perspectives and moving towards social action. By accelerative approaches we mean programmes like Reading Recovery and instructional strategies like guided reading that are centrally intended to move the slowest developing students, through focused attention to problem-solving within instructional level texts, to catch up with their grade-level counterparts. Melissa used a guided reading approach to literacy instruction (Fountas and Pinnell 1996). Melissa worked with small groups of children to support each reader's effective strategy use for processing texts at increasingly challenging levels of difficulty. We refer to Melissa's instructional approach as 'critical' guided reading because of her use of children's literature that was at an instructional level for each of her students within a guided reading framework.
4   RR refers to Rebecca Rogers and MM refers to Melissa Mosley in the transcripts.
5   By the end of the unit, the students demonstrate an awareness of racism – both historical and present day conditions. They wrote letters to Martin Luther King Jr., they made a list of 100 ways to honour Martin Luther King Jr. In their play writing they constructed scenes that reflected the racism before Brown v. Board as well as after. They also extended their understanding of racism to the current day political climate when they talked about how people of Middle Eastern descent are treated in the United States.
6   TPing is a form of vandalism where people throw toilet paper (TP) on property.

Part III

Learning in community settings

Introduction to Part III

These chapters demonstrate how necessary it is to move beyond school and family settings to understand the broader sociocultural and historical contexts in which literacies are constructed. In this part, we see prolepsis in action, as whole communities acting as mediators draw on the past and create activities in the present to teach children the knowledge and skills they will need to participate fully in the future. Sociocultural practices are syncretized in the process. The nurturing of children's social and emotional skills as well as their cultural expertise is interwoven with the development of multiple languages and literacies. Critically, such rich practices are described for communities whose young children are often labelled 'at risk of reading failure' because they are thought to arrive at school with few resources or literacy experiences.

Chapter 12, by Alessandro Duranti, Elinor Ochs and Elia K. Ta'ase, was originally published in the journal *Educational Foundations* in 1995. This classic article describes the process of teaching Samoan to Samoan American children, 5 years old and younger, in a church school in California. The children's participation in this context extended the socialization process of their homes as they learned how to be Samoan. The authors provide a thought-provoking discussion of the complexities of syncretic literacy as represented by the teacher's use of a literacy tool, a Samoan alphabet chart.

In Chapter 13, Leena Helavaara Robertson analyzes the bilingual learning and language use of 5- to 7-year-old British Pakistani children in a community school class located in their regular school. She describes the skill of their Pakistani teacher, who drew on the children's knowledge as a group to foster learning in Urdu and English simultaneously and to attend to the children's social, emotional and cultural development. Helavaara Robertson also describes the advantages of this multilingual group process for the children's literacy learning, their sense of agency that emerged and the knowledge and skills they developed that were beyond those typical for children of their age.

In Chapter 14, Gwendolyn McMillon and Patricia A. Edwards discuss in rich detail the literacy learning of 4- to 6-year-old African American children in an African American church. Within the historically significant learning environment of the church and within a community of caring and supportive adults, the

children developed specific literacy skills and understandings needed to participate in their community. This chapter also includes a discussion of the culturally
relevant strategies of the teachers and the reflections of older children who describe
the value of what they learned in church when they were younger.

Chapter 15, by Wendy L. Haight and Janet Carter-Black, is an illuminating
analysis of the ways in which the competence and learning of young African
American children are supported within an African American church. Insights
into child-rearing practices are based on an oral history with a church 'mother'.
Drawing lessons for teachers from their experience running a church computer
club, the authors describe both the role of the church in nurturing resilience
and spirituality as well as the characteristics of a distinctive, 'child-sensitive and
growth-oriented' approach to teaching and learning within a meaningful web of
relationships.

Chapter 16 deals more broadly with cultural literacy as Mary Eunice Romero
develops a clear picture of young Pueblo children learning from family and
community caretaker-teachers how to be members of the Pueblo worlds. As in
all the chapters in this part, this proleptic process is characterized by an emphasis
on individuals growing up as community members and by syncretism as religions,
calendars, oral and written languages and socialization practices are blended and
reinvented. Romero also discusses some of the strategies used by the caretaker-
teachers to share cultural knowledge and nurture children's growth.

Chapter 12

Change and tradition in literacy instruction in a Samoan American community

Alessandro Duranti, Elinor Ochs and Elia K. Ta'ase

Ancient Polynesians have captured the imagination of the west with their adventurous voyages in outrigger canoes across hundreds if not thousands of miles of ocean. Filled with pigs, fowl, taro roots, breadfruit and a rich oral tradition, these canoes carried Polynesian culture to islands throughout the Pacific (Howard and Borofsky 1989). Over a period of 3,000 years, settlers adapted to the new environments, producing the variety of cultures that comprises Polynesia (Kirch 1984). Today, despite European and American colonization, the dissemination of Polynesian cultures has not ended. Polynesians migrate in large numbers to the countries of their colonizers – Australia, New Zealand and the United States. With them, they continue to bring taro, breadfruit, fine mats and their oral tradition. These days they also bring a literate tradition, introduced to them by Christian missionaries. They carry with them their Bible and their memories of how they learned to read it. This is a story of how these memories organize community and school among people of Polynesian descent now living in an urban setting. We follow the voyage of a literacy tool from the Samoan Islands to a Samoan community in Los Angeles. Samoans call this tool the *Pi Tautau*.

In the 1830s, the London Missionary Society established itself in the Samoan Islands. They created a Samoan orthography and a Samoan language version of the Christian Bible (Williams 1832; Turner 1861; Huebner 1987). They established pastors' schools to transmit literacy skills necessary to read this important religious text. These schools survive to this day. Nearly every village has a pastor's school run by the Congregational Christian Church, the local successor to the London Missionary Society.

This historical phenomenon is by no means unique. For centuries, religion has promoted literacy. Jews, Muslims and Christians alike rely on written scriptures and instruct their congregations how to read passages within them. The transition to adulthood among Jews is marked by demonstration that the child can read a portion of the Holy Torah. For Muslims and Christians, religion is synonymous with the written Word and missionization with spreading the Word. For Christians spreading the Word is achieved primarily through diffusion and translation of the Bible, creating new orthographies and new literate populations throughout the world. Far more than public schools, religious schools serve as the cornerstone of literacy across nations.

Church literacy in a Western Samoan village

Imagine yourself a child growing up in a Samoan village. From infancy you are carried on the hips and backs of your older siblings to church services. Your older sibling holds on to you with one hand and with the other holds up the Bible or Book of Hymns. Starting around the age of 4, you walk to the church compound several afternoons a week to learn how to read letters and numbers.

For over 150 years, in every pastor's school, this initial literacy instruction has been accomplished in exactly the same way, through what is called the *Pi Tautau* (Figure 12.1). Published by the Congregational Christian Church, the *Pi Tautau* is a large poster displaying the Samoan alphabet, with Arabic and Roman numerals along the bottom. Each letter is accompanied by a picture of an object beginning with that letter. As the literacy lesson begins, you sit cross-legged on the floor with the other children in front of the teacher, who is seated on a chair, holding the *Pi Tautau* on her lap. Over time you come to understand what is expected of you. Each lesson the teacher points to the picture on the top left corner and asks the class to collectively recite first the letters and their corresponding images, then the letters alone and finally the Arabic and Roman numerals from one to ten.

Excerpt 1: Pastor's school class, Western Samoa, September 1989

Teacher: faitau fa'atasi le tātou Pî, e::,[1]
(let us) read together our Pî (Tautau), *okay?*
Children: ((start early)) 'a:: 'ato
a (for) ato (basket)...
Teacher: faitau- fa'atali-fa'atali faitau.
read- wait-wait read.
((she hits the first letter/image on *Pi Tautau* with ruler))
Children: ((in unison)) 'a:: 'ato, 'e:: 'elefane, 'i:: ipu, 'o:: ofu, 'u:: uati
a (for) ato (basket), e (for) elefane (elephant), i (for) ipu (cup), o (for) ofu (dress), u (for) uati (watch)
fa:: fagu, ga:: gata, la:: logo,
f (for) fagu (bottle), g (for) gata (snake), l (for) logo (bell),
mo:: moa, no:: nofoa, pi:: pusi, sa:: solofanua,
m (for) moa (chicken), n (for) nofoa (chair), p (for) pusi(cat), s (for) solofanua (horse)
ti:: ta'avale, ((raising pitch)) vi:::↑ va'a!
t (for) ta'avale (car), v (for) va'a (boat)
he:: Herota, ka:: kirikiti, ro:: rapiti,
h (for) Herota (Herod), k (for) kirikiti (cricket), r (for) rapiti (rabbit)
((teacher continues to point with ruler to the rest of the chart))

While a few of these images are familiar to you, for example, the chicken, the horse and the car, many of the images are new. You have never seen an elephant, a rabbit, a snake, or an ocean liner and you don't know who Herod is. Even the

Figure 12.1 The Samoan alphabet chart, known as the *Pi Tautau*

images you can identify are not common ones. The image for the word *'ato* (basket) is not the one you see your siblings carry, but rather the basket sold in the capital to tourists. The image for the word *'ofu* (clothes) is not the traditional *'ie lavalava*, the sheet of cloth villagers wrap around their lower body, but rather a western style of dress reserved for special occasions.

The *Pi Tautau* in this sense introduces not only the alphabet and the numbers, but also images associated with a way of life that is peripheral to village life. In a Samoan village, the experience of the *Pi Tautau* opens a door to worlds associated with Christianity and foreign objects (Duranti and Ochs 1986).

Samoan communities in the United States

While most Samoans do not leave their villages, thousands have emigrated (Shankman 1993). Within the United States, Hawaii and California house large Samoan communities (Franco *et al.* 1993). Currently more than 90,000 ethnic Samoans live in California, most born and raised there (Pouesi 1994). Like other ethnic communities in the United States, Samoans are proud of their culture and grapple with the problem of transmitting their heritage to their children – children who have never experienced life in a Samoan village and have limited knowledge of Samoan language. In this struggle for language and culture maintenance, the *Pi Tautau* plays a major role.

Wherever Samoans have moved in large numbers, they have formed strong local communities based around a Samoan church. An important component of these churches is the religious school, where, like in a Samoan village, very young children are introduced to the Samoan alphabet and numbers. It is important for researchers concerned with the relation between community and school to recognize that religious school may have an entirely different relation to a community than public school (Cohen and Lukinsky 1985; Zinsser 1986). Indeed, religious schools are far more continuous with the values and social organization of the Samoan community than are public schools. Researchers working on literacy have focused predominantly on the relation between home and public school (e.g., Philips 1972; Leichter 1974; McDermott and Gospodinoff 1981; Heath 1983; McDermott *et al.* 1984; Chandler *et al.* 1986) rather than on the relation between home and religious schools. In this chapter we consider the complex social and historical intersection of home, school and community as represented by and constituted through church literacy.

In an urban environment in which the Samoan children are in daily contact with members of so many other ethnic communities, the church compound provides a haven for the preservation of what their parents and grandparents define as the 'Samoan way of life' or *fa'aSâmoa*. In the Samoan Congregational Church in Los Angeles, language and culture maintenance among Samoan children is accomplished through several means. Unlike public schools, all the teachers in the religious school are ethnic Samoans. Inside the church compound, adults often wear a formal style of clothes common in Samoa: the pastor wears a tailored sarong called *pocket 'ie* and women wear long white dresses or elegant sarong-like suits called *puletasi*.

Children are also likely to see visitors from the Samoan Islands – perhaps a guest pastor or a church group from Western or American Samoa.

On Sunday and during the week the church involves neighbourhood children in diverse activities that resonate with life in the Samoan Islands. Children witness weddings, funerals and other rites of passage where fine mats are distributed and traditional oratory can be heard. Children practise Samoan dances for fundraising festivities. Children and adults sing Christian songs in both Samoan and English. They accompany songs in both languages with traditional Samoan body movements. In this manner English code interfaces with Samoan expressive gesture. The actual church service is almost completely in Samoan.

For the many children who have never been to a Samoan village, the church experience augments the home in socializing children into what it means to be Samoan. The church compound is in fact called by some the *nu'u lotu*, literally 'church village' and by others the 'urban village'. In Los Angeles, the village metaphor is reinforced by the layout of the church compound, which resembles the plan of a typical village with buildings circling a central ceremonial ground or *malae*. In this case, the *malae* is a parking lot and the buildings that surround it are the church and a large hall that houses the Sunday school as well as a number of other educational and recreational activities.

Church literacy in a Samoan American church

Before the Sunday service, children 5 years old and younger attend religious school. As part of their lesson, these children are expected to recite and master the very same *Pi Tautau* used in pastors' schools throughout the Samoan Islands. Just like children in traditional villages, Samoan children in Los Angeles recite the letters, words and numbers represented in the *Pi Tautau*.

Excerpt 2: Sunday School in southern California, February 28, 1993

Teacher:	Okay? Everybody real loud. ((points to the alphabet chart))
Girl:	((softly)) a:::
Teacher:	o::ne . . . two:: . . . three:: . . .
Teacher:	a//::: ato
	a (for) basket
Students:	ato
	ato (basket)
Students:	e::: elefane
	e (for) elefane (elephant)
Students:	i::: ipu
	i (for) ipu (cup)

Students:	o::: //ofu
	o (for) ofu (clothes)
Teacher:	ofu
Students:	u::: //uati
	u (for) uati (watch)
Teacher:	uati
Teacher:	//fa::: fagu
	f (for) fagu (bottle)
Students:	fa::: fagu
	f (for) fagu (bottle)
Teacher:	//ga::: gata
	ga (for) gata (snake)
Students:	ga::: gata
	g (for) gata (snake)
Teacher:	//la::: logo
	l (for) logo (bell)
Students:	la:::logo
	l (for) logo (bell)
Teacher:	//mo::: moa
	m (for) moa (chicken)
Students:	mo::: moa
	m (for) moa (chicken)
Teacher:	nu::: nofoa
	n (for) nofoa (chair)
Students:	nu::: nofoa
Teacher:	//pi::: pusi
	p (for) pusi (cat)
Students:	'pi::: pusi
	p (for) pusi (cat)
Teacher:	//sa::: solofanua
	s (for) solofanua (horse)
Students:	sa::: solofanua
	s (for) solofanua (horse)
Teacher:	//ti::: ta'avale
	t (for) ta'avale (car)
Students:	ti::: taavale
	t (for) ta'avale (car)
Teacher:	//vi::: va'a
	v (for) va'a (boat)
Students:	vi::: va'a
	v (for) va'a (boat)
Teacher:	//he:: ka:: ro::
	h, k, r
Students:	he::: ka::: ro:::

Teacher:	he::: ka:: ro:::
Girl:	I got a:-
Teacher:	ta::/ /si:,
	one,
Students:	ta:si::.
	one,
Teacher:	//lua::,
	two,
Students:	lu:a:,
	two,
Teacher:	((points to number on poster))
Students:	to:lu:, fa::, lima::, o:no:, fi:tu:, va:lu:, i:va:, sefu:lu:
	three, four, five, six, seven, eight, nine, ten,
Teacher:	((looks up)) okay. I'm gonna turn you over to Annette now and Annette is going to give you guys your Bible lesson ((folds poster)) okay?
Girl:	okay.
Boy:	okay.

At first this routine looks much the same as the one performed in the Samoan village. The *Pi Tautau* is thus an instrument and a symbol of continuity and even more. It is a tangible and safe anchor for keeping the children of Samoan descent in southern California connected to the language of their parents and grandparents. But a closer look at the recitation of the *Pi Tautau* belies important discontinuities with its village counterpart. The context of the *Pi Tautau* has changed and it is context that gives meaning to what we do and say.

Most importantly, the linguistic repertoires of the children in Los Angeles and in the Samoan village are not the same. Whereas children who go to the village pastor's school speak Samoan before they are exposed to the *Pi Tautau*, Samoan children in Los Angeles typically have only rudimentary knowledge of Samoan when they begin attending religious school. Some of the teachers as well do not speak Samoan as their first language, but rather have learned it later in life to more fully participate and gain status in the local Samoan community. This explains how at times certain Samoan American children might know more than their teacher. In one of the videotaped interactions, a child corrects a teacher who mispronounced the name of the letter 'r'— she said 're' instead of 'ro'. This would be unthinkable in Samoa.

Partly as a consequence of such linguistic insecurity, teachers in southern California use English to introduce and explain the *Pi Tautau*. Only the actual recitation of the *Pi Tautau* is carried out in Samoan. This code-switch from English to Samoan marks the *Pi Tautau* as linguistically distinct from other genres of discourse that comprise the Bible lesson. This linguistic shift is absent in village pastors' schools, where Samoan is the sole language of instruction.

These differences in linguistic repertoire shape the meaning and function of the *Pi Tautau*. Whereas in the Samoan village, the *Pi Tautau* is used to instruct literacy, in southern California it is used to teach children how to speak as well as how to read Samoan. Thus, while the tool – the *Pi Tautau* – is constant across Samoa and southern California, the instructional activity is not.

That in southern California the *Pi Tautau* is a tool for teaching spoken Samoan is manifest in certain instructional practices. The most striking is that the teachers sometimes ask the children to recite the *Pi Tautau* without visual access to the chart itself, which is often unavailable. As the next example illustrates, at these moments the children are not engaged in reading but rather are reciting from memory the sequence of letters and words that comprise the *Pi Tautau*.

Excerpt 3: Sunday School in southern California, May 30, 1993

((Two teachers and five students sitting at a table in the hallway are reciting the alphabet without the poster, the second teacher is the same teacher as in Excerpt 2, but here she is acting as an assistant))

All:	mo::: moa, nu::::: nofoa, pi::: pusi
	m (for) moa (chicken), n (for) nofoa (chair), p (for) pusi (cat)
	sa::: solofanua, ti::: ta'avale, vi::: va'a
	s (for) solofanua (horse), t (for) ta'avale (car), v (for) va'a (boat)
	he:: Herota, ka:: kirikiti, ro:: rapiti
	h (for) Herota (Herod), k (for) kirikiti (cricket, the game), r (for) rapiti (rabbit)
Teacher-1:	What is 'rapiti'? What is that word class?
Student:	Rabbit
Teacher-1:	What is it Sikē?
Sikē:	Rabbit.
Teacher-1:	Everybody what is that word?
Students:	RA:BBIT!

As shown in the last part of this segment, the activity of reciting the *Pi Tautau* can become a second language more than a literacy lesson. Whereas pastors' school teachers in Samoa ask the children to label objects depicted in the *Pi Tautau*, teachers in the Los Angeles religious school ask the children to translate words referring to objects in the *Pi Tautau* from Samoan to English. In the segment just shown, the teacher asks the class 'What is "rapiti"?', to which one child responds in English 'rabbit'. Thus while village teachers point to a picture and ask, 'What is this?', Los Angeles teachers ask, 'What does this mean in English?'

The *Pi Tautau* differs across communities in other ways as well. In our earlier work (Duranti and Ochs 1986), we saw the *Pi Tautau* and the activities that surround it as an instrument of westernization. Not only does the *Pi Tautau* chart depict objects such as Cola bottles and ocean liners, but also *Pi Tautau* instruction introduces village children to patterns of adult–child interaction associated with Euro-American societies. For example, the interaction around reading in the pastor's school is not only text-centred, but also child-centred and, as the children become older, individual oriented. This type of interaction is illustrated in Excerpt 4 from a pastor's school class in Western Samoa.

Excerpt 4: Pastor's school, Western Samoa, April 1981: children are asked to read a verse each from the Bible

Pastor: Luka luasefulu ma le tolu, faia'upu sefulumaletolu . . .
    Luke twenty-three, verse thirteen . . .
    ia' amata . . . faitau . . . amata iā Teresa.
    So starts . . . reading . . . Teresa starts.
Teresa: ((reading)) ona fa'apotopoto lea e Pilato le 'aufaitaulaga sili,
    and when Pilate had called together the chief priests
    ma le faipule, ma le nu'u'.
    and the rulers and the people

((after several children have each read one verse, it is Pato's turn))

Pato: ((reading slowly)) ona toe tau//tala-
        and spoke again-
Pastor: leo tele Pato.
        speak loud Pato.
Pato: ((reading)) ona toe tau- . . . tala . . . atu ai lea 'o Pilato . . .
        Pilate . . . spoke . . . again then . . .
        ina . . . ina 'ua fia . . . ((stops))
        in . . . order . . . to . . .
Boy: ((whispers something))
Pastor: sipela le 'upu.
        spell the word.
Pato: ((spells the word)) ti-a-ti-a-la-a-i-nu-a.
        t-a-t-a-l-a-i-n-a.
Pastor: 'o le ā?
        What is it?
Other students: ((whispers various words))
Pastor: ti-a . . . ti-a . . . -la-a-i-nu-a. 'o le ā? . . .
        t-a . . . t-a . . . -l-a-i-n-a. What is it? . . .
        'aua le pisa fo'i le isi.
        the rest (of you) be quiet.
Pato: ((reading)) ta-la-ina. . . . tala//ina
        release. relea//se
Pastor: fai.
        say (it).
Pato: talaina atu . . . Iesū
        release . . . Jesus

Individual children must be able to read a letter, a number, a word, or a verse, without relying on the help of their peers. When a child cannot complete the task, other children cannot come to her rescue. In contrast to other village contexts, in the pastor's school other children's contributions in the form of whispers or prompts are neither rewarded nor encouraged.

What is striking about the activity of reading the *Pi Tautau* is that what we had seen in the village as predominantly an Anglophile practice has become conceptualized in California as a powerful symbol of Samoan culture. Samoan children in Los Angeles are exposed to the *Pi Tautau* as part of a larger effort to bolster the Samoan side of their identity. The *Pi Tautau* is part of the discourse of nostalgia, of bringing a piece of 'home' to children here in the United States.

The relation between the *Pi Tautau* and Samoan tradition is made explicit in this excerpt, where a teacher articulates the reasons for learning the Samoan alphabet.

Excerpt 5: Sunday School in southern California, February 28, 1993

((Teacher is holding an alphabet table while kids are sitting listening))

Teacher: Okay you guys now, why do you guys think it's important to learn our uh . . . our alphabet, uh?

. . .

Teacher: What are you? What's your nationality? ((another teacher comes to take a box from the table.)) Samoan . . . Okay? And you have to learn your culture, ((leans down to pick up an envelope dropped by the other teacher)) it's important for us to learn our culture as we grow up . . . because as we grow older, . . . if you're like me::, it took a long time to lea:rn . . . how to speak the language . . . oka:y? Meanwhile you have an advantage right now you're only – you're you:ng . . . and we start teaching you guys the alphabets right now? . . . Then you will grow up and you will know how to talk how to p-put the words together and it will be easier for you to talk in your own language . . . And carry the American language at the same time . . . okay?

Does it work? It depends on what we see as the task at hand. As a strategy to teach children of Samoan descent to speak and read Samoan, it does not seem to be effective. The children eventually learn the *Pi Tautau* routine but they do not necessarily learn the individual words and their meanings. It is hard for most of them to recognize or remember the words in the *Pi Tautau* out of sequence.

Among other difficulties, the children are exposed to a variety of Samoan that is rarely used in their home, a variety called 'good speech' (*tautala lelei*) strongly associated with literacy and the church (Shore 1982; Duranti and Ochs 1986; Ochs 1988). When the children go beyond the words and numbers of the *Pi Tautau* to articulate whole Samoan utterances, they do so in the context of memorizing

Bible verses, which are written in an esoteric register, full of special words, borrowed from the Samoan rhetorical tradition.

Nonetheless we have witnessed moments of pure pleasure and laughter while memorizing a verse whose meaning could not possibly be understood by the children. Such pleasure suggests that when Samoan children in Los Angeles enter the 'church village', they know that they are entering safe grounds where they will find not only adult instructors, but also other children of their age who are undergoing similar experiences, who are struggling in similar ways with their multiethnic identity. The 'church village' is the place where one does not need to explain oneself to outsiders. For a brief and yet exhilarating moment, while singing a song or shouting the letters of the Samoan alphabet, home, community and school come together. In fact, for the time that one stays within the boundaries of the church village, everyone seems to share the same meaning of 'home' (Kondo 1996). The rest of the world is kept on hold.

Conclusion

In this chapter, we have followed the history of a literacy tool, the Samoan *Pi Tautau*, over the last century and a half as a way of gaining insights into the relationship between 'home' and 'school' in a Samoan American community in southern California. We have shown how a tool that we had previously analyzed as a vehicle of westernization has been transformed into a symbol of tradition and an instrument for cultural continuity. Our comparative data on Samoan literacy instructions in two different settings – a Western Samoan village and an urban environment in the United States – suggests that one of the main functions of language maintenance practices is the reproduction of cultural identity. The children of Samoan descent who participate in the religious school classes in southern California are taught to recognize the Samoan alphabet and the words that represent the sounds of the Samoan language to provide them with a link with an important part of their cultural heritage.

This study also suggests that educational research needs to reconfigure the relation between home and school and between home and community. The boundaries of home need to be expanded historically and geographically to include places of origin conveyed in expressions such as 'back home'. For many Samoan Americans, home is both here and there. Similarly, for Samoans and other groups, the boundaries of school go beyond the public school to include religious school and community extends beyond the neighbourhood to embrace the 'church village', a place where change and tradition can be safely negotiated.

Acknowledgments

An earlier version of this chapter was presented at the 1995 Annual Meeting of the American Education Research Association, San Francisco, CA, April 18. The work presented here has been made possible by many people in (Western)

Samoa and the United States who generously gave their time to our projects on child language acquisition and socialization. Special thanks to Rev. Fa'atau'oloa Mauala and his late wife Sau 'iluma from the village of Falefâ, on the island of 'Upolu in (Western) Samoa, for their kind assistance in recording literacy activities and other kinds of adult–children interactions since the early 1980s. In Los Angeles, we benefited from the help and advice of many people from the Samoan American community, some of whom joined our research team. In particular, we are grateful to the late James Soli'ai and to Edgar Ta'ase for their careful transcription and interpretation of the video-recordings and for their insights on language use and change. We also discussed the main topics of this chapter with two other members of our team, Jennifer F. Reynolds and Jennifer Schlegel, who generously shared their intuitions and observations. The research on the Western Samoan community was sponsored by the National Science Foundation and the research on the Samoan American community was sponsored by the US Department of Education through a grant to the National Center for Research on Cultural Diversity and Second Language Learning, University of California, Santa Cruz.

Note

1   We have used here traditional Samoan orthography. The letter 'g' represents a velar nasal and the apostrophe stands for a glottal stop. The macron on vowels indicate length, that is, a is a short [a] and ā is a long [a:]. The colons are used for the emphatic lengthening of sounds, e.g. a::: ato. The vertical arrow indicates pronounced rising intonation.

Chapter 13

Multilingual flexibility and literacy learning in an Urdu community school

Leena Helavaara Robertson

Monday midday, Watford Garden School.[1] Lunch is over and the majority of the school's pupils have gone out to play. About 20 children of Pakistani origin,[2] all aged between 5 and 7 years, stay in and settle down for their weekly Urdu class. Mrs. Gani, the teacher and the children greet each other in Urdu and switch between English, Urdu and Pahari, the children's home language. Mrs. Gani wipes the English words off the board and writes the Urdu alphabet from right to left. The children wait; some are talking in English and comparing pictures of American TV cartoon characters on the plastic lunch boxes. Mariam watches Mrs. Gani very carefully and comments in English: 'You forgot to do the dot there'. Mrs. Gani smiles, nods approvingly and corrects the mistake. 'Let's start', Mrs. Gani says in English and continues in Urdu and soon the whole class is reading the alphabet in unison. 'Let's do it faster', Mrs. Gani says and repeats and extends the instructions in Urdu.

In this chapter I explore young bilingual children's early literacy learning that takes place in an Urdu community school in England. The focus is on a group of 5- to 7-year-old British Pakistani children who attend the same mainstream English school, the host of this Urdu school. The children's experiences raise questions about the kinds of literacy-learning advantages that learning to read *simultaneously* in two or more languages may bring about. I examine the children's multilingual flexibility, that is their ability to operate within different literacy events and practices and work out and separate a diverse range of characteristics between these. In essence the emphasis here is not just on the general advantages *of* bilingualism, but also on the advantages that these multilingual processes may bring about *for* literacy learning and for young children who are at their initial stages of learning to read. Thus I consider the ways in which multiliteracy promotes and supports emergent bilingual children's general literacy learning process.

The questions raised here arise from a broader study which explores young bilingual children's early literacy experiences in three different types of schools in Watford, Britain: English literacy lessons in a mainstream school, classical Arabic/Qur'anic lessons in a local Mosque and Urdu lessons in a community school – the sole focus here. The larger study follows six children – five of Pakistani and one of Bangladeshi background, four boys and two girls – from their Reception class (4–5 years) to Year 2 class (6–7 years) in a Watford Garden school. Around 15 percent of this school's pupils are of second generation Pakistani background and were born in Watford. Urdu, the national language of Pakistan, is rarely the first language for these children. The children's main home language, and their first language, is Pahari, sometimes described as the Mirpuri dialect of Punjabi, which is distinctively different from Urdu. The overall methodology of this broader study includes ethnographic research methods ranging from field notes, participant observations, audiotapes and videotapes to interviews with teachers and parents.

Urdu community school

Here the term 'community school' is intended to cover a wide range of schools and classes that exist outside the general English, National Curriculum-driven 'mainstream' education and which are generally initiated and organized by different non-dominating linguistic or cultural minority groups. The Urdu school in Watford Garden School was initiated a year ago by Mrs. Gani, the Urdu teacher, and the two new mainstream teachers, head and deputy head. It takes place once a week during lunchtimes and although it happens within the normal 9 a.m. to 3 p.m. school day and operates inside the walls of this mainstream school, it retains its distinctive identity. The lessons, separate from the rest of the school curriculum, are planned and taught by Mrs. Gani, who teaches in local schools and acts as a home-literacy coordinator for the local education authority and its surrounding area. She uses her own lunchtimes for this and receives no funding for this kind of home-literacy work. She remains hopeful that soon someone else from the community will take over the running of this school.

The classes, often lasting around 30–40 minutes, are open to everyone (one non-Pakistani English boy also attends) and all Pakistani parents have requested that their children attend regularly, even when outside play activities seem to be the more favourable option to the children themselves. From week to week 17–25 Pakistani pupils attend and when observing these children it soon becomes evident that on the whole the parents' concern is unnecessary: the children arrive with a sense of security, enjoyment and positive anticipation.

According to Mrs. Gani this Urdu school has three broad overlapping aims:

- social-emotional development
- cultural development
- linguistic development.

It is interesting to note that Mrs. Gani raises the need for shared social and emotional experiences as the first aim. She emphasizes the need for time and place for the children to 'feel at ease' and 'comfortable within themselves' by using their own languages and talking about their specific learning experiences during a normal mainstream school day: a bit of respite from the main school work and overall concentration. The second aim is concerned with the cultural knowledge and according to Mrs. Gani the children 'need help in learning their own culture'. Otherwise there is a possibility that they will grow up without knowing and understanding their own background or culture. Finally, Mrs. Gani aims to teach Urdu language and literacy. She feels strongly about the need for these children to learn the national language of their 'other home', that of Pakistan, and this is, as Mrs. Gani puts it, 'almost like teaching a foreign language, the children do not yet know many Urdu words'. Therefore, given the time constraints Mrs. Gani aims to teach basic Urdu vocabulary, Urdu alphabet and a few written words, the main emphasis remaining on spoken language and 'having fun and enjoying it like a club'. The children, on the other hand, learn far more than these basic areas of knowledge.

Some theoretical considerations

The aim here is to integrate non-dominating language and literacy practices into educational theory that deals with early literacy. There is a pressing need for this as learning to read in two or more languages *simultaneously* is largely absent in research, even though the number of young children for whom this is everyday reality is increasing. I also aim to discover the types of advantages this simultaneous multilingual process in formal classroom learning situations brings about for literacy learning.

On discovering advantages

For all children talking around learning is important. In fact classroom talk is accepted as inseparable from school learning. Vygotsky (1962) emphasized the role of talk in organizing our view of the world and therefore in learning. When learning to read, young children need opportunities to construct the world of reading for themselves and to make sense of texts, what their functions are – and might be later on in their lives – and about sound–symbol relationship, genres, different audiences and purposes. This type of learning is socially shared and socially organized and cannot be deposited in children in a ready-made form. All learners need space, time, experiences to talk about these, so that these complex literacy concepts can grow in their minds and become their own. The joint social interactions with other, more knowledgeable and experienced readers facilitate the 'making of a reader' (Cochran-Smith 1984). And when listening to children talking about their different types of reading, how they make sense of the overall practices and their specific conventions, their knowledge and understanding becomes evident. But could it also be possible that experiencing and talking about two sets of literacy concepts aids the overall process as bilingual children come to view these as complex systems and systems that can be manipulated, controlled and responded to with creativity, imagination and personal interest?

The inclusion of previous learning experiences – starting from what the child knows and avoiding decontextualized learning situations – is generally seen as an effective staring point for enabling young children to learn (Donaldson 1978). With all novice readers then, it is important to find out about *their* prior knowledge and to build on their previous reading knowledge. Through talk and participating in a range of real reading experiences, children learn to belong to a school's 'literacy club' (Smith 1985). In addition, talking about home and community reading experiences has the potential of enabling all children to feel closer, socially and emotionally, to other readers in the 'club' and thereby to the general practice.

This is important for all, but crucially so when children's early literacy experiences at home have been very different from those that schools cherish and esteem (see for example Heath 1983; Gregory 2000). This learning to belong to any literacy practice includes learning the explicit and implicit rules, ways of interacting with texts and mediating values. The learning process, learning through 'guided participation' (Rogoff 1990), takes place when children use and watch others use texts in real-life events. It also includes the more specific written language systems and the corresponding reading strategies, some of which are highly specific to the particular phonic and graphic conventions of a language, while others may be more common to all. With all written languages (from Braille to Chinese) reading includes decoding abstract symbols and establishing meaning, but what counts as beginning to learn to read in a meaningful way varies between different languages, scripts, cultures and times.

Literacy-learning advantages

While languages such as Welsh or French are often viewed in Britain as 'advantageous' to young children's learning (see the Welsh National Curriculum or the Primary Languages Strategy: summaries can be found on www.bbc.co.uk), there are far fewer studies that reveal the benefits of all literacy learning *per se*. But could it be that a multilingual literacy-learning process, regardless of languages, results in specific advantages?

A number of studies that have explored the benefits of bilingualism have found increased metacognitive and metalinguistic knowledge and heightened communicative sensitivity (Ben-Zeev 1977; Bialystok 1991). A positive link between children's bilingualism and concept formation, classification, creativity, analogical reasoning and visual-spatial skills (e.g. Diaz and Klingler 1991) has also been discovered. But there are far fewer studies that have focused specifically on the literacy-learning advantages, that is the advantages that a multilingual process may bring about for very young children and for their initial stages of literacy learning. In addition, studies, like Cummins (1984; 2000) in his influential work on 'thresholds' (or age-appropriate levels of language competence leading to advantages), have also discussed a connection between some children's 'low level' of bilingualism (lower than age-appropriate levels of competence) and their academic school learning which is seen to lead to disadvantages.

In his work Cummins has used reading as a way of establishing benefits of bilingualism and in effect bilingual children's ability in learning to read and write in a new school language is allowed to stand for these more general cognitive 'academic' advantages and disadvantages (Edelsky 1996). There are various critiques of this study (e.g. Frederickson and Cline 1990) focusing on the difficulties of measuring any level of language competence. Moreover, with all children, but particularly with young children who at the age of 5 are starting school, it is problematic to perceive any level of bilingualism as a static, or complete process. Similarly in terms of beginning to learn to read *all* children of that age are in the early stages, regardless of language competencies, therefore the connection between fast or slow academic progress and the level of bilingualism depends on which languages are used for teaching and on how and what aspects of the progress are measured.

The children in my study are beginners in terms of learning Urdu and English; they have not yet gained the age-appropriate levels of competence in Urdu or in English. All of them are also beginning to learn to read in three languages. But could it be that this multilingual learning process benefits and supports their overall progress in learning to read and results in specific advantages?

The research into bilingual children's literacy learning process in the English context has characteristically focused on various approaches that have aimed to take English school-literacy experiences into bilingual homes (see Wolfendale and Topping 1996, for examples). This one-way movement – from schools into homes – is generally based on a deficit view. The fact that in some homes children do not have school-type reading experiences is seen as disadvantageous to the general school learning process. The resulting approaches aim to change the homes, rather than find out what types of reading experiences are important to the families. It is rare to find two-way approaches – from homes to schools and back to homes – or research studies in which the schools are also expected to change and to begin to welcome and build on other types of language and literacy practices and to acknowledge that bilingual learners may have a different set of strengths (Gregory 1998; Gregory and Williams 2000; Kenner 2000a).

So, what types of strengths, or additional advantages, might these emergent bilingual children have? For the purpose of my discussion I have categorized the possible advantages under the following sections which arise from the types of knowledge that in literature have been put forward as prerequisites in learning to read (see Robertson 2002 for a summary of these).

- *Linguistic advantages:* knowledge and understanding of language and writing systems, including metalinguistic awareness of lexicon, syntax, phonology and orthography.
- *Psycholinguistic advantages:* knowledge and understanding of book/text conventions and presentational devices.
- *Sociocultural advantages:* knowledge and understanding of learning to read as

a rule-governed practice; sensitivity to appropriateness; syncretic literacy, infusing and blending skills and approaches from different languages and literacies (rather than keeping them separate).

- *Situated and procedural advantages:* knowledge and understanding of class-specific approaches, rules and rituals; understanding how reading is done and what the roles of learners and teachers are.

Multilingual flexibility and advantages for literacy learning

The lesson continues. As in the mainstream literacy lesson, the children sit on the carpet and focus their attention on a large book which rests on a stand in front of the class. The book, *Lima's Red Hot Chilli* (Mills 2000), is a dual language book; Urdu and English texts accompany illustrations, though in terms of pagination it follows the left-to-right conventions of English. Mrs. Gani asks in both languages 'Who can tell me what "illustration" means?' – a familiar question from the mainstream English literacy lesson. 'Tell me in Urdu', she prompts in both languages. 'Can you see anything in the picture that begins with a /b/?', she asks, points to the corresponding Urdu letter and begins to accept words in Urdu, Pahari and English. 'What about /d/?' The children offer words and all are accepted as long as they begin with the correct sound. The sound /d/, however, proves to be complicated (in Urdu there are two separate /d/ sounds: alveolar and post-alveolar) and the children discuss this and repeat the different sounds. 'Ice-cream' is accepted both as an English and an Urdu word as this word has made an entry into modern Urdu and replaced the old Urdu version; the Urdu word 'mirsh' (for 'chilli') may well also disappear as 'chilli' gains acceptance. Monsoor is invited to write 'ice-cream' on the board while Mrs. Gani writes it in Urdu. 'There are no straight lines in Urdu', Monsoor says as he completes the word. Ikram comments on right-to-left direction, 'You just got to do it like this'. He also shows that he can recite by heart 'the proper alphabet' and he means the classical Arabic alphabet. This language is briefly discussed and contrasted with Urdu because they share many similar characteristics. (Classical Arabic is the language of Qur'an and the third language these children are learning to read in, but one that they do not speak or understand.) Some Urdu words are new to the children, so Mrs. Gani continues to translate these into Pahari and English. Many of the examples given are briefly discussed and related to children's everyday experiences. 'Do you eat chillies, mirsh?', she asks the children.

Together, layer by layer the teacher and her pupils peel off the different aspects of learning to read. Their overall interaction, the ease of switching from one language to another, is perhaps better described as multilingual flexibility. The children demonstrate flexibility in operating within different languages and commenting on and working out characteristics of reading and writing systems which they use to analyze aspects of reading.

At the age of 5 these emergent bilingual children examine, translate and reflect on words in different languages and how they are written in different scripts. They also contrast sound systems in different languages. They acknowledge different kinds of reading strategies, like memorization or practising by repeating and accept the rule-governed nature of reading. They practice decoding different words in two languages and aim to memorize high-frequency words. In essence they are able to discuss their literacy learning in highly analytical and complex terms and are developing a wide range of skills, knowledge, understanding. In fact, much more than the basic Urdu words.

Linguistic advantages

The children have an awareness of different aspects of language learning: lexicon, phonology, grammar, semantics and orthography. They are used to switching from one language to another and demonstrate metalinguistic awareness and knowledge. They are highly accustomed to talking about semantics ('What does that mean?') and show that they know that all languages have words which generally are very different, but occasionally they can also be the same ('ice-cream').

This gives them a good springboard for focusing on reading. Answers to questions like what begins with /d/ – typical also in English mainstream literacy lessons – allows them to identify similarities between words, practise segmenting initial phonemes and also enables them to find similarities and differences between languages. The languages familiar to them all have words that begin with /b/ and /d/. Words can be broken down into individual phonemes, some of which are the same, but not all languages have the same sets of phonemes. Monsoor's evaluation of the two scripts, Urdu and English, 'there are no straight lines in Urdu' is an apt conclusion and reveals understanding of the overall characteristics of these two writing systems.

Psycholinguistic advantages

The children's responses also reveal understanding of book-languages, text and presentational devices, which are heightened by their diverse sets of experiences. For example, directionality of print clearly has a role to play in shaping their understanding of the wide range of arbitrary writing conventions. The children demonstrate an ability to 'switch systems' as they follow their finger from right-to-left on the Urdu alphabet and left-to-right with English words. They take these conventions in their stride. Ikram's comment 'You just got to do it like this' sums up their overall approach. This kind of starting point, viewing highly complex writing systems as something arbitrary, will support them in gaining control of these systems and responding to them to with imagination and personal interest.

Sociocultural advantages

The children's literacy lessons share many similar characteristics. In both Urdu and English literacy lessons the focus is on learning phonics in context (generally on segmenting and blending phonemes) and on big books with large texts which are used for reading aloud together. This may be because Mrs. Gani teaches in both types of lessons. In the first vignette she asks 'who can tell me what "illustration" means?' and many of her other reading rituals, for example beginning each lesson by talking about the title, cover page, author, are also formal national requirements for the English lesson. This is an example of syncretic literacy: Mrs. Gani is infusing techniques, approaches and strategies from different literacy practices. The Urdu alphabet is recited and repeated a few times and this practising, or repetition, is a strategy which the children are familiar with from their Qur'anic lessons. The repetition needs to be accurate and fluent, 'let's do it faster', she says.

In effect, Mrs. Gani is enabling children to build on their prior reading knowledge. The children themselves, too, blend in different elements of reading. They view reading as a rule-governed practice and their comments reveal sensitivity to appropriateness. They talk about how you 'got to do it'. This kind of sensitivity, understanding reading as an activity which needs to take on board 'appropriateness' will provide them with heightened knowledge about audiences and purposes.

Situated and procedural advantages

That reading is a highly culture and language-specific activity is obvious to these children. But they are also tuned to the finer details of classroom practice. Moving from one literacy class to another they demonstrate very explicitly how reading can be done differently. Rather than finding it confusing, it seems a powerful force in their approach to learning. For example Ikram has learnt what is appropriate and where. Reading in the Qur'anic class includes an ability to recite long sections by heart and Ikram takes pride in demonstrating that he can do this. This is his goal and he works towards it conscientiously. In Urdu and English classes his goals are different, but he displays similar pride and interest in achieving these.

Some implications for teachers

The overall context for language and literacy learning in this Urdu community language school raises some interesting points. By bringing in and building on the whole range of previous reading experiences, the teacher allows this kind of multilingual flexibility to flourish. She activates it. Then she develops it further. This provides the children with opportunities to switch between different languages and literacies and to talk, translate, reflect on and evaluate these. They do this switching effortlessly – it is the stuff of their everyday life – while the teacher also expects them to do it with an increasing vocabulary, more complex syntax and deepening understanding of the subject matter. They are expected to contrast written language systems and to acknowledge and practise different kinds of reading strategies. They also know that there is a need to develop their knowledge of the more specific grapho-phonic systems and practise applying these with different kinds of texts in different languages.

This kind of multilingual flexibility has three highly important consequences. First, it speeds the overall process of language learning. There is now enough evidence, from different parts of the world, that shows that using bilingual children's home/first languages in the teaching/learning process accelerates the learning of school language (see for example Linguistic Minorities Project 1985; Collier 1995). Second, it enables children to build on their prior knowledge and to consolidate and develop their knowledge, skills and understanding of reading further. Cummins' (1984) model of Common Underlying Proficiency is highly useful here; consolidating common reading concepts in two or more languages deepens children's overall understanding. Third, in syncretic use multilingual flexibility itself evolves into a useful tool for beginning to analyze and examine what reading is, how readers go about it and how it is done in different classrooms. For example the joint, shared and very concrete process of writing 'ice-cream' in English, next to Mrs. Gani's Urdu word, facilitates Monsoor's conclusion 'there are no straight lines in Urdu'. Without this kind of syncretic context and use the opportunities for discovering links, similarities, differences and common strategies within systems would remain limited.

In learning situations like these the children themselves are active in finding ways of connecting home and school literacies. The Urdu lessons are also a good example of an 'additive practice' (Lambert 1974). Different kinds of reading practices are all built upon each other, added on, and each one is used to clarify the different types of scripts and overall reading in children's lives. It is also a real-life example of an inclusive practice and, thus, fulfills some of the broader statutory expectations of the mainstream National Curriculum for England (DfEE 1999).

This is invaluable for the children here and now. It supports their overall early literacy learning. It will undoubtedly also have a knock-on effect on their later progress, on their self-esteem, self-perception and general construction of identity and, therefore, their later life. When observing these children it is clear that they feel at ease and comfortable within themselves, as their teacher suggested. They consolidate their cultural knowledge and understanding, which allows a stronger sense of identity to be constructed and maintained. In these lessons they seem both emotionally and culturally secure.

It is precisely the shared group experience and this joint shared construction of reading knowledge that facilitates the development of advantages. The more specific early literacy-learning advantages can be summarized as:

- easy identification of similarities and differences between lexicon, phonology and orthography in different languages

- understanding writing systems as something arbitrary
- ability to switch between different reading and writing systems
- ability to process words and to identify and segment initial phonemes simultaneously in different languages
- knowledge and understanding that all languages have phonemes, but that not all languages have the same sets of phonemes
- knowledge and understanding of reading as a rule-governed practice
- heightened sensitivity to appropriateness.

These advantages are very different from the general English age-appropriate expectations of early reading progress (DfEE 1999). They also sit uncomfortably with Cummins' (1984, 2000) threshold hypothesis and his notion of age-appropriate levels of language competence leading to the advantages of bilingualism. The key factor in the accumulation of these advantages is the need to understand and operate within different language and literacy practices. The children's multilingual flexibility is a direct result of their varied syncretic language and literacy experiences.

The advantages provide a highly analytical starting point for learning to read increasingly complex texts and a range of genres. It prepares young readers for retrieving some very different types of information for strongly contrasting purposes. At the age of 5, children are capable of demonstrating how different literacies are important to them in their very different ways. For example learning Urdu cannot take the place of learning English; learning English cannot do for reading the Qur'an and becoming a Muslim. On the whole children are keen to learn them all.

The Urdu teacher's expectations of these children and their literacy-learning abilities, are clearly very high and different from those mainstream teachers who view children's lack of English knowledge as a disadvantage, or an obstacle in learning to read. In effect all community language schools and classes, such as this Urdu one, are a significant language and literacy resource. Using them directly, collaborating with their teachers and pupils and learning *from* them, can significantly enhance and deepen the understanding of the early literacy-learning process. Moreover, allowing bilingual children to bring along their languages and literacies into school reading lessons can reveal what young children are really capable of. Building on the kinds of analytical knowledge and understanding that these 5- to 7-year-old bilingual children have gained can also serve to raise expectations of all children's literacy-learning abilities.

Conclusion

In the light of this study it is important to continue to consider the following:

- What are teachers' views of bilingual children as readers?
- How can teachers maintain high expectations of *all* beginning readers?

- How can bilingual children build on their previous language and literacy knowledge and understanding in all classrooms?
- How can bilingual children demonstrate their expertise in literacy lessons and how can this expertise be of benefit for all young readers?
- How can the work of community language teachers be integrated into general educational theory that deals with early literacy and into mainstream literacy lessons?

The lesson is over. The mainstream teacher, together with other non-Pakistani children, arrive and they begin to prepare the classroom for the next lesson. The teacher wipes the Urdu words off the board. 'So, what did you learn today?' she asks Monsoor. Monsoor, with the typical nonchalance of a 6-year-old and already busy eavesdropping his classmates' stories from the playground, replies, 'Urdu words'.

Notes

1   All the names in this chapter – the school, children and their teacher – have been changed.
2   These Pakistani British children were born in Watford, but in most cases their parents were born in Azad Jammu and Kashmir (northern Pakistan) and its Mirpur district. The language they speak in the hills of Mirpur is often referred to as Pahari, which is a dialect of Punjabi. Sometimes Pahari is also referred to as Mirpuri. Pahari has no written form, therefore Urdu (the official national language of Pakistan) is considered important for the children's literacy development.

Chapter 14

The African American Church

A beacon of light on the pathway to literacy for African American children

*Gwendolyn Thompson McMillon and
Patricia A. Edwards*

For years researchers have attempted to address the academic difficulties that African American students experience in US classrooms. Many of these students are considered at-risk in their school environment based on various factors, such as free or reduced lunch and low test scores. Those who attend urban schools often participate in programmes such as Head Start and all-day kindergarten, which were developed to address the problems of at-risk students. Although these programmes successfully impact upon many students, the gap between African American students and their White counterparts continues to exist (Edwards 1995). One of the most visible ways that researchers have attempted to improve the success rate of African American students has been through a shift towards a more socio-cultural view of literacy in order to closely examine their academic problems and look for possible solutions.

A sociocultural theory of learning and development (Luria 1976; Vygotsky 1978; Scribner 1985; Wertsch 1985) focuses upon the ways in which learning takes place within cultural contexts and addresses the importance of looking beyond the classroom to examine institutions that may influence classroom experiences. In recent years, several researchers have emphasized the importance of considering the literacy practices of outside institutions in order to understand the literacy crisis within the classroom (Heath 1983; Resnick 1990; Purcell-Gates 1995; Edwards *et al.* 1999; McMillon and Edwards 2000).

As African American researchers, we believe that educators have paid little or no attention to the African American Church as a literacy environment. Based on our personal experiences, we know that African American children begin school with multiple literacy experiences emerging from home, church and community activities. Furthermore, as we have found at church, children participate in rich literacy experiences that may affect their initial literacy acquisition and development, the way they think about literacy and ultimately their literacy development at school (McMillon and Edwards 2000).

In order to move beyond our personal predictions and experiences, we conducted a formal research study to closely examine the types of literacy experiences provided by African American churches and consider ways to build upon this knowledge in classrooms at school. The purpose of this chapter is to share the findings of our research project. In particular, we give specific examples of students' learning experiences and teachers' instructional methods at a Midwestern African American Church. The chapter ends with 'voices of students' who express significant ways that their church has provided a beacon of light on their 'pathway to literacy'.

The African American Church

When studying children, or assessing the current status of a group of people, it is extremely important to consider their history – the historical events, people and institutions that may have influenced their present state (Elder *et al.* 1993). One must understand the culture, cultural values, artifacts, beliefs and idiosyncrasies of a group of people, in order to understand the people within the culture (Heath 1983; Elder *et al.* 1993). The African American Church was created from a combination of beliefs and was specifically designed to meet the multifaceted, complex needs of African Americans (Lincoln and Mamiya 1990). It has historically been the most influential institution in the Black community (Proctor and Watley 1984) and was the site of the first formal learning environment organized specifically for African Americans. Worship service was held in the church on Sunday and the church building was utilized as a school during the week (Cornelius 1991). At church, the importance of literacy skills has historically been emphasized and continues to be a focus today (Lincoln and Mamiya 1990).

The African American Sunday School, in many cases, provides the first formal learning environment for African American children (Frazier 1974). Additionally, the church often provides the only social outlet for young children, where they interact extensively with people outside of their family circle (McMillon and Edwards 2000). When developing educational strategies for African Americans it is imperative that the African American Church be included in the conversation.

Many African Americans' cultural dispositions are reflected in the learning environment of the African American Church, where the human side of literacy (Edwards *et al.* 1999) is often emphasized through the establishment of meaningful relationships. In this setting, adults are respected for wisdom acquired from life experiences regardless of social status or educational background (Proctor 1995). Many teachers and other adult role models enjoy intergenerational relationships with parents and hold high expectations for student performance (Edelman 1999). Students often have close relationships with teachers and other adult role models who scaffold their efforts and expect them to succeed (Hale-Benson 1986; Edwards *et al.* 2001). It is within these social interactions that learning and development takes place (Van Dijk 1997). Based on a *positive* self-fulfilling prophecy, most students achieve (Edwards *et al.* 2001). In this environment, there lies an opportunity for educators to begin to understand multiple literacy practices within the African American Church and identify ways to improve classroom literacy experiences in the school environment for African American children.

Our project

We conducted a case study that focuses on the literacy experiences of children who attend a Midwestern, African American Baptist church (a member of the largest African American organization in the world – the National Baptist Convention, USA, Inc.- which has 8.7 million members: Billingsley 1992). The church is located in an impoverished urban neighbourhood and provides several programmes that can influence children's literacy development including Sunday School, midweek Bible Study and Children's Church for ages 2–6 (Sunday mornings during worship service). These classes were observed for four weeks in their natural setting. Teachers were interviewed concerning their instructional methods and pedagogical beliefs. Observations were videotaped and interviews were audiotaped. Discourse and narrative analyses were used to find patterns and organize data into themes and categories (Cazden 1988; Tannen 1989; Riessman 1993; O'Connor and Michaels 1996).

Our observations focused on preschool, kindergarten and first grade levels. Students in the classes ranged from 4 to 6 years old and were African American or biracial. Teachers in the classes observed were female African American, middle-class women. Three were married and one was single.

The 'student voices' data were collected through personal taped interviews with older students who previously participated in the classes that were observed. We were especially interested in hearing students talk about the various ways that they believed their literacy experiences at church influenced their literacy experiences at school.

What we learned

Although some students may have limited literacy experiences at home, when children attend the African American Church, they participate in varied, rich literacy experiences. During our observations, we found that Sunday School, midweek Bible Study and Children's Church took place in a classroom environment, divided according to students' ages. Teachers utilized literature that was age/grade specific. At church, teachers and students share cultural values and instruction is often based on unique, African American learning styles (Hale-Benson 1986). These students are given ample opportunities to practise their literacy skills and learn from their mistakes. A forum is also provided for students to display their talents in a nurturing, supportive, all-inclusive environment.

Students' literacy experiences

Literacy practices during Sunday School, midweek Bible Study and Children's Church focused on two specific areas: pre-reading/reading skills and oral language development. While participating in these classes, students acquired and developed various skills, which could be utilized in their classrooms at school.

Pre-reading/reading skills included print awareness, concepts of print, sight-reading, vocabulary building, comprehension and application. Oral language development was emphasized while learning Bible stories and memorizing scriptures. Most of these literacy experiences reinforced religious and/or cultural values.

Learning to read at church

In the church setting, print awareness is developed when students have experiences with print in the Bible, songbooks, class literature and weekly church bulletins. Students understand the importance of print in the cultural community of the African American Church. They see many adult role models utilizing these tools and are taught from a very young age to 'read' their bibles and bring them to church to use while in class and during worship service. In class, students receive take-home literature each week. Teachers have been taught to use the literature as an evangelistic tool to encourage students to attend classes, remind them to apply their lessons during their everyday lives and as a way to keep parents informed concerning what their children are learning in class.

The Lesson Sheet for preschoolers, kindergarteners and first graders usually has a beautiful picture on the sheet that is related to the lesson. Under the picture is a Bible scripture (called the 'memory verse') which students are expected to memorize during class. The scripture is often short and students follow along with their fingers as the teacher reads it first. Concepts of print, such as directionality and spoken/written word correspondence, are reinforced during this activity. Teachers often ask if a student knows any of the words in the Bible verse. The students have an opportunity to decode the words with scaffolding from the teacher. All students repeat the verse several times, as if reading the words. Each week students have an opportunity to learn sight words, which they are expected to *read* to their parents when they get home. Their vocabulary increases tremendously over a period of time and they become very familiar with words that are related to various Bible stories. To reinforce this activity, the Sunday School teacher places large poster size Lesson Sheets on the classroom wall, allowing students to see pictures and *read* words from previous Lesson Sheets. The posters assist the teacher with content continuity by helping students remember past lessons and understand how lessons are interrelated within a specific unit. Additionally, 'requiring students to memorize scripture passages from the Bible helped them to develop print awareness and concepts of book print' (McMillon and Edwards 2000: 113). Concepts of book print are important pre-reading skills that are being developed each time students reference scriptures in the Bible, especially when they are encouraged to find the scriptures for themselves – an activity in which they participate often during midweek Bible Study.

In addition to Lesson Sheets, students also receive Activity Sheets to complete each week, which relate to the Bible lesson. Students are expected to utilize various literacy skills when completing the Activity Sheets, which are given after the Bible lesson is completed. For example, during a Children's Church observation, the Bible lesson was about Jesus going to the temple as a boy to study with the people who were assembled (Luke 2: 41–47). The Activity Sheet for this lesson displayed approximately twelve small pictures. The instructions were to circle the items that Jesus may have seen when he was on his way to the temple. This whole language activity required students to utilize skills (e.g. vocabulary and understanding time differentials) gained from life experiences to identify the pictures and determine the correct answers. One of the students suggested that they cross out the pictures that did not belong. The teacher praised her idea and told the other students to follow her suggestion. Pictures on the sheet included a cinema, a bird, a boy with a donkey and a girl on a skateboard. Because all of the students were non-readers, the teacher assisted them with the activity by asking them to identify each item in the picture and then asking if the picture should be circled or crossed out. The cinema was initially mistaken for a shop. The teacher responded to the mistake by scaffolding the students' efforts. During this session, two teachers were team teaching. The more experienced teacher (Mrs. Jackson) modelled several important teaching strategies for the other teacher (Mrs. McCray), who displayed a well-developed understanding of the importance of creating a nurturing, safe learning environment for the students. Mrs. Jackson makes the best possible use of an opportunity to teach several literacy skills during the following conversation:

Mrs. McCray:	What's this a picture of?
Tina:	A store!
Mrs. McCray:	Is that a store?
Shara and Deb:	Yes, a store.
Mrs. McCray:	Are you sure?
Mrs. Jackson:	Look, that's not a store because the word on the front of the building begins with a . . .
Shara:	a 'M'!
Mrs. Jackson:	Right!!! That word is mmmooooovvvvv . . .
Students:	Mmmmooooovvv . . .
Shara and Tina:	Movie!
Deb:	It's a movie theatre.
Mrs. Jackson:	That's right! It's a movie theatre.
Mrs. McCray:	Wow! That's excellent! Deb is the youngest one here today and she knew the right answer! Good job Deb. You are really smart!
Mrs. Jackson:	She sure is smart. All of our students are smart.

During the activity, the teacher modelled word-decoding strategies that gave students an opportunity to practise their phonics skills. After being told that the object in the picture was not a store, but a 'mmmmooooovvvvvv . . .', students were able to think about another type of building that may look like a store, but begins with the sound that the teacher was making. Various types of activities required students to utilize different literacy skills during each class period.

Oral language development: a tradition in the African American Church

Great emphasis is frequently placed upon oral language development skills. In the tradition of the African American Church, students are expected to speak clearly and articulately with voice inflection and emotion. The oral tradition of the African American Church often requires members to give extemporaneous prayers, testimonies and speeches. Sunday School, midweek Bible Study and Children's Church offer numerous opportunities to develop and refine oral language skills and prepare students to participate in worship services with the adults.

The importance of memorization is emphasized when Bible stories are frequently retold and students memorize the stories after hearing them repeatedly. The Sunday School teacher in this study utilized storytelling as a way to help students understand abstract concepts. Two difficult-to-understand concepts are Jesus dying on the cross to save the world (John 3:16) and Jesus' return for his people (also called the *Rapture*) (1 Thessalonians 4:16, 17; Revelations 21, 22). In order to scaffold student learning and comprehension, the teacher involved students in an ongoing project in which she required them to learn the 'Story of Jesus Dying on the Cross' and the 'Story of the Rapture'. Approximately two to three times per month after the Activity Sheet is completed, students are asked to retell these two stories utilizing a poster board and 'heaven box' (a cardboard box created as a replica of heaven based on the biblical description) as mnemonics to assist with details of the stories (McMillon and Edwards 2000). Regular class members are expected to remember these stories and be prepared to share them with younger students and new students until they learn them also. Requiring students to memorize and retell stories helps develop oral language as a bridge to reading (Searfoss and Readence 1985) and it fosters the beginning of metacognitive strategies for reading comprehension (Mason *et al.* 1986). Students are able to ask questions that address specific issues about the story. Teachers provide clarification on these issues and help students think about ways to apply the story to personal circumstances.

Storytelling activities also build confidence by giving students opportunities to share their knowledge with others. During the storytelling activities students utilize storybook terms that are a part of the *teacher-talk register* (Cazden 1988). The teacher-talk register is the unique words and terms that teachers use to communicate with their students during specific activities. For example, during storytelling activities, teachers use terms such as: 'Now let me tell you the story of Jesus'; 'When they put the thorny crown on Jesus' head, did they smash it hard? . . . or did they smash it soft? They smashed it hard!' or 'When we get to heaven there will be no more pain and no more sorrow; no more sickness and no more dying! Won't that be a glorious day?' When students retell the story, they use the same terms and voice inflection that they often hear the teacher using. Appropriately using the teacher-talk register indicates their ability to code-switch between casual conversation and formal classroom discourse (McMillon and Edwards 2000).

Students learn the purpose and relevance of Bible stories and scripture memorization through listening to teachers and other adult role models share their personal stories. Teachers in the classes addressed many difficult to talk about issues, such as death, chronic illness and single parenthood. The teachers feel that it is their responsibility to prepare their students for all circumstances in life. They discuss these issues and share Bible verses to support their comments. The memorized scripture and personal stories provide students with standards of reference (values) that they are expected to remember and apply in their daily lives.

Teachers' instructional methods

Teachers often utilized similar instructional methods based on foundational cultural beliefs, supported by scripture and perpetuated in the African American Church environment. They have high expectations of students in this learning context and students respond accordingly. To assist students in reaching these high expectations, teachers displayed a commitment to creating a positive, nurturing, all-inclusive environment in their classrooms, which we found that they accomplished through structure, repetition, their unique response to mistakes and by utilizing common communication patterns.

Classroom structure increases participation

Teachers provide a structured class environment, which followed a weekly pattern, very familiar to the students. The pattern was Opening Period, Bible Lesson, Learning Activity and Closing Period. The Opening Period included a song, scripture and prayer, similar to the Opening Period (called 'devotion') conducted during adult worship services and other meetings. This activity instills within the children the importance of honouring God through song, reading His Word (the Bible) and praying to God, before doing anything else. All students are expected to participate in the Opening Activity and usually did so enthusiastically. Teachers often allow more than one student to pray, sing or read the scripture, if there are many volunteers. Students are invited to participate when they do not volunteer. The teachers stress the importance of an all-inclusive participatory environment and ensure that students feel comfortable by scaffolding their efforts if needed.

The Bible Lesson is usually teacher-oriented. The teacher passes out the literature for the day and reads the lesson to the students, often with animated voice inflection, changing tones to indicate different characters' voices. Teachers ensure that students are paying attention by interacting with them while reading. Probing techniques were often used to interact with students and as assessment tools to evaluate student comprehension.

The Learning Activity immediately follows the Bible Lesson and is usually directly related to the weekly Bible story. Learning Activities include various ways to help with comprehension and application of the Bible story. The Closing Period includes cleaning up by storing the materials that were used during the Learning Activity, lining up to wash hands, eating a snack and sharing a closing prayer.

The important role of repetition

Repetition plays a vital role in this context. Because students were familiar with the structured patterns of the class they were able to participate in a greater variety of activities that supported their literacy development. Students volunteered to participate by praying, assisting the teacher with the lesson and helping younger or new students with their Activity Sheets. In this setting, peer tutoring was common and expected from the regular and older students. We found that repetition also increased the confidence level of the students. As they became familiar with the structure of the class and the teacher's instructional style they became more willing to take risks. Students would answer questions, make comments and ask for clarification concerning the lesson. They often shared personal experiences that were related to the lesson. The teachers made a special effort to include students' comments and showed that they valued them by referring to the comments throughout the class period. Teachers displayed a unique ability to *think on their feet* by being able to find a common thread that connected the students' comments to the lesson.

Turning mistakes into teachable moments

While familiarity with structured repetition may be the impetus that motivated students to participate on many levels in class, teachers' responses to mistakes created the nurturing environment that encouraged students to continue to participate and assured them that it was *safe* to take risks in class. A common instructional tool used by teachers in this study was their response to mistakes. Teachers were careful not to embarrass or discourage students by telling them that an answer or statement was *wrong*. Instead, teachers utilized revoicing and scaffolding techniques to assist students (O'Connor and Michaels 1996). Whenever students made an error, teachers would often ask a question to help the student give a clarifying statement. This type of scaffolding improved students' ability to articulate their own ideas. Teachers also utilized revoicing techniques in which they would simply restate student comments, adding specific details for clarification. We believe that students perceived this unique response to mistakes as mechanisms to ensure a safe, welcoming environment where their efforts were valued and praised. An example of one teacher's response to mistakes especially stood out because Lashawn was a first time student. The other students were familiar with the Opening Period and the type of prayer that is appropriate during that time, but Lashawn was not. Several of the regular students wanted to pray and the teacher decided to let each one pray. After they finished, Lashawn (age 6) raised her hand:

Lashawn:	Teacher, I want to pray too.
Mrs. Nettles:	Lashawn, you would like to pray this morning too? [smiling]
Lashawn:	Yes, I want to pray!
Mrs. Nettles:	OK everybody. Let's fold our hands and close our eyes so Lashawn can pray. She wants to pray too. [Everyone obeyed].
Lashawn:	God is great. God is . . .
Chris:	No! [yells, as Joshua sniggers].
Mrs. Nettles:	Now we don't interrupt anyone when they are praying, do we students?
Students:	No!
Mrs. Nettles:	All right Lashawn please continue.
Lashawn:	God is great. God is good. Lord, we thank you for our food. [Several students laugh quietly. Lashawn looks at them sadly].
Mrs. Nettles:	Great job Lashawn! Lashawn just blessed the snack that we're going to have a little later. We always need to remember to thank God for our food before we eat. Thank you so much Lashawn!
Lashawn:	You welcome! [smiles brightly]
Several students:	Ooooo! I want to pray for the food. I want to . . .
Mrs. Nettles:	No. Right now we need to do our lesson. Lashawn already took care of the prayer for our snack.

At this particular moment Lashawn became an accepted member of the class because of the teacher's ingenuity. Although Lashawn said the wrong type of prayer, the teacher recognized the importance of making her feel safe and welcome in her new learning environment. The teacher was aware of the ridiculing in which several students were engaging and wanted to model the type of attitude that they should have towards a newcomer. Her reaction to Lashawn's mistake was creative. She reassured Lashawn that she valued her participation and encouraged her to continue to take risks. She also reinforced a nurturing environment (free of ridicule). After this experience, Lashawn continued to participate freely and displayed a level of comfort unlike most students in a new environment.

Cultural classroom management, techniques and communication

We believe that similar values, learning styles and communication patterns between the teachers and students make success a greater possibility in this environment. Classroom management was not a problem because teachers usually enjoyed close relationships with students and parents. When students misbehaved, they were not ridiculed or singled out, but addressed by the teacher in general terms. For example, the Bible study teacher stated: 'Now I know everyone understands what he or she should be doing right now and I expect you all to get it done'. Mrs. Jackson, one of the Children's Church teachers, utilizes a puppet as an innovative classroom management tool. The puppet's name is George, who often welcomes the students to class in order to get them to calm down and become attentive. He welcomes newcomers and makes students feel better when they are not having a good day. George has become a regular class member and students look forward to seeing him every Sunday.

All of the teachers agreed that students rarely misbehave when they are engaged in learning and they challenged themselves to develop creative ways to retain student attention. For example, teachers helped students learn their scripture verses by conducting memorization exercises that cater to African American learning styles. Students were often taught with rhythmic phrases and given opportunities to march in step, clap and sway from side to side as a means of keeping the beat to assist with memory. During Bible Study Class, as the students learned the scripture below, they clapped after each phrase and applauded at the end to *act out* the word *victory*:

Ms. Stuckey: With God . . . [clap]
Students: With God . . . [clap]
Ms. Stuckey: we will gain . . . [clap]
Students: we will gain . . . [clap]
Ms. Stuckey: the victory!
Students: the victory! [applause]
(Psalms 60: 12, NIV)

By allowing students to learn in rhythm with movements, teachers were catering to students with musical and kinesthetic learning styles. Students who are musically inclined and students who need to move around learn exceptionally well when they are allowed to learn to a beat, clap, dance, march or sway. Students and teachers smiled, laughed and became quite enthusiastic during the activities, but most importantly, the students learned the scriptures.

We found that teachers and students utilized Black Vernacular English when conversing. However, during the Bible Lesson and Learning Activities, teachers code-switched into standard, teacher-talk language, which was usually grammatically correct, Standard English. When communicating with students, teachers often used gestures, hugs, smiles, eye gaze and hand shakes. Several times when a student had the floor, teachers gave affirmation grunts and/or nods to let the student know that they were listening intently. It was also common for teachers to use terms of endearment such as *honey*, *sweetie*, *buddy* and *baby* when addressing their students. Communication in this environment was not strained, but was laid back and natural. Students were seldom corrected when speaking. If they did not use correct grammar, it was not offensive to the teachers. The teachers seemed more interested in the meaning of the speaker's message, rather than the words utilized in the message.

Students' voices

We believe that one of the most important aspects of the African American Church is their commitment to children. The value of children and emphasis on their development is illuminated in a traditional cliché often utilized in the church environment when discussing children's issues: 'Our children are the *Church of Tomorrow*.' Church teachers and adult role models spend a tremendous amount of time preparing students to become leaders in the Church community. Biblical training and explicit instruction of cultural values are an integral part of all church activities organized for students, especially Sunday School, midweek Bible Study and Children's Church. This section highlights students' voices in response to the question: 'Looking back, how have your learning experiences at church influenced your "pathway to literacy"?' The students speaking in this section have participated in the classes observed.

Joshua (age 10 – fourth grader)
Participating in church activities helped improve my behaviour at school and especially helped me in my decision-making process. By going to church and having a connection with God, I feel like I don't get in as much trouble at school. I'm influenced to do good because I know you have to be good in public. It gives you a good foundation to be good. Rules are similar everywhere. If you go to church and learn, then you can be a good boy who everyone respects. I learned to be a good leader in Sunday School. I wasn't old enough to be in another class, so I was the teacher's assistant. Mrs. Nettles helped me become a better leader. I had to make sure that class was in order. I was given special responsibilities. The children would get upset when I had to tell on them, but I still thought that it was most important to tell Mrs. Nettles the truth. I had a really hard time obeying the teachers at school when I was younger [see McMillon and Edwards 2000] and I still have to work hard to remember to act appropriately, but I know that being given extra responsibilities by Mrs. Nettles in Sunday School helped me understand the importance of trying to follow classroom rules. But most important, Mrs. Nettles helped me realize at a very young age that I am a leader and not a follower.

David (age 12 – seventh grader)
One of the greatest benefits of participating in activities at church is that I have been able to identify and develop many of my talents. Learning and presenting Christmas and Easter speeches helped me with memorization and my oratorical talents. I learned how to speak with authority, clearly, legibly, so everyone could understand me. I was taught to use hand motions and I understand how they correlate with what I'm saying as I'm doing a

speech. My memorization skills help me at school with vocabulary tests, study skills, math formulas and especially when I'm studying to compete in the County Spelling Bee. I think that I have done exceptionally well in Science Fair competition because when I'm talking with my judges I am comfortable speaking about my project because I'm accustomed to interacting with adults and conversing with them about important topics.

Language arts skills such as my listening skills are really well developed from listening to the pastor's (my dad's) sermons. When they are interesting to me, I really get into those sermons. I've learned that words can be deep and powerful when used in the right combination. Being exposed to good preaching and the writings of the Bible has really helped my writing ability.

When the people at church compliment me, it makes me feel 'at the top'. It increases my self-esteem and confidence; and confidence builds competence, which is especially needed at a school like mine. You have to believe that you can; and you can. It also makes me feel really good when they are supportive. I am thankful for them. They make me feel like more than a regular person; I feel really special.

Morgan (age 14 – eighth grader)

The people at church encourage me in my school activities. I get recognized for doing well at school and people encourage me to continue doing well. The Sunday after I won the County Spelling Bee, I received a standing ovation. The church members were so proud! I really believe one of the reasons that I won was because I developed a good memory from memorizing scriptures and speeches at church when I was young. Speaking at church has given me lots of practice using a microphone and feeling calm in front of an audience. At school, my concentration is Music and I'm not nervous when I have to perform. At church, I've been given a lot of opportunities to do things, such as speaking, praying, talking and teaching. With so much practice, I've gotten really good at doing a lot of things. For example, by working with the musicians at church, I've improved my skills and learned how to play several different instruments, including the piano, keyboard, drums and saxophone. These experiences helped me be better prepared to compete at school for performances.

In Sunday School, all the students relate. We're taught many lessons that can help us in our daily lives. We can talk about anything, such as our individual problems. The teachers also share their experiences and explain mistakes they've made, so we can learn from them. One of the most important lessons that I've learned at church is to respect my elders. Even if I was upset and didn't like what an adult was saying, I still respected them because I didn't want to get in trouble. It's important to show respect to the elders. I think that's one of the most important lessons that we all learn at church – to show respect.

Conclusion

As African American researchers, we were excited to conduct a study in an environment in which we learned and developed as young children. We were given ample opportunities to develop and practise literacy skills that continue to be useful for us today. The African American Church has much to offer in terms of considering time-tested and proven ways of effectively teaching African American students. We hope that the literacy experiences described in this chapter provide the impetus for educators to look beyond their classrooms to learn about and attempt to understand outside cultural contexts in which their students learn and develop. We believe that this information can assist teachers by helping them more fully understand the literacy practices within the African American Church. It is crucial for teachers of African American children to become knowledgeable about the African American Church – a cultural context within which many literacy skills are acquired and developed. Classroom teachers can utilize this information to create innovative ways to build on the knowledge acquired from literacy practices and values taught at church thereby improving the literacy learning experiences of African American students at school. Additionally, we hope that this study encourages *all* teachers to help *all* students make connections between their in-school and out-of-school literacy experiences.

Acknowledgements

The authors gratefully acknowledge the support of the research reported in this chapter from the Michigan State University Spencer Research Training Grant and the Spencer Dissertation Fellowship for Research Related to Education.

Chapter 15

His eye is on the sparrow
Teaching and learning in an African American church

Wendy L. Haight and Janet Carter-Black

Why should I feel discouraged,
Why should the shadows come,
Why should my heart be lonely,
And long for Heav'n and home?
When Jesus is my portion,
My constant friend is He:
His eye is on the sparrow,
And I know He watches me;
　　　(C. D. Martin and
　　　Charles H. Gabriel)

In September 1991, I sat observing a group of primary school-aged children and their teacher during Sunday School at an African American Baptist church. Tanisha (all participants' names are pseudonyms) stood and recited all 27 books of the New Testament from memory. Other children discussed with their teacher, Sister Justine, the meaning of the metaphor, 'fisher of men' and whether they too, like Jesus' disciples, could become fishers of men. Jared refused to complete the accompanying written worksheet. Sister Justine pointed out that his grandmother would not approve and Jared continued to misbehave. Then, Sister Justine told a funny story of a time when she and Jared had been rebuked by his formidable grandmother and the class all laughed together. Jared, still laughing, completed his worksheet. Later, Jeff debated with Sister Justine how God's love for all his children was relevant to his own situation at school.

What was remarkable to me was that many of these obviously intelligent, loving, motivated and feisty children were having difficulties in school. On the same week that Tanisha recited the books of the Bible from memory, she failed her spelling test. On the Friday prior to his debate with the Sunday School teacher, Jeff had been harassed by a school bully. Earlier, Jared's mother has asked the pastor to intervene with the principal in a conflict between Jared and a teacher. By understanding a context in which children succeed, I wondered if we could better understand, and eventually improve, the contexts in which they were struggling. What might educators, social workers and others concerned with supporting children's development learn from First Baptist Church?

These questions motivated what was to become a decade-long research programme exploring teaching and learning within First Baptist Church in Salt Lake City, Utah. This programme included an ethnographic study of African American children at church (Haight 2002), an oral history of a church mother (Hudley *et al.* 2003) and the development and assessment of an educational intervention for community members (Haight *et al.* 2001). Observational methods were combined with in-depth interviews and historical analysis to understand adults' socialization beliefs and practices and children's participation. A variety of themes emerged that are highly relevant to educators and others seeking to enhance children's success. These themes include an emphasis on creating community, respecting the child, teaching culturally significant material and relating it to children's everyday lives.

Spiritual belief systems and the African American Church: a conceptual framework

Scholars of human development increasingly recognize the importance of context in human development. The research programme described in this chapter focused on patterns of socialization and participation within the Black church that may promote the development of resiliency in children. The concepts of risk and protective factors were used to understand how individuals develop well despite profound, ongoing stress (Fraser 1997). Risk factors, such as poverty, can increase the probability that psychological problems will develop, progress and become chronic. Protective factors, such as positive relationships with adults, can moderate the effects of risk factors so that more positive developmental outcomes may occur (Fraser 1997). Understanding the nature of risk and protective factors requires that they be embedded within their sociocultural context. Risk factors vary, depending on where children are positioned in the sociopolitical world. For African American children and many other children of colour, racism is a significant risk factor that can limit opportunities for development and undermine motivation, confidence and self-esteem. For European American children who do not carry the burden of membership in a devalued group, racism operates differently as a risk factor. It can limit opportunities for cultural enrichment, for self-understanding and for awareness of the detrimental effects of privilege on their own lives. Yet, the role of oppression in the lives of children and youth has received little attention from developmental researchers (but see Fisher *et al.* 1998).

Scholars of African American history and culture have argued, essentially, that spiritual belief systems are protective factors for many African Americans. Randolph Potts (1996) defines spirituality as 'the direct, personal experience of the sacred; the awareness of a higher power, a causal force beyond the material or rational, that operates in all aspects of existence' (p. 496). Spirituality has to do with life's ultimate significance. Spiritual belief systems have been portrayed as a common cultural value, a strategy for coping with adversity and an agent of socialization for African Americans from the time of slavery through to the present (see Haight 2002 for review). During slavery, responding to evil and other challenges of life while remaining a moral person was viewed as an important opportunity for spiritual development (Sobel 1988). In twentieth-century North America, spiritual belief systems also have been portrayed as a key factor in African American families' abilities to cope with and thrive despite stressful lives (Hale-Benson 1987). Robert Coles (1990) described children and families who called upon their rich spiritual traditions to deal with the trials of their own everyday lives, for example, racial hatred during forced school desegregation. The social sciences literature, however, is sparse in the area of children's spiritual beliefs.

Historically, the African American Church has been a key context within African American communities. Throughout its history, the African American Church has played a significant role in the provision of social support services. Historically, strong involvement in churches has been one of the means through which African American families have coped with adversity (see Haight 2002 for review). Within the African American Church, Sunday School has been a particularly significant context for children's socialization (Mitchell 1986).

The African American Church is an important context for the acquisition of a culturally distinct, alternative identity and view of reality (see Haight 2002 for a review). This alternative system of beliefs is not a simple imitation or derivation of European American Christianity (C. H. Long 1997), but evolved in relation to a distinct, African heritage, shaped by experiences in North America (Smitherman 1977; Hale-Benson 1987; C. H. Long 1997). Several general characteristics of this meaning system and related practices seem particularly relevant to children's resilience. First, African American religion has been described as the pragmatic intertwining of the sacred and the material (Smitherman 1977). Consistent with both a traditional African world view and with the experience of racism within the United States, a key to the African American notion of spirituality is its importance in facilitating survival (Hale-Benson 1987). African American religion addresses specific human needs and experiences and it helps individuals to cope with more traumatic aspects of human existence (Lincoln 1999). A second feature of African American religion is an emphasis on community. Community is central to African American culture (e.g. Stack 1974) with religious underpinnings (Hale-Benson 1987), for example, in the preoccupation in spirituals with the threat of loneliness and despair to disrupt the community of faith. A third feature, viewed by some as a cornerstone of contemporary African American theology, is the belief in the inherent dignity and worth of each individual. Each child, each individual, is special because he or she was created by God (Hale-Benson 1987). The belief that God recognizes African Americans as equal to European Americans – each personally as one of his children – has given many the inner resolve to 'keep on keeping on' (Hale-Benson 1987).

One of the contexts in which systems of belief are co-constructed is storytelling. Storytelling appears to be a cultural universal and is particularly prominent in African American culture (Gates 1989). Stories of personal experience, in which past events personally experienced by the narrator are related – have been observed in the language of children and adults from a wide variety of cultural communities including African American. Several scholars, however, have argued that the study of socialization through stories should be expanded to include more than just past events. For example, Linda and Doug Sperry (1996) found that at home, young children within a rural African American community preferred telling stories about fictional events, rather than past events as is common, for example, in European American families.

How we learned about children's socialization and participation

The methods employed in this research programme reflect an emerging interest in the integration of developmental, ethnographic and other qualitative methods. The intent of such methodological pluralism is to strengthen both developmental and ethnographic approaches in order to better understand development in a variety of sociocultural contexts (Jessor *et al.* 1996). Developmental methods include the systematic, often microscopic, description of children's participation in everyday activities and changes in participation over time. Ethnographic and other qualitative methods include the interpretation of the meanings of social behaviour from participants' perspectives through analyses of broader contexts of beliefs and practices. Thus, the intertwining of developmental and ethnographic and other qualitative methods allows identification both of the regularities inherent in everyday life and an interpretation of what such regularities may mean to the participants themselves (Sperry and Sperry 1996).

An ethnographic portrait of First Baptist Church

The research programme began with the collection of developmental and ethnographic materials over a four-year period (1991–5) within an African American, Baptist community in Salt Lake City, Utah. The goal was to understand, in-depth, the coherence and diversity of adults, socialization beliefs and practices and children's emerging participation within this specific cultural context. In the long run, the complex, differentiated portrait emerging from this case-based strategy provides a basis for meaningful comparisons with other communities. In the short run, it highlighted and perhaps challenged culturally based assumptions about educational practices and social service interventions with children and families.

First Baptist Church (a pseudonym) is an important case for at least two reasons. First, the African American community in Utah shares many similarities with African American communities in other parts of the United States. Many African American Utahns experience racial discrimination in employment, housing, education and everyday social interactions (Coleman 1981). The developmental literature, however, is virtually silent with respect to the impact of racism on children's development (Fisher *et al.* 1998). Second, the African American Utahn community has characteristics distinct from many other African American communities. For example, the overwhelming majority of African American Utahns find themselves in the religious as well as the racial minority. In contrast to the predominantly Baptist African American community, most of the population of the state of Utah belong to the Church of the Latter Day Saints (whose members are commonly known as 'Mormons'). Despite the diversity present across African American communities, there remains an unfortunate tendency in some of the developmental, educational and social service literatures to minimize such complexities. This case provides an important illustration of adaptation and development within a particular African American community in relation to a geographically and culturally distinct larger community.

This study focused on socialization practices, including storytelling, verbal conflict and role-playing, through which adults, particularly Sunday School teachers and their students, aged from 3 to 15 years, constructed personal meanings from an important cultural resource, the Bible. These observations focused on Sunday School. I audiotaped and took notes in a total of 40 Sunday School classes for children ranging in age from 3 to 16. From these materials, I reconstructed detailed, verbatim transcripts of Sunday School classes and descriptions of non-verbal contexts. These observations were contextualized by multiple, in-depth, semi-structured interviews with the pastor, the Sunday School superintendent and Sunday School teachers. These interviews also were audiotaped and transcribed. Practices and beliefs associated with Sunday School were further contextualized through description of yearly events such as Vacation Bible School, monthly events such as 'youth emphasis day', weekly events such as the pastor's sermons for children, a variety of other special occasions focusing on children, adult Sunday School classes and weekly Sunday School teachers' meetings. Observations and interviews were further contextualized through historical and social background information obtained from a variety of sources including local newspaper articles, historical documents and church publications.

Mother Edith Hudley's oral history

A 'mother' of First Baptist Church and master storyteller, Edith Hudley, provided an in-depth, oral history (Hudley *et al.* 2003). Mrs. Hudley was born in 1920 on a small family farm in Kennard, Texas. The sixth of eight surviving children, Edith was her mother's helper and apprentice. When Edith was 10 years old, her mother died from complications of childbirth and she was called upon to help her father raise her younger brothers. Her father realized that he would have to be both father and mother to Edith, but fortunately did not face this challenge alone. When Edith brought her father questions that he found inappropriate for a father to answer, he sought out his older sister, cousins and other female community members. He also encouraged Edith to form relationships with the 'mothers of the church', the ones with experience who would keep her to the right path. The oral history tells the story of Edith's life, largely in her own words. Because Mrs.

Hudley has spent much of her life caring for children – her brothers, sons, grand-children and 'adopted' offspring – the oral history is also about child rearing.

There is a growing awareness that children cannot be understood apart from the cultural and historical contexts that shape their lives. This is true of all children, but because African American children and other minorities have been underrepresented in studies of child development, the need to imagine the contexts of their lives is especially urgent. Edith Hudley's story stimulates our imaginations and prompts us to question, enlarge, or reaffirm certain assumptions about child rearing. For example, Mrs. Hudley's strong opinions about child rearing are grounded in the messages that she received from the family and community into which she was born: religious faith is the most important force in life, the compass by which all conduct is oriented.

Mrs. Hudley recounted her life story during several days in the fall of 1998 and the winter of 1999. Although she had never narrated so much of her life story in a single sitting, her stories had a shape that had been honed over multiple tellings. We tried to respect the integrity of her tellings by not interrupting or redirecting her talk. Twenty-three hours of audio recordings were transcribed verbatim, yielding 346 typed, single-spaced pages. The transcripts were edited to retain the essence of Mrs. Hudley and the conviction of her telling.

Contributing to the community

Information and insights gained from Mrs. Hudley and from the ethnography were used to inform the development of an educational intervention for children. This intervention had two goals. First, community members identified computer literacy as a weak area in the education of many children who had little access to computers either at home or in their relatively poorly funded public schools. As the pastor expressed, adults worried that children would be 'behind the 8 ball' (i.e. they would be at a disadvantage academically to other children) in their secondary school education and beyond if they did not receive some meaningful computer experience. Second, community members identified multicultural education as a relatively weak area of preparation in local teacher education programmes. Experience at First Baptist Church could provide a context for White, middle-class students, especially those who intended to go on in education, social work or other helping professions, to learn from the local African American community.

In collaboration with community members, we developed a Computer Club for children aged 3–18. We received donated computers from the local university and housed them in the church basement. The Computer Club operated on Thursday evenings and Saturdays. It was staffed by university students taking my child development class. These students were made aware of research findings regarding adult–child interaction in church (described later) and supervised in their interactions with the children by university staff and community members (see Haight 2002 for further discussion of the Computer Club).

Lessons we learned

Spirituality is a lifeline

At First Baptist Church, religious beliefs – such as the inherent worth of each individual and the value of freedom, justice and forgiveness – are viewed as lifelines both to healthy spiritual development and also to effective coping with the challenges of everyday life. The primary goal of Sunday School teachers is to 'Bring that child to God' for spiritual salvation. In addition, they argued that children must be familiar with religious beliefs so that they may reach for them in times of need. In the words of one Sunday School teacher, children must know how to 'Put on the armour of God'. This protection can be carried inside of each child to school, to work and in the community (Haight 2002).

Consistent with this emphasis on spiritual protection, Mrs. Hudley provided numerous illustrations of how her faith provided her with a coherent framework for coping with life's challenges including racism, poverty, violence and, in the following excerpt, death:

> I was a little girl and they was building a chimney . . . And Mama had this baby. It was a pretty baby and I was in the house . . . they let me stay in the kitchen and Mama was in the room when the baby was born. That was the prettiest baby. It had a full head of hair. And the baby died . . . And I went and I was lookin at the baby and Papa had to stop buildin the chimney to build a little box to go bury the baby. And I was just lookin for the baby to say somethin. And I said, 'Mama, the baby ain't sayin nothin!' I was listenin for the baby to cry. And Mama said, 'Well the baby won't be sayin anything. The baby's goin back to Jesus,' she said. That's the way she told me the baby's dead.
>
> (Hudley *et al.* 2003: 11)

Meaningful involvement in community

Consistent with the literature in African American studies, a key finding from the ethnographic research and the oral history concerns the emphasis on community. The significance of community as it relates to the African American Church is exemplified in the common reference to one's 'church home', indicating membership in a particular church. At First Baptist Church children are valued members of a cultural community stretching back in time and including members of the church highly esteemed for their wisdom and spirituality. Each child participated in meaningful ways beside these esteemed community members, for example, ushering worship services, leading devotions, singing in the choir, or providing service to families in need. In describing her own participation as a child with adults at church, Sister Irma noted: 'I gathered my spirit from them. I saw what they did. I saw them pray. I saw them read the Bible. I saw them sing and they would sing joyously' (Haight 2002: 69).

Adults also described the necessity of knowing the child's family and community in order to teach effectively. For example, during Sunday School, teachers often referred to individuals and events that class members knew. When Jared misbehaved, Sister Justine reminded him of their mutual connection to his grandmother. A sense of community also was fostered during the Children's Story, a part of the regular Sunday morning worship services, when the pastor or other church leaders would tell the children stories relating biblical concepts to the lives of famous African Americans or to African or African American folktales. These stories encouraged a sense of pride in being African American and also connected the child to a broader African or African American heritage.

Community ties also were seen as central to survival. For example, when Mrs. Hudley told the story of her rural home burning down when she was a child, it was neighbours and community members who provided the family with shelter, food and clothing (Hudley *et al.* 2003).

The inherent worth of each individual: love and respect

Another key concept to emerge from this research programme is the inherent worth of each individual. This worth exists independently of material success and social status. In the words of a popular hymn, each individual is a 'child of the King' with unique, God-given gifts. As such, each child is entitled to love and respect and with opportunity and effort will go far. As elaborated within the stories told in Sunday School, Vacation Bible School and other church contexts, however, the journey will be difficult. Just as many were blind to Jesus – a powerful, personal role model for many African American children – many will not see the Black child's inner resources and strengths. Just as the Egyptians enslaved and oppressed Moses' people, some will attempt to oppress the Black child. These and other stories told to children, however, also stress that through faith, effort and community, they too, like the Hebrew people, eventually, can prevail. The challenge is to remain a loving and moral person throughout the journey and to maintain a deep optimism in the ultimate rewards of a successful journey.

A love of children pervaded the narratives collected in this research programme as well as the practices observed. For example, when asked what made a good Sunday School teacher, adults at First Baptist Church did not refer to intellectual qualities or professional achievement. A good Sunday School teacher loves children. In describing her life's work, Mrs. Hudley repeatedly emphasized, 'I love children, period'. This love provides a basis for a relationship that was viewed as prerequisite to effective socialization.

A respect for children also pervaded adults' beliefs and practices. At First Baptist Church, children were seen as the hope of the future, but also respected as models for spiritual salvation. For example, the pastor exhorted the congregation to 'learn to be more childlike', that is, to trust and have faith in God. Furthermore, children's spiritual experiences were taken seriously. For example, Mrs. Hudley's belief that the dead remain available to the living was introduced and reinforced through relationships with her parents and other adults, but it was she, not they, who as a child actually witnessed the spirits of her dead grandmother and, later, her own mother.

Appropriate adult–child relationships

Love and respect for the child and the child's spiritual experiences, however, did not lead to dissolution of generational boundaries. Haight (2002) described the nature of adult–child relationships as 'child sensitive and growth oriented'. Sunday School teachers and Mrs. Hudley clearly were sensitive to children's emotional, social and cognitive immaturity. On the other hand, they demanded respect and took very seriously their charge to pass down spiritual lifelines to children. In a narrative relating a conversation with her son, Mrs. Hudley emphasized, '"Honor your mother and father that your days may be longer." I say, "God gave ya'll to me to raise and if I fail to raise you, I have failed God." And I said, "I have to suffer the consequences"' (Hudley *et al.* 2003: 158).

Adults' leadership roles, however, did not result in children's passivity. Sunday School classes clearly were led by the teachers who initiated narratives, posed questions and made demands on children's behaviour and performance. Children, however, were not passive. They actively contributed by responding to questions, debating issues and putting forth their own interpretations, for example, of how scriptures related to their own lives.

Storytelling

Another key finding from this research programme has been the importance of storytelling to relating new and complex concepts to children's own lives and experiences. Helping children to understand and then to apply biblical concepts in their everyday lives was described by every informant as a central goal of Sunday School. When asked how they accomplished their goals, adults consistently discussed storytelling. For example, Pastor Daniels explained:

> We are convinced that it is out of life that the best applications of any kind of principles can be found. And, certainly if you're going to make sense of it, you have to relate it to life. And, when we tell our own personal stories, there's almost an immediate connection with the youngsters.
>
> (Haight 2002: 83)

Observations of Sunday School classes revealed that storytelling was a central part of lessons. Children's formal Sunday School lessons included reading extended excerpts from the King James Bible, which children struggled to understand. It was through the stories that accompanied or followed these texts that the ideas really came to life. These stories had several characteristics. First, these stories frequently contained comments that explicitly linked the biblical texts to children's everyday lives. For example, Sunday School teachers routinely concluded a story with challenges such as, 'And how is this lesson relevant to our lives today?' Such stories sometimes contained deeply personal, spiritual meanings. In her oral history, Mrs. Hudley related numerous stories told to her over 75 years ago by her own parents that have provided guidance during difficult times and remain a touchstone for her life.

Second, narratives related a variety of types of events. Consistent with adults' emphasis on the significance of biblical text, many narratives involved retelling the biblical text. Stories also related personal experiences and elaborated hypothetical events. These stories always followed the biblical text and were used by teachers to illustrate and elaborate key points from the text. For example, Sister Irma ended a particularly dramatic story from her own life with the explicit comments, 'Now I share that with you not that you need to be worried about it . . . , but that's something that happened to me that's in line with today's lesson' (Haight 2002: 96).

Typically, adults used stories of personal experience to relate their own experiences to children. Through stories of personal experience, adults seemed to communicate to children that biblical principles are important to their lives and how. For example, after discussing with her class several examples from the New Testament of storms at sea, Sister Justine challenged the 8- to12-year-old children to understand the metaphorical meaning of 'storm'. Embedded within this discussion was Sister Justine's personal story of recovery from alcoholism, the 'major storm' in her life 'calmed by Jesus'.

Although stories of personal experience can be very powerful, they also have limitations. First, teachers are concerned about keeping children, particularly young children, focused on the biblical text – and children's own personal experiences can be highly distracting to them. Second, teachers are concerned with respecting the privacy of families and young children are not always discrete in relating their stories. On the other hand, teachers also needed to check children's abilities to apply the lesson to their own lives. Hypothetical talk referring to temporally sequenced, hypothetical events within narratives was common in Sunday School. Like stories of personal experience, hypothetical stories provided children with concrete instances of how biblical concepts relate to modern, everyday experiences and elaborated upon biblical text. For example, Sister Justine routinely asked the 8- to 10-year-olds, 'If Jesus was walking with us today, what would he want you to do?' Unlike personal narratives, however, they frequently cast a child in the role of protagonist. Interestingly, by the time they were 8- to 12-years-old, some children began to initiate hypothetical narratives. The follow excerpt involves 9-year-old Latasha and Sister Justine (SJ):

Latasha: If, if you were good and – say you were really good.
SJ: Ahha.
Latasha: And an angel when you were a child, but you got up and when you got grown up you were just mean in a gang – but then turned back over

to God and then when you die – say you were shot by a gang member
. . . So where would they go then? Because their sins were there?

SJ: All you have to do is ask for forgiveness! You're saying this person went
to church, came back hard-headed, then came back to church and
then got accidentally killed in the line of fire of a gang member? . . . All
it takes is believing . . .

Latasha: [Interrupting] Yeah, but you believe yes and you believe no.

SJ: You can't waiver in your faith.

(Haight 2002: 99)

Clues to facilitating competence and motivation in children

Despite the strong value African American communities historically have placed
on academic achievement and educational attainment (Comer 1988), educational
underachievement in public schools remains a sad reality for many African
American children and youth. Yet, the context of the African American Church
appears to facilitate competence and motivation in children who tend to experience
much difficulty in the public school setting, including in relationships with teachers
and administrators as authority figures. The findings presented in this chapter,
in conjunction with those of Robin Jarrett (1995), Jan Carter-Black (2001) and
others, provide several clues for educators, social workers, researchers and others
concerned with supporting children's development.

Respect the inherent worth of every individual

The Sunday School teachers at First Baptist Church taught the children to
believe in the inherent dignity and worth of each individual. Regardless of racism
and other indignities in the world, they are always 'Children of the King'. Crucial
to the development of African American children are curriculums, programmes
and services that incorporate strategies for dealing with racism in ways that diminish
the experience as a risk factor. In other words, adults must display beliefs and
practices that promote children's healthy racial identity and awareness of and
constructive responses to racism, without promoting hatred or discrimination
toward members of other racial groups (Sanders 1997).

Gain familiarity with culturally normative styles of adult–child interactions

Adult–child interactions at First Baptist Church were described as 'child-sensitive
and growth-oriented' (Haight 2002). Adults prioritized their relationships with
children and their families and they also held very high standards for conduct and
achievement. As is not uncommon for Sunday School teachers in African American
churches, teachers at First Baptist Church presented in a manner that conveyed

strong conviction, absolute authority and clear generational boundaries. While these teaching techniques may vary from the norm of middle-class White strategies, educators must realize that the meaning that African American children and their families attach to diverse teaching strategies may in fact be quite different from their own. Within the African American community, teachers who love children and feel a personal calling to teach are easily identified. European American educators may respond negatively to tone of voice, volume, or cadence of speech and relatively authoritarian demeanour and affect. African American children and their families, however, may be more likely to pay attention to the teacher's motivation and intentions. Does she care about the children? Is she able to convey that caring? Is she willing to be nurturing and encourage children to be strong, competent and ambitious, yet conform to church community and parental values and goals? Does she love the children?

Recognize the centrality of spirituality

Spirituality was the central value at First Baptist Church and a lifeline for Mrs. Hudley. Certain values expressed in public schools, however, may be in conflict with the strong spiritual orientation (e.g. Jarrett 1995) of many African American families. Awareness by educators of a family's spiritual orientation may minimize misunderstanding and facilitate home–school relations. For example, adults at First Baptist Church seemed less concerned with concepts such as individuality, competition or personal achievement – considerations more reflective of the analytical learning environment in schools, and more concerned about instilling in children the importance of placing God first in their lives.

Understand community

At First Baptist Church children participated as valued members of the community. Social workers and public school educators need to be cognizant of the meaning of *community* as programmes and services are being developed that will enhance the resilience in African American children. For example, the inclusion of members of a child's extended kinship system, including fictive kin, in planning and decision-making resonates with the construction of 'family' within the African American Church and larger social community.

Utilize storytelling to engage children in learning

Storytelling is an historically and culturally prescribed strategy for passing along to children lessons for living from which educators may draw. Mrs. Hudley and teachers in Sunday School use stories to bring the biblical meanings to life and relate central concepts to everyday life. Stories provide a venue for engaging children's imaginations. The use of strategies such as hypothetical talk keeps children focused on the lesson and minimizes opportunities for childish indiscretions.

Furthermore, stories provide powerful and coherent frameworks for interpreting even the most difficult experiences.

Conclusion

In conclusion, educators, social workers and those engaged in community-based youth programmes who have some knowledge of the ethos and principles of the African American Church will understand how the church, especially Sunday School, functions as a significant context for children's socialization. This increased knowledge can be called upon as a guide in the development of education and various community-based youth programmes that support rather than conflict with the characteristics of the African American alternative system of beliefs. Programmes designed to reach children and youth might even consider modelling effective child development strategies employed by the church as they seek to develop schemes that are tailored to meet specific, culturally relevant programmes. Similarly, academic and extramural school-based schemes that reflect dimensions of the relationships and interactions between African American children and their Sunday School teachers, pastors, mothers' boards and other significant church leaders may find that children exhibit competencies where previously they were struggling.

> I sing because I'm happy,
> I sing because I'm free,
> For His eye is on the sparrow,
> And I know He watches me.
> (C. D. Martin and
> Charles H. Gabriel)

Acknowledgements

This chapter is based, in part, on Haight, W. (2002) *African-American Children at Church: A Sociocultural Perspective*, New York: Cambridge University Press and Hudley, E., Haight, W. and Miller, P. (2003) *Raise Up a Child: Human Development in an African-American Family*, Chicago: Lyceum Press.

Chapter 16

Cultural literacy in the world of Pueblo children

Mary Eunice Romero

It is a cool winter morning. People sit in the plaza wrapped warmly in Pendleton blankets waiting for the buffalo dance to begin. Suddenly, high-pitched melodies along with white puffs of cold air come from the north end of the plaza. Twenty-plus singers are in Plains Indian attire and regalia, customary dress for this dance. In front of the choir of men are ten children dressed accordingly and singing the traditional buffalo songs. As the singing and drumming echo through the plaza, two male and two female buffalo dancers and a 'hunter' enter the plaza.[1] One of the youngest children in the choir, a 4-year-old boy, is dressed as a tiny buffalo dancer. When the signal is given, the drummers begin a rhythmic beat and the adult buffalo dancers begin dancing. The tiny buffalo dancer stands in a trance watching the dancers carry out the complex choreography. Before long he starts to dance too, no longer conscious of the many onlookers around the plaza. He raises his feet high in the air mimicking the adult buffalo dancers. He frequently looks down at his feet as if instructing them how to move. He glances back up at the adult dancers and follows their motions, sometimes off beat. Amazingly, this tiny buffalo dancer does this for the entire day.

In this vignette, we have witnessed one of many traditional winter dances performed by Pueblo people. Here the focus is on a young Pueblo boy who is deeply immersed in learning through participation, a customary teaching method in the socialization of children from Pueblo communities. Although collectively known as 'Pueblo Indians', each of the nineteen Pueblos of New Mexico in the south-west are autonomous nations and are considered to be one the least changed tribal groups in North America; 'their languages, governments, social patterns and cultural components remain uniquely Pueblo' (Suina 1994: 116). Like others around the world, the Pueblo people have developed distinctive ways to socialize their children into the beliefs, values and practices that will insure the continuation of their cultural worlds. In these complex worlds, adults must take on roles and responsibilities crucial to the perpetuation of the community's life and ways of knowing. These roles and responsibilities require extraordinary skills and preparation on the part of each community member. Consequently, children from these communities must be well prepared to assume these critical roles and responsibilities in adulthood. The vignette provides a glimpse of the means by which Pueblo people prepare and teach children the essential components of their cultural worlds, a process that begins before they enter mainstream schools and continues into adulthood.

In US societies, ensuring that children start school 'ready to learn' is of prime importance and is viewed as a prime responsibility of schools and families. 'Readiness', in the minds of mainstream educators and parents, includes introducing literature to young children by reading to them, working with them on number, letter and shape recognition, engaging them in verbal expression and so forth. Much of the current research examining school readiness focuses on the importance of families in this process and the promotion of these valued activities as being crucial for school success (Bohan-Baker and Little 2002). Furthermore, school success is equated with life success. Thus, middle-class American families and educators work hard at providing children with this 'before-school' curriculum. While most educators and parents concur that preparing young children for school is a fundamental obligation, there are many others who 'believe that the most important thing to teach children early in life is how they are related to the other people in their world and what kind of obligations they have as members of a family or community' (Fillmore 2000: 2). For many culturally and linguistically diverse peoples, such as those found in the New Mexican Pueblos, the goals for children reach far beyond those shaped and promoted by formal schooling. In each of these cultural communities, there are blueprints, or cultural plans, on how things should be done, including how children are inculcated and socialized. In that socialization process, which is part and parcel of a culture, are methods for imparting all that a community or a people truly believe children ought to learn. This chapter explores what Pueblo people believe about children and what they should learn. How do Pueblo children learn these things? Who teaches them? This discussion is based on my dual roles as cultural 'insider' – a member of the Pueblo of Cochiti and as a researcher of Pueblo communities (Romero 2003).[2] Before moving into this discussion, however, it is important to have a basic understanding of the Pueblo world. Therefore, a general description of the Pueblos is provided in the following section.[3]

The Pueblos of New Mexico

Over 52,000 members reside in the nineteen New Mexican Pueblos (New Mexico Office of Indian Affairs 2000). Also known as the Rio Grande Pueblos because of their position along the Rio Grande river, they range in population size from fewer than 170 in Picuris Pueblo to close to 9,000 in Zuni Pueblo. The Pueblos are categorized into two groups, Northern and Southern Pueblos. The eight Northern Pueblos are Taos, Picuris, Nambé, Pojoaque, San Ildefonso, Tesuque, San Juan and Santa Clara. The eleven Southern Pueblos are Jemez, Cochiti, Sandia, San Felipe, Santa Ana, Santo Domingo, Zia, Isleta, Ácoma, Laguna and Zuni.

Popularly known for their adobe terraced dwellings, today Pueblo people live in agrarian, communal villages and modern homes. Even though subsistence farming is no longer practised in the majority of Pueblos, it continues to be central to daily and ceremonial life. Familial and societal clans play key roles in upholding customs and traditions. The purity of Native religion has been retained, though signs of Catholicism are present in some of the traditional dances and rituals. As will be discussed later, both Native and Catholic religions play important roles in the socialization of Pueblo children.

While the Pueblos share general sociocultural characteristics such as history and geographic proximity, distinct differences exist among them. One major difference is language. There are three distinct language families represented by the Pueblos: the Keresan, Tanoan and Zunian. The Tanoan family is further subdivided into the Tewa, Tiwa and Towa dialects. Although closely related, the seven Keresan-speaking Pueblos have dialectical differences that make communication between some of them quite difficult if not impossible. Tewa-speaking Pueblos present a similar situation. Since the early twentieth century, a gradual shift from the indigenous languages to English has been occurring in nearly all of the Pueblos.

Differences among the Pueblos are also found in tribal governments. Each pueblo is governed by a bipartite system consisting of traditional and secular governing bodies. Each body serves separate and distinct functions and both are ultimately responsible for the welfare of the entire Pueblo community. The secular leadership is responsible for all external transactions, including educational, judicial, political and economic matters. Serving as the foundation for the secular government is the ancient governing system comprised of traditional leadership positions, the *cacique*,[4] warchiefs and their officials. It is responsible for maintenance of the ceremonial calendar and annually appoints the secular leadership for the community. This unique theocratic organizational structure assures that the traditional and contemporary needs of the Pueblo community are met and protected. Today the majority of the Pueblos maintain this bipartite governmental structure. However, in the 1930s, diversification of Pueblo governments resulted in the adoption of a constitutional form of government by some Pueblos.

In many respects, the Pueblo worlds of today resemble the Pueblo worlds of the past. They remain highly oral collectivist societies that emphasize group solidarity, interdependence, cooperation and social relationships (Greenfield 1994). In the traditional Pueblo world, community is given precedence over the individual. Thus, there is a profound belief in the value and act of 'giving back' to one's community. 'Giving back' is described as an inner desire to contribute to the well-being of one's people and community and to the perpetuation of the Native culture and lifestyle. Fundamentally, giving back extends beyond individual actions and desires and spans into the realm of Pueblo spiritual beliefs, as explained here by a Pueblo leader:

I want to be a part of the event because I think as an Indian, you're already taught the specifics of those events . . . so it's up to the individual wanting to be a part of it. If you don't want to be, then if somebody forces you to go over there, your heart and your mind is not gonna be pure. You got to have that genuine feeling, not only for yourself . . . you're there for the people and for the world.

(cited by Romero 1994)

The value and reverence given to each human being creates a society in which relationships and cooperation rather than individualism and competition are emphasized; where community contribution and helping others rather than self-promotion and self-interest are encouraged; and where individuals are equally valued rather than differentiated and separated. It is from this sociocultural framework that Pueblo children develop an understanding of themselves and others in their community – and beyond.

Socialization of children

People of different cultural worlds have developed ways to socialize children according to their own realities, assumptions and beliefs of their communities. Through everyday social interactions with experts in speech contexts, children simultaneously acquire the cultural, social and linguistic (and non-linguistic) knowledge and develop the cognitive skills for becoming competent members of their world (Schieffelin 1995). During these social interactions, the young mind is tacitly, yet actively, absorbing social knowledge and internalizing what he/she acquires from such external activities to make it his/her own. Vygotsky referred to this socio-cognitive process whereby an external interaction is transformed into internal mental functioning as *internalization* (Wertsch 1985). In his view, through sociolinguistic interactions with experts (adults), children come to know who they are in relation to others in a social world (Vygotsky 1978). For instance, in Japan, children are socialized primarily by their mothers who, through the Japanese communicative style, teach them the group values of empathy and conformity (Clancy 1986). Japanese children, by learning socially appropriate language, come to internalize the beliefs about an individual's responsibility to uphold the interests of the group. Similarly, in Samoan (Ochs 1988) societies, through the process of language acquisition, young children learn to use language in ways that acknowledge the hierarchical relations that constitute the core of their social and cognitive worlds.

Socialization of Pueblo children

Like other cultures around the world, the Pueblo societies of New Mexico have their own distinctive cultural plan for socializing their children, albeit they have been influenced in more recent times by the wider mainstream society. In Pueblo societies, the unwritten language has patterned various forms of knowledge into intricate designs earlier referred to as cultural plans. Early in this plan, through various settings of ritual and ceremony, the sacredness of children is impressed on everyone. Pueblo children, from birth, grow up surrounded by familial and communal caretaker-teachers;[5] throughout their lives they will experience a number of special events that will collectively contribute to the development of their self and communal identities. The development of 'self' begins within the first days of a child's life with the naming rite,[6] the time when a child receives a Pueblo name. The following naming rite took place in a Keresan Pueblo:

> Family, relatives and friends gather at the home of the newborn infant. As the sun rises in the east, the baby, wrapped in a blanket, is carried outside where she is surrounded by those present. The baby's face is uncovered and she is exposed to the first rays of Sun. The grandparent, parent, or respected elder presents her to the Sun and in the Native language asks Father Sun to welcome and guide the new person into the physical world. With an offering of cornmeal, he gives the infant her Keres name(s) and identifies her by her maternal clan. Others give the newborn names as well. The baby is covered and taken back inside. Adults take turns holding the infant and address her by her new names. They informally discuss the meanings of the names; some are names of ancestors whom one wants to honour while others were chosen for their aesthetic sounds and/or meanings. Gradually, good-byes are given and the parents and their daughter are left alone.
>
> (Home observation)

As weeks pass, through a natural selection process, one of the names will emerge from amongst the rest to become the infant's publicly known Keres name. The other names will be primarily remembered and used by those who gave them to the child. In addition to their Pueblo name(s), children will come to know themselves by the maternal clan into which they are born. Clans, a sociocultural organization reserved for ceremonial purposes, are powerful means for socializing children.

Another of the earliest socialization events is the baptismal ceremony, an event welcoming a new member (the newborn) into the community. In the baptismal ceremony, two primary parties, the newborn's and the godparent's families, are united into one familial unit with the responsibility for the child's upbringing. The baptism involves an intense day of Catholic and Pueblo ceremony in which the entire community participates. An important part of this ceremony is the 'acceptance of the child' ritual that takes place in the home of the newborn after the baptismal mass. The following is a description of such an event:

> The house is filled with people waiting for the arrival of the newly baptized baby and her Godparents. After a short wait, the family and friends of the Godparents arrive with the infant; there is standing room only in the house. The Godparents and parents with the newborn make their way to the centre

of the crowded room. Everyone surrounds them and gently places their hand on the shoulders of the person in front of them. They bow their heads to listen. In the Native language, the infant's grandfather begins the prayers by giving the infant's Pueblo name and the maternal clan. Prayers ask for a healthy, happy and safe life for the newborn and for her acceptance as a new member of the families, community and the world. Additional prayers are exchanged between the two families and the newborn is handed back to her parents.

(Community observation)

Godparents serve as 'guardian' parents, who monitor the well-being of their godchild through a special relationship equivalent to that of the parents. Godparents have the right and responsibility of disciplining and guiding their godchild throughout his or her life – even into adulthood. Godparents play a peripheral but nonetheless important role in the socialization of children.

Multi-calendar world of Pueblo children

In mainstream US society the home and school are the primary settings for the socialization of children, whereas in Pueblo society it is the home and community. Additionally, whereas home and community are considered separate socialization settings in US mainstream society, home and community are intricately linked together to serve as the context for socialization of children in the Pueblo world. This interrelationship can be seen in the religious and social life of Pueblo people, which evolves around a rich and complex ceremonial calendar. In this calendar, as exemplified in the naming and baptismal events, the Native and Catholic religions are juxtaposed in a unique relationship. Additionally, the American calendar of celebrations is also observed. Collectively, the three calendars create a year permeated with activities and ceremonies (Suina and Smolkin 1995). Through their participation in the various communal activities guided by the Pueblo calendar, children are taught fundamental cultural values of sharing, compassion and respect as well as their roles and responsibilities as members of a community. For example, prior to the observance of the Catholic All Souls Day, Pueblo children participate in the typical American holiday ritual of Halloween. After an evening of trick-or-treating, families prepare for two days of observance and veneration of spiritual visitors, their ancestors and deceased loved ones. During this period, the entire community is tranquil. In homes, everyone is advised to be patient, respectful and observant of the practices and children are instructed to avoid anger and to keep their voices down while they play. On the final day of veneration, families gather at the church. They bring baskets of native foods (e.g. Indian corn, oven bread, tamales, *piki* bread,[7] Indian corn, melons, chilli, etc.) and store-bought treats (chips, sodas, candy, fruits) and place them on the floor in the centre of the church. When the church is filled with people (and baskets of food), the *fiscales* begin their public orations in the Native language, asking for another year of bountiful crops and a peaceful community.[8] Everyone is silent, including the youngest of children. At the conclusion of the prayers, the children's bags are filled with the food and treats. The families return home where the children scramble through their bags in search for their favourite treats.

A world of caretaker-teachers

From the day they are born, Pueblo children are surrounded by influential caretaker-teachers who play vital roles in their daily care and in the shaping of their individual, social and communal beings. This elaborate network of socializers, although weakened through the years, remains a crucial and central force in the lives of children.

Whereas in mainstream families, parents are the central players in socialization (Ely and Gleason 1995), in Pueblo families the primary socializers are parents, grandparents and siblings. In the home setting, where a Pueblo child's earliest socialization experiences occur, the care of the infant is primarily the responsibility of the mother, but this responsibility is also shared by a multitude of other caretakers – father, siblings, aunts, uncles, cousins and godparents. Through various interactions inside and outside of the home (e.g. visitations, communal activities, etc.) children will come to intimately know their various caretaker-teachers. In particular, grandparents are vital holders and transmitters of knowledge in Pueblo societies; they are also central socializers of children. In the first two years of life, grandparents take a minor role in the physical care of grandchildren, but begin to play a major role in socializing them when they are 2 or 3 years old. At that age, grandchildren may spend extended periods of time with their grandparents. Often a young grandson will accompany grandfather to the practice house (a community building for social and ceremonies activities) where the men's singing society gather to compose and refine songs. The greetings that the child has heard since birth are heard from the men in the practice house. If the shy grandson refuses to respond, grandfather will quietly whisper to him, 'My grandson, he is calling you' and urge him to give the greeter a gentle handshake. Similar routines are taught to girls who, like boys, frequently accompany their grandmothers and mothers to social activities or engagements in the home and community contexts. In many Pueblo communities, it is the custom for women to gather at a home to 'help' a family prepare for a certain event (e.g. wedding, family meeting, ceremony, etc.). During these times, children are welcomed yet closely supervised participants.

Older siblings also play important and active socialization roles. They are responsible for the care of their younger siblings, including teaching them proper behaviour and social discourse and cultural knowledge. In addition, they serve as role models and mentors to them. Older siblings are given rudimentary responsibilities for the care (e.g. holding, rocking, feeding, playing) of their younger sibling, under adult supervision. Siblings are given more responsibility for looking after their brother or sister during the toddler period. They may watch the toddler while mother is busy in the kitchen or make sure that the little one does not wander off or create a disturbance (crying, fighting others, etc.) during a community activity. As the child grows older, older siblings take on mentoring roles, especially for siblings of the same gender. In this mentoring role, an older sibling will demonstrate to a younger sibling how to dress appropriately in traditional attire and, if appropriate, will take the younger sibling with him to a communal event, such as the buffalo dance in the opening vignette. Older sisters will teach younger siblings how to make tortillas or tamales.

In the cultural world of Pueblo children, there is a third group of caretaker-teachers. As mentioned earlier, a unique theocratic body of secular and traditional leaders governs the Pueblos. These caretakers are responsible for the guidance, welfare, safety and harmony of the entire community. Furthermore, they can advise and discipline fellow community members (children and adults) whenever necessary. Elders and godparents have this same responsibility. Thus, children are taught to heed the advice of any these individuals and to give them the utmost respect.

Additionally, each Pueblo has a traditional social organization comprised of moieties and clans that have key functions in the community's religious life and its ceremonies. A moiety is a sociocultural organization that subdivides the community into two parts or groups, a winter group and a summer group. Moieties are patriarchal. It is common for families to take infants and young children to the moiety houses for community functions where they will learn crucial cultural knowledge and discourse through participation and observation. Through the moiety and other traditional realms of Pueblo society, children are exposed to an elaborate network of human interrelationships and teachers.

Learning social and cultural values

Kinship is the heart the Pueblo society. Therefore, fundamentally, one must be aware of the social, familial, religious (Native and/or Catholic) and cultural webs connecting individuals in the community. A part of 'knowing one's people' includes respecting them. Consequently, the teaching of *respect* – respect of others and the Pueblo ways of life – begins early in infancy. In home and community contexts, the socialization of children into respectful behaviour and discourse is quite evident. For instance, when interacting with their grandchild, grandparents model politeness discourse for the infant. As she holds her grandson, the grandmother will greet and respond for the infant using gender-specific language. After a few moments of smiling and talking to the infant, he is handed over to the grandfather who follows the same routine. Thus, in addition to learning social discourse, the child is learning gender-specific language and interrelationships. As the child grows older, speech modelling continues. Additionally, there will be an abundance of peripheral opportunities for him to learn appropriate behaviour and social discourse through listening and watching others. Another example of learning proper social discourse and relationships follows. The interaction occurs between a 5-year-old girl, her mother and others in a home where preparations for a Pueblo wedding are taking place:

> Upon entering the house, the adults extend the customary greetings. Immediately, the adults give special attention to the young girl, greeting her with smiles and verbal delight. The young girl does not greet them back, so her mother instructs her to greet her aunt who is sitting close to the door. The young girl hides shyly behind her mother and does not greet the aunt. Then the mother walks her over to the aunt and models the proper verbal and nonverbal (a hug or a handshake) greeting. With her mother's assistance, the young girl greets everyone present in the house.
>
> (Home observation)

Through this type of guided practice, children learn proper acknowledgement of others through greetings as well as important familial and communal relationships.

Learning how to show respect through behaviour and social (and ceremonial) discourse is essential for Pueblo children. Furthermore, they must also know when and where to demonstrate it. In each Pueblo there is a plaza, the physical centre of the village and the core of ceremonial activity. Children are taught to regard the plaza and other particular physical areas and structures (e.g. kiva, moiety house, etc.) as places of reverence where respectful behaviour is expected of all individuals. In these settings, adults indirectly model and directly communicate to children the appropriate and expected verbal and non-verbal behaviour. For instance, crying infants are quickly quieted and young children are instructed not to shout and to restrain from unruly behaviour or intrusive loud play. A caretaker observing a traditional dance will rhythmically rock and quietly sing to an infant or will speak to children in whispers or use facial gestures unobtrusively to express approval or disapproval of behaviour (e.g. smiling, frowning).

Pueblo ways of learning and teaching

On a daily basis Pueblo children interact with their primary caretakers, and on a less frequent but still important basis, they interact with their secondary and communal caretakers. All these individuals are holders and transmitters of knowledge, values, beliefs and principles of the Pueblo way of life; they are the children's teachers. In this section, *some* of the means by which these caretaker-teachers transmit to Pueblo children essential cultural knowledge and contribute to their cognitive and social growth are examined.

Teaching by doing

A key strategy in the socialization of Pueblo children is 'teaching by doing'. Children are exposed to various stages of interaction in which teaching by doing plays a crucial role in their learning. These stages are illustrated below in the process of bread making. Guided practice, silent learning and active participation are also seen in this example.

> Pueblo bread is made in large, outdoor, earth ovens called *hornos* and heated by a wood fire. Hornos bake 25 to 60 loaves of bread at one time. Usually two or more women work together to make the bread. Children from an early age observe the bread making process, which takes place in the home. When making bread, an infant is often positioned near the activity (e.g. in a highchair) so that he/she is kept in place and in sight. As a bystander (or by-sitter), he/she can watch the bread makers at work. When the infant is older and able to hold and manipulate objects, he/she is somewhat more directly involved in the activity. Again, the infant is positioned near the activity, however he/she is now given a small piece of dough to handle (or 'to play with'). As he/she handles the dough, the adults will praise the youngster for his/her 'attempts' at rolling out a ball of dough even though that is not his/her intention. Nevertheless, in this manner of encouragement and praise, young children are included in activities like bread making. When the child is adept enough to manipulate dough purposely, usually about 2 or 3 years of age, he/she is directly included in the activity. He/she is positioned next to someone who models the action for him/her. When a child begins to mould (or play) with the dough, he/she is praised for helping and told he/she is a 'good helper'. If the child does not attempt the task, an adult (or older sibling) will assist the child in completing the task by demonstrating through a collective effort. At 4 and 5 years of age, children are expected to participate in the activity without much coaxing. At each stage, public praise and encouragement are continuously given to the child who is told about the wonderful job he/she is doing in helping. In this way the values of helping others, cooperation and contribution are instilled in children. By age 8 or 9, the bread making becomes a task more associated with girls than boys.
>
> (Field notes)

Active participation

'The best way for them [children] to learn is to be there and to participate', explained a Pueblo grandfather about Pueblo children's learning. In the Pueblo world, participation is a crucial form of learning and includes the physical, cognitive, social and more importantly the affective domains. Participation is linked to one's desire and willingness to be a part of an activity. Thus, if a person – young or old – desires to participate, he/she is encouraged to do so (force or coercion are atypical). Consequently, novice dancers who are barely able to keep pace with the adult dancers (such as the tiny buffalo dancer) will partake in the dancing until they tire.

Silent learning

Another prevalent form of socialization found in Pueblo societies is 'silent learning'. Silent learning takes place by being around individuals engaged in a certain task or activity. The observer or learner is an active participant in the activity even though he/she may not be directly engaged in it. Basically, learning occurs through direct and indirect social interactions with experts. Lave and Wenger (1991) call this type of learning 'legitimate peripheral participation' (LPP). In Pueblo home and community contexts, children engaged in silent learning, watch, listen and internalize the events and interactions occurring. In the interview excerpt below, a young mother describes the manifestation of her son's silent learning.

> But it's so funny too because I like remember when he started going with his dad to practise. He just, like I said, they just pick up everything around them. He'd get his little drum and walk like an old man and sit on a little stool and start beating his drum. The funny thing is for the longest time his crayons were his cigarettes. He would walk around with his crayons doing this and he would want to go to town with his crayons [laughing]. He did this for a long time. He picked up a lot just by going with his dad and seeing the older men. I don't know for some reason that's always been with him or in him. We would go to town and he would sing all the way going and all the way back. And he still does it. That's how I know he's content. Like if we're eating and he's real happy with his food, he'll be humming or singing. We'll just be looking at him. He's funny.

This particular young boy has been accompanying his father to the moiety house since he was an infant. Apparently, during these times he had been watching and listening to the older men in this context and internalizing their interactions which focused on singing and drumming, and smoking. Consequently, as described above, he often imitated the behaviours of the older men, including their smoking habits. In addition to silent learning, the above example also illustrates another powerful form of socialization and learning that occurs in Pueblo societies, 'teaching by example' or role modelling.

Teaching by example (role modelling)

Pueblo children learn proper social behaviour and discourse by observing adults. Boys watch their fathers, grandfathers and/or uncles in home interactions and in leadership roles. Girls observe their mother, grandmothers and other females performing their respective roles in the home and community. As illustrated in the following account, teaching by example is a strong method for socializing child:

> A non-native man who was visiting a Pueblo family was trying to interact with his friend's 5-year-old son. He asked the Pueblo boy a question typically

asked to children: 'What do you want to be when you grow up?' The boy did not look up to acknowledge that he heard the man; he continued playing with his truck. So the visitor asked the question again. This time the boy stopped playing, looked up at him and responded in the Native language, 'A traditional leader'.

(Personal communication, J. H. Suina, 1999)

The child's response had to be explained to the visitor who expected the boy to reply with a common mainstream occupation (e.g. fireman, doctor, etc.). The boy, who has witnessed both his father and grandfather in traditional leadership roles, responded that he aspired to be like them.

Mentoring

Mentoring, a form of expert–learner education, is different from silent learning in that both parties acknowledge the teaching–learning relationship and it takes place over an extended period of time. The extent of mentoring depends on the maturity of the learner, the task to be learned and the purpose of the mentorship. Earlier it was explained that older siblings demonstrate behaviours or tasks in ways that will assist their younger siblings' abilities to eventually perform them on their own. In a higher level of mentorship there is a special type of relationship between expert and learner. In this relationship people interact in ways that will eventually result in the acquisition of skills and knowledge by the learner and ultimately his/her successful completion of the task on his/her own (Vygotsky 1978). Take, for example, the art of pottery making. Pottery making is passed down within the family and is considered an adult activity. However, in the homes of potters, children observe the pottery maker, usually a mother or grandmother, making pottery and are thus exposed to the pottery-making process. Sometimes they will accompany the pottery maker on excursions to the mountains to acquire clay or other materials needed for making pottery. If a child shows an interest in making pottery, she/he will be given a piece of clay to mould. Simply instructions may be given, but the main purpose for involving the child is to encourage his interest and interaction. As the child looks on, some verbal instruction may be given if the child asks questions, but mainly the child is an onlooker. It is not until the teenage years or older that an apprentice will intentionally attempt to learn through structured performance. It is then that the maker will seriously model and teach essential skills and knowledge solely to promote the growth of the learner. Higher, sophisticated levels of mentoring are reserved for the arenas of Native religion and ceremony.

Conclusion

This chapter has provided a modest glimpse of how cultural forces transform the natural and social development of children into the ideals of Pueblo people.

Clearly, for Pueblo children, learning the language they need for literacy in the Pueblo world requires continual linguistic and social interactions with many caretaker-teachers. Although their early experiences differ from those of mainstream children, Pueblo children are provided with many rich and meaningful opportunities to acquire the cultural symbols (Benjamin *et al.* 1997) and intellectual traditions important in and vital for the perpetuation of their cultural worlds.

Notes

1   The hunter dresses in a buckskin shirt and leggings and carries a leather sheath across his back; he and the buffalo dancers represent the traditional hunting excursions conducted years back.
2   The core of information (i.e. observations, interviews and field notes) comes from my dissertation research.
3   See Sando (1998) for further information on the New Mexico Pueblos.
4   Top religious leader and caretaker of the entire Pueblo.
5   In Pueblo societies, 'caretaker' and 'teacher' are synonymous terms and are used interchangeably or combined into 'caretaker-teacher'.
6   Variations of this rite exist among the Pueblos.
7   *Piki* bread, also called 'paper bread', resembles paper; it is thin and light. *Piki* is made of blue or white corn mix and is smeared by hand on a hot stone slab heated underneath by a wood fire.
8   *Fiscales* are men appointed to oversee and care for the church and Catholic needs of the community (i.e. baptisms, marriages, etc.).

Many pathways

Implications of Syncretic Literacy Studies for practice and research

Eve Gregory, Susi Long and Dinah Volk

The contributors to this book provide powerful demonstrations of the generative activity of young children and their mediating partners – family members, peers and community members – as they syncretize languages, literacies and cultural practices from varied contexts. Through studies grounded in real world settings of homes, schools, community schools, nurseries (preschools), senior centres and churches, we see children's learning expertly scaffolded and children expertly scaffolding the learning of others, in ways that are not typically recognized, understood or valued in schools. By paying close attention to interactions in the contexts of day-to-day lived experiences, researchers illuminate the work of the invisible teachers in children's lives.

These representations of teaching and learning are rooted in convictions about overturning stereotypes, redefining what counts as literacy, expanding notions about who counts as teachers of literacy, capitalizing on children's ability to negotiate meaning and take control of learning, learning from and through first languages while developing bilingual and bicultural capabilities, nurturing home and community networks of teaching and learning and seeking to understand others by looking beyond surface attempts to appreciate culture and language.

What does this mean for teachers?

Calls for transformation in education often focus on the central role of the teacher and the need for parents to become more involved in their children's schooling. Without minimizing the importance of these figures, we argue that change efforts must help teachers understand the power of the other mediators in children's lives as well, particularly in the areas of language and literacy learning. The consideration of these other mediators shifts our exclusive focus from the school to the children and the many contexts in which they are active participants.

When we confront the invisibility of these mediators and contexts, recourse to the broader cultural, political and historical contexts of children's communities is needed to explain why these many teachers and sites for learning have been overlooked, disparaged, or rejected. A commitment to social justice that leads to meaningful collaboration with families and communities in school reform projects becomes essential. When we observe the skills of these mediators and the varied ways they co-construct literacy with children, our understanding of the social construction of multiple literacies is strengthened as is our understanding of the need to bring these mediators and these literacies into classrooms (or to recognize and value those that already occur there). This requires us to rethink both the curriculum and the pedagogies that we praise and select as most appropriate. When we immerse ourselves in these learning interactions and come to see the many sources and resources on which participants draw, we further our understanding of the process of syncretism and of the social and cultural mediation of cognitive development.

To accomplish such reform, we recognize that a critical stance, an understanding of education for the purpose of affecting social change, is required. Such a stance leads us to examine deficit perspectives and to vigorously critique the status quo. It requires us to question 'universal truths that should be imposed on all human beings' (Cannella 1997: 61) and to recognize that 'all of us emerge from local cultures set in global contexts where language from multiple sources shapes us' (Shor and Pari 1999: 2). Teachers who construct learning environments from a critical perspective open their classrooms to previously invisible mediators and literacies and to the syncretic practices created in the process. They construct classrooms that are learning communities where children are supported as questioners and learners who seek to hear and understand voices that are typically marginalized (Edelsky 1999).

Embracing this critical stance, we present a compilation of recommendations for classroom practice generated by the studies in this book. All are based on the assumption that children and their communities 'have something to offer which is relevant to what is taught' (Olmedo, Chapter 6 in this volume). We advocate that teachers and teachers-in-training:

- Observe children and members of their communities in school and out. Visit families and interact with them in places where they are the experts (Ladson-Billings 1995) and in collaborations they have developed (Haight 2002). Develop 'ethnographic eyes' (Frank 1999).
- Learn about and value insiders' voices. Work with community members to recognize the value of *their* knowledge and practices while supporting their efforts to understand, work with and challenge mainstream perspectives. Work together with community members to develop syncretic perspectives that build on your expertise and theirs (Compton-Lilly 2003).
- Understand that the teacher is a mediator of young children's learning and just one member, though an important one, of children's learning communities (Nieto 1999).
- Begin with the assumption that children have had relevant and valuable experiences with literacy before and outside of school. Work with family members and fictive kin to learn about, understand and participate in such

literacy events. Respect and tap into the social matrices in which funds of knowledge are shared in children's communities (Moll *et al.* 1992).

- Explore ways to link mandated curriculum and standards to local funds of knowledge.
- Learn about the cultures and political histories of children's communities from a critical perspective. Analyze and appreciate children's developing literacy and language as embedded in these contexts.
- Nurture learning communities within classrooms and schools (Rogoff *et al.* 2001). Build on and create opportunities for children to teach and learn from each other within and across age groups and ability levels. Nurture the expertise of peer teachers and learners and the synergy that can be generated in their interactions. Look for and support a variety of learning relationships within children's zones of proximal development.
- Make a commitment to the maintenance of children's first languages. Create bilingual contexts in schools in which English language learners can work with children and adults who are native speakers of their language to jointly construct understandings of language and literacy. Create opportunities for children to be experts in their own language(s) and culture while broadening the worldviews of those who speak only English.
- Support the social development of English language learners. Provide children with opportunities to engage in play and informal learning interactions with others who speak the same language as well as with those whose language they are learning.
- Weave literacies from children's interests, families, communities and popular culture into a classroom culture (Kenner 2000b; Dyson 2003). Do the same with styles and forms of communicating, such as storytelling, that are familiar to the children. Use the juxtaposition of these literacies as learning opportunities (Gregory 1997).
- Create opportunities for children to help shape their own learning and to co-construct it with others, both children and adults.
- Consider the desired ends of your change efforts. Certainly children's learning is a central one. Creating a democratic classroom and '[p]reparing students for active membership in a democracy' (Nieto 2002: 41) may be others.

Looking further: new directions for research

Further research is needed. Ethnographic approaches grounded in sociocultural theory seem most suited as methods of investigation, though there is also much to learn methodologically about the study of children's cognition in an array of complex social contexts. Following are a selection of research questions raised by the studies described in these chapters.

- What are the characteristics of literacy practices constructed in children's communities? What are the ideologies of children, parents, families and community leaders and elders that underpin their literacy practices?

- How do children and their mediators syncretize the multiple literacies in their lives? How do we understand young children's agency in this process?
- What is the role of community mediators and institutions in supporting the literacy learning process? In what ways might these mediators and institutions be more successful than schools in engaging and teaching children and why?
- What does the study of teaching/learning interactions among children and their mediators have to teach us about conceptualizing such relationships? What conceptual tools can be used to analyze peer teaching as a negotiated exchange of knowledge?
- What is the role of play in young children's construction of syncretic literacy?
- What is the role of culturally significant literacy tools in literacy learning in the classroom and in community settings?
- How do children learn to mediate other children's learning? Where, how and by whom is their developing expertise as mediators nurtured?
- What are the advantages and disadvantages of simultaneous bilingual language use for literacy learning and for the development of metacognitive and metalinguistic abilities?
- What strategies work for bilingual adults teaching bilingual children and how might these strategies differ from and be similar to those used by monolinguals?
- How do teachers successfully build on communities' funds of knowledge to create learning communities as well as a multicultural curriculum that integrates content areas and facilitates inquiry? How do teachers do so at the same time as they work to meet current standards and mandates about curriculum and testing?
- What is the teacher's role in the organization of peer problem-solving and how might it change over time? What kinds of classroom environments support peers' interactions that foster the language and literacy of native English speakers and English language learners?
- How do educators use the juxtaposition of the approaches they advocate with those valued in children's homes and communities to nurture their own learning and that of children and community members?
- In what ways do the political and historical contexts of researchers' work facilitate or impede efforts to make visible the literacy lives of young children from diverse backgrounds?

The studies in this book represent 'active involvement in and with the multiple worlds of the child, expanding from the narrow confines of preschools [nurseries], elementary schools [primary schools] and child care programmes' (Cannella 1997: 163). They provide a deeper and broader look at invisible mediators, the more knowledgeable others beyond teachers and parents who, with young learners, co-create contexts in which literacy is used and learned. Drawing energy and insight from these studies, we urge readers to think critically about practice and create opportunities for all children to use and value the literacies of school, home and community. To do this requires a firm commitment to question assumptions and challenge stereotypes as well as accepted practices and beliefs; to engage in dialogue with colleagues and urge them to question and challenge also; to begin dialogues and interact with children, families and community members while listening, observing and learning; to make the many pathways to literacy visible and valued.

References

Adult Literacy and Basic Skills Unit (1993) *Parents and their Children: The Intergenerational Effect of Poor Basic Skills*, London: ALBSU.

Agar, M. (1996) *The Professional Stranger: An Informal Introduction to Ethnography*, San Diego, CA: Academic Press.

Allen, J. (ed.) (1999) *Class Actions: Teaching for Social Justice in Elementary and Middle School*, New York: Teachers College Press.

Allen, K. (1987) 'Promoting family awareness and intergenerational exchange: an informal life-history programme', *Educational Gerontology*, 13.1: 43–52.

Almasi, J. and Gambrell, L. (1997) 'Conflict during classroom discussions can be a good thing', in J. Paratore and R. McCormack (eds) *Peer Talk in the Classroom: Learning from Research*, Newark, DE: International Reading Association.

Apter, A. (1991) 'Herkovits's heritage: rethinking syncretism in the African diaspora', *Diaspora*, 1: 35–260.

Atkinson, P. and Hammersley, M. (1998) 'Ethnography and participant observation', in N. K. Denzin and Y. S. Lincon (eds) *Strategies of Qualitative Inquiry*, Thousand Oaks, CA: Sage.

Baghban, M. (1984) *Our Daughter Learns to Read and Write: A Case Study from Birth to Three*, Newark, DE: International Reading Association.

Baker, C. (2001) *Foundations of Bilingual Education and Bilingualism*, 3rd edn, Clevedon, UK: Multilingual Matters.

Bakhtin, M. M. (1981) *The Dialogic Imagination*, trans. M. Holquist and C. Emerson, Austin, TX: University of Texas Press.

Banks, J. A. and Banks, C. A. M. (eds) (1997) *Multicultural Education: Issues and Perspectives*, Boston, MA: Allyn & Bacon.

Barker, R. and Wright, H. (1955) *Midwest and its Children*, New York: Harper & Row.

Barton, D. and Hamilton, M. (1998) *Local Literacies: Reading and Writing in One Community*, London: Routledge.

Bateson, G. (1979) *Mind and Nature*, London: Wildwood House.

Baum, W. (1980) 'Therapeutic value of oral history', *International Journal of Aging and Human Development*, 12.1: 49–53.

Baynham, M. (1995) *Literacy Practices: Investigating Literacy in Social Contexts*, London: Longman.

Bearne, E. (ed.) (1998) *Language across the Curriculum*, London: Routledge.

Benjamin, R., Pecos, R. and Romero, M.E. (1997) 'Language revitalization efforts in the Pueblo de Cochiti: becoming "literate" in an oral society', in N. H. Hornberger (ed.)

Indigenous Literacies in the Americas: Language Planning from the Bottom Up, Berlin: Mouton de Gruyter.

Benmayor, R., Juarbe, A., Alvarez, C. and Vazquez, B. (1987) *Stories to Live By: Continuity and Change in Three Generations of Puerto Rican Women*, New York: Centro de Estudios Puertoriqueños.

Ben-Zeev, S. (1977) 'The influence on cognitive strategy and cognitive development', *Child Development*, 48: 1009–18.

Berger-Gluck, S. and Patai, D. (1991) *Women's Words: The Feminist Practice of Oral History*, New York: Routledge.

Berk, L. E. and Winsler, A. (1995) *Scaffolding Children's Learning: Vygotsky and Early Childhood Education*, Washington, DC: National Association for the Education of Young Children.

Bialystok, E. (1991) 'Metalinguistic dimensions of bilingual proficiency', in E. Bialystok (ed.) *Language Processing in Bilingual Children*, Cambridge: Cambridge University Press.

Billingsley, A. (1992) *Climbing Jacob's Ladder: The Enduring Legacy of African-American Families*, New York: Touchstone.

Bissex, G. (1980) *GYNS at Work: A Child Learns to Write and Read*, Cambridge, MA: Harvard University Press.

Bodrova, E. and Leong, D. (1996) *Tools of the Mind: The Vygotskian Approach to Early Childhood Education*, Englewood Cliffs, NJ: Prentice Hall.

Bohan-Baker, M. and Little, P. (2002) *The Transition to Kindergarten: A Review of Current Research and Promising Practices to Involve Families*, available http://www.gse.harvard.edu/d~hfrp/ (accessed February 3, 2003).

Bolton, E. (1998) 'Introduction: why books matter', in B. Cox (ed.) *Literacy is Not Enough*, Manchester: Manchester University Press and Book Trust.

Bourne, J. (1989) *Moving into the Mainstream: LEA Provision for Bilingual Pupils*, Windsor, UK: NFER Nelson.

Bretherton, I. (1984) 'Representing the social world in symbolic play: reality and fantasy', in I. Bretherton (ed.) *Symbolic Play and the Development of Social Understanding*, New York: Academic Press.

Britton, J. (1972) *Language and Learning*, Harmondsworth, UK: Penguin.

Brown, A. (1994) 'The advancement of learning', *Educational Researcher*, 8: 4–12.

Brown, A. and Campione, J. C. (1994) 'Guided discovery in a community of learners', in K. McGilly (ed.) *Classroom Lessons: Integrating Cognitive Theory and Classroom Practice*, Cambridge, MA: MIT Press.

Brown, R. (1970) 'Three processes in the child's acquisition of syntax: the child's grammar from I to III', in R. Brown (ed.) *Psycholinguistics: Selected Papers by Roger Brown*, New York: Macmillan.

Browne, A. (1996) *Developing Language and Literacy 3–8*, London: Paul Chapman.

Browne, N. (1999) *Young Children's Literacy Development and the Role of Televisual Texts*, London: Falmer.

Bruner, J. S. (1981) 'Intention in the structure of action and interaction', in L. P. Lipsitt (ed.) *Advances in Infancy Research*, vol. 1, Norwood, NJ: Ablex.

—— (1983) *Child's Talk: Learning to Use Language*, New York: Norton.

—— (1986) *Actual Minds, Possible Worlds*, Cambridge, MA: Harvard University Press.

Bryant, B. K. (1990) 'The child's perspective of sibling caretaking and its relevance to understanding socio-emotional functioning and development', in P. G. Zukow (ed.) *Sibling Interaction across Cultures: Theoretical and Methodological Issues*, New York: Springer-Verlag.

Bryant, P. and Bradley, L. (1985) *Children's Reading Problems: Psychology and Education*, Oxford: Blackwell.

Bullock Report (1975) *A Language for Life*, London: HMSO.

Cambourne, B. (1988) *The Whole Story: Natural Learning and the Acquisition of Literacy in the Classroom*, Auckland, New Zealand: Scholastic.

Cancelada, G. (2001, 13 January) 'Ford's workers think they have a better idea', *Post Dispatch*, pp. 1/13.

Cannella, G. (1997) *Deconstructing Early Childhood Education: Social Justice and Revolution*, New York: Peter Lang.

Carter-Black, J. (2001) 'The myth of "the tangle of pathology": resilience strategies employed by middle-class African-American families', *Journal of Family Social Work*, 6.4: 75–100.

Cazden, C. (1988) *Classroom Discourse: The Language of Teaching and Learning*, Portsmouth, NH: Heinemann.

Chall, J. (1967) *Reading: The Great Debate*, New York: McGraw-Hill.

Chambers, I. (1994) *Migrancy, Culture, Identity*, London: Routledge.

Chandler, J., Argyris, D., Barnes, W. S., Goodman, I. F. and Snow, C. E. (1986) 'Parents as teachers: observations of low-income parents and children in a homework-like task', in B. B. Schieffelin and P. Gilmore (eds) *The Acquisition of Literacy: Ethnographic Perspectives*, Norwood, NJ: Ablex.

Chang-Wells, G. L. M. and Wells, G. W. (1993) 'Dynamics of discourse: literacy and the construction of knowledge', in E. A. Forman, N. Minick and C. A. Stone (eds) *Contexts for Learning: Sociocultural Dynamics in Children's Development*, New York: Oxford University Press.

Childs, C. P. and Greenfield, P. M. (1982) 'Informal modes of learning and teaching: the case of Zinacenteco weaving', in N. Warren (ed.) *Advances in Cross-Cultural Psychology*, vol. 2, London: Academic Press.

Cicirelli, V. (1995) *Sibling Relationships across the Lifespan*, New York: Plenum.

Clancy, P. M. (1986) 'The acquisition of communicative style in Japanese', in B. B. Schieffelin and E. Ochs (eds) *Language Socialization across Cultures*, Cambridge: Cambridge University Press.

Clarke, P. (1996) 'Investigating second language acquisition in preschools: a longitudinal study of four Vietnamese-speaking children's acquisition of English in a bilingual preschool', unpublished thesis, La Trobe University, Bundoora, Victoria, Australia.

Clay, M. (1973) *Reading: The Patterning of Complex Behaviour*, Auckland, New Zealand: Heinemann.

Cochran-Smith, M. (1984) *The Making of a Reader*, Norwood, NJ: Ablex.

Cochran-Smith, M. and Lytle, S. (1999) 'The teacher research movement: a decade later', *Educational Researcher*, 28.7: 15–25.

Cohen, B. and Lukinsky, J. (1985) 'Religious institutions as educators', in M. D. Fantini and R. L. Sinclair (eds) *Education in School and Nonschool Settings*, Chicago: National Society for the Study of Education.

Cole, M. (1985) 'The zone of proximal development: where culture and cognition create each other', in J. A. Wertsch (ed.) *Culture, Communication and Cognition: Vygotskian Perspectives*, Cambridge: Cambridge University Press.

—— (1996) *Cultural Psychology: A Once and Future Discipline*, Cambridge, MA: Harvard University Press.

Coleman, R. (1981) 'Blacks in Utah history: an unknown legacy', in H. Z. Papanikolas (ed.) *The Peoples of Utah*, Salt Lake City, UT: Utah Historical Society.

Coles, R. (1990) *The Spiritual Life of Children*, Boston, MA: Houghton Mifflin.

Collier, V. (1995) *Promoting Academic Success for ESL Students: Understanding Second Language Acquisition for School*, Union, NJ: New Jersey Teachers of English to Speakers of Other Languages/NJ Bilingual Educators.

Collins, J. (1995) 'Literacy and literacies', *Annual Review of Anthropology*, 24: 75–93.

Comer, J. (1988) *Maggie's American Dream: The Life and Times of a Black Family*, New York: New American Library.

Compton-Lilly, C. (2003) *Reading Families: The Literate Lives of Urban Children*, New York: Teachers College Press.

Cooper, C. R., Marquis, A. and Edward, D. (1986) 'Four perspectives on peer learning among elementary school children', in E. C. Mueller and C. R. Cooper (eds) *Process and Outcome in Peer Relationships*, San Diego, CA: Academic Press.

Cornelius, J. D. (1991) *When I Read my Title Clear: Literacy, Slavery and Religion in the Antebellum South*, Columbia, SC: University of South Carolina Press.

Crook, C. (2000) 'Motivation and the ecology of collaborative learning', in R. Joiner, K. Littleton, D. Faulkner and D. Miell (eds) *Rethinking Collaborative Learning*, London: Free Association Books.

Crystal, D. (1987) *Child Language, Learning and Linguistics*, London: Arnold.

Cummins, J. (1981) 'The role of primary language development in promoting educational success for language minority students', in California State Department of Education (ed.) *Schooling and Language Minority Students*, Los Angeles: Evaluation, Dissemination, and Assessment Centre.

—— (1984) *Bilingualism and Special Education: Issues in Assessment and Pedagogy*, Clevedon, UK: Multilingual Matters.

—— (1991) 'Interdependence of first and second language', in E. Bialystok (ed.) *Language Processing in Bilingual Children*, Cambridge: Cambridge University Press.

—— (1996) *Negotiating Identities: Education for Empowerment in a Diverse Society*, Ontario, CA: California Association for Bilingual Education.

—— (2000) *Language, Power and Pedagogy*, Clevedon, UK: Multilingual Matters.

Damon, W. (1984) 'Peer education: the untapped potential', *Journal of Applied Developmental Psychology*, 5: 331–43.

D'Arcy, C. (2002) 'Children teach languages at Birmingham University', *Community Languages Bulletin*, Autumn, London: Centre for Information on Language Teaching.

Datta, M. (ed.) (2000) *Bilinguality and Literacy: Principles and Practice*, London: Continuum.

Delgado-Gaitan, C. (1994a) '*Consejos*: the power of cultural narratives', *Anthropology and Education Quarterly*, 25.3: 298–316.

—— (1994b) 'Socializing young children in Mexican-American families: an intergenerational perspective', in P. M. Greenfield and R. R. Cocking (eds) *Cross-Cultural Roots of Minority Child Development*, Hillsdale, NJ: Lawrence Erlbaum.

Delpit, L. (2002) 'No kinda sense', in L. Delpit and J. Dowdy (eds) *The Skin that We Speak: Thoughts on Language and Culture in the Classroom*, New York: The New Press.

Delpit, L. and Dowdy, J. (eds) (2002) *The Skin that We Speak: Thoughts on Language and Culture in the Classroom*, New York: The New Press.

Denzin, N. K. (1997) *Interpretive Ethnography: Ethnographic Practices for the 21st Century*, Thousand Oaks, CA: Sage.

Department for Education and Employment/Qualifications and Curriculum Authority (1997) *The Implementation of the National Literacy Strategy*, London: DfEE/QCA.

—— (1999) *The National Curriculum Handbook for Primary Teachers in England*, London: DfEE/QCA.

—— (2000) *Curriculum Guidance for the Foundation Stage*, London: DfEE/QCA.

Department of Education and Science (DES) (1963) *English for Immigrants*, London: DES.

Dewey, J. (1916) *Democracy and Education*, New York: Macmillan.

Diaz, R. and Klingler, C. (1991) 'Towards an explanatory model of the interaction between bilingualism and cognitive development', in E. Bialystok (ed.) *Language Processing in Bilingual Children*, Cambridge: Cambridge University Press.

Dodd, L. (1983) *Hairy Maclary from Donaldson's Dairy*, Milwaukee, WI: G. Stevens.

Donaldson, M. (1978) *Children's Minds*, New York: Norton.

Drury, R. (1997) 'Two sisters at school: issues for educators of young bilingual children', in E. Gregory (ed.) *One Child, Many Worlds: Early Learning in Multicultural Communities*, London: David Fulton and New York: Teachers College Press.

Dulay, H., Burt, M. and Krashen, S. (1982) *Language Two*, New York: Oxford University Press.

Dunn, J. (1990) 'Siblings and the development of social understanding in early childhood', in P. G. Zukow (ed.) *Sibling Interaction across Cultures: Theoretical and Methodological Issues*, New York: Springer-Verlag.

Duranti, A. and Ochs, E. (1986) 'Literacy instruction in a Samoan village', in B. B. Schieffelin and P. Gilmore (eds) *Acquisition of Literacy: Ethnographic Perspectives*, Norwood, NJ: Ablex.

—— (1997) 'Syncretic literacy in a Samoan American family', in L. B. Resnick, R. Saljo, C. Pontecorvo and B. Burge (eds) *Discourse, Tools, and Reasoning: Essays on Situated Cognition*, Berlin: Springer-Verlag.

Duranti, A., Ochs, E. and Ta'ase, E. K. (1995) 'Change and tradition in literacy instruction in a Samoan American community', *Educational Foundations*, 9.4: 57–74.

Durkin, D. (1966) *Children Who Read Early*, New York: Teachers College Press.

Dyson, A. H. (2003) *The Brothers and Sisters Learn to Write: Popular Literacies in Childhood and School Cultures*, New York: Teachers College Press.

Edelman, M. W. (1999) *Lanterns: A Memoir of Mentors*, Boston, MA: Beacon.

Edelsky, C. (1996) *With Literacy and Justice for All: Rethinking the Social in Language and Education*, 2nd edn, London: Taylor & Francis.

—— (1999) *Making Justice our Project: Teachers Working toward Critical Whole Language Practice*, Urbana, IL: National Council of Teachers of English.

Edwards, P. A. (1995) 'Connecting African-American parents and youth to the school's reading curriculum: its meaning for school and community literacy', in V. L. Gadsden and D. Wagner (eds) *Literacy among African-American Youth: Issues in Learning Teaching and Schooling*, Cresskill, NJ: Hampton Press.

Edwards, P. A., Pleasants, H. M. and Franklin, S. H. (1999) *A Path to Follow: Learning to Listen to Parents*, Portsmouth, NH: Heinemann.

Edwards, P. A., Danridge, J., McMillon, G. T. and Pleasants, H. M. (2001) 'Taking ownership of literacy: who has the power?', in P. R. Schmidt and P. B. Mosenthal (eds) *Reconceptualizing Literacy in the New Age of Pluralism and Multiculturalism*, San Francisco, CA: Jossey-Bass.

Edwards, V. (1998) *The Power of Babel: Teaching and Learning in Multilingual Classrooms*, Stoke-on-Trent: Trentham.

Egan, K. (1992) *Imagination in Teaching and Learning Ages 8–15*, London: Routledge.

Elder, G., Modell, J. and Parke, R. D. (1993) 'Studying children in a changing world', in G. Elder, J. Modell and R. D. Parke (eds) *Children in Time and Place*, New York: Cambridge University Press.

Ellis, S. and Rogoff, B. (1986) 'Problem solving in children's management of instruction', in E. C. Mueller and C. R. Cooper (eds) *Process and Outcome in Peer Relationships*, Orlando, FL: Academic Press.

Ellis, S. and Whalen, S. (1990) *Cooperative Learning: Getting Started*, New York: Scholastic.

Ely, R. and Gleason, J. B. (1995) 'Socialization across contexts', in P. Fletcher and B. MacWhinney (eds) *The Handbook of Child Language*, Oxford: Blackwell.

Emerson, R., Fretz, R. and Shaw, L. (1995) *Writing Ethnographic Fieldnotes*, Chicago: University of Chicago Press.

European Communities (EC) (1977) *Council Directive on the Education of Children of Migrant Workers*, Brussels: EC.

Farver, J. A. M. (1993) 'Cultural differences in scaffolding pretend play: a comparison of American and Mexican-American mother–child and sibling–child pairs', in K. MacDonald (ed.) *Parent–Child Play: Descriptions and Implications*, Albany, NY: SUNY Press.

Fillmore, L. W. (2000) 'Beyond baby-sitting and chocolate chip cookies: grandparents and the socialization of children', paper presented at La Choseca Conference, Albuquerque, NM.

Finn, P. (1999) *Literacy with an Attitude: Educating Working-Class Children in their Own Self-Interest*, Albany, NY: SUNY Press.

Fisher, C. B., Jackson, J. F. and Villarruel, F. A. (1998) 'The study of African-American and Latin American youth', in I. Sigel and K. Renninger (eds) *Handbook of Child Psychology*, 5th edn, vol. 4, New York: John Wiley.

Florida, R. (2002) *The Rise of the Creative Class and How It's Transforming Work, Leisure, Community, and Everyday Life*, New York: Basic Books.

Foley, D. (1990) *Learning Capitalist Culture: Deep in the Heart of Tejas*, Philadelphia, PA: University of Pennsylvania Press.

Foot, H., Morgan, M. and Shute, R. (eds) (1990) *Children Helping Children*, Chichester, UK: John Wiley.

Fountas, I. and Pinnell, G. (1996) *Guided Reading: Good First Teaching for All Children*, Portsmouth, NH: Heinemann.

Franco, R., Aga, T. and Keene, D.A. (1993) 'From houses without walls to vertical villages: Samoan housing transformations', paper presented at the Association for Social Anthropology in Oceania, Hawaii.

Frank, C. (1999) *Ethnographic Eyes: A Teacher's Guide to Classroom Observation*, Portsmouth, NH: Heinemann.

Fraser, M. W. (ed.) (1997) *Risk and Resilience in Childhood: An Ecological Perspective*, Washington, DC: NASW Press.

Frazier, E. F. (1974) *The Negro Church in America*, New York: Schocken.

Frederickson, N. and Cline, T. (1990) *Curriculum Related Assessment with Bilingual Children*, London: University College London.

Freire, P. (1973) *Education for Critical Consciousness*, New York: Continuum.

—— (1993) *Pedagogy of the Oppressed*, New York: Continuum.

Gates, H. L. (1989) 'Introduction', in L. Goss and M. E. Barnes (eds) *Talk that Talk: An Anthology of African-American Storytelling*, New York: Simon & Schuster.

Gee, J. P. (1996) *Social Linguistics and Literacies*, London: Routledge.

—— (1999) *An Introduction to Discourse Analysis*, NewYork: Routledge.

—— (2000) 'New people in new worlds: networks, the new capitalism, and schools', in B. Cope and M. Kalantzis (eds) *Multiliteracies: Literacy Learning and the Design of Social Futures*, London: Routledge.

Geertz, C. (1973) *The Interpretation of Cultures: Selected Essays*, New York: Basic Books.

Giroux, H. (1992) *Border Crossings: Cultural Workers and the Politics of Education*, New York: Routledge.

Goncu, A. (1998) 'Development of intersubjectivity in social pretend play', in M. Woodhead, D. Faulkner and K. Littleton (eds) *Cultural Worlds of Early Childhood*, London: Routledge.

Goncu, A., Tuermer, U., Jain, J. and Johnson, D. (1999) 'Children's play as cultural activity', in A. Goncu (ed.) *Children's Engagement in the World: Sociocultural Perspectives*, Cambridge: Cambridge University Press.

González, N., Moll, L., Tenery, M. F., Rivera, A., Rendon, P., Gonzáles, R. and Amanti, C. (1995) 'Funds of knowledge for teaching in Latino households', *Urban Education*, 29.4: 443–70.

Goodman, K. (1965) 'A linguistic study of cues and miscues in reading', *Elementary English*, 42: 639–43.

—— (1996) *Ken Goodman on Reading: A Common-Sense Look at the Nature of Language and the Science of Reading*, Ontario, Canada: Scholastic.

Goody, J. (1968) *Literacy in Traditional Societies*, Cambridge: Cambridge University Press.

Greenfield, P. M. (1984) 'Oral or written language: the consequences for cognitive development in Africa, U.S. and England', in B. V. Street (ed.) *Literacy in Theory and Practice*, Cambridge: Cambridge University Press.

—— (1994) 'Independence and interdependence as developmental scripts: implications for theory, research and practice', in P. M. Greenfield and R. R. Cocking (eds) *Cross-Cultural Roots of Minority Child Development*, Hillsdale, NJ: Lawrence Erlbaum.

Gregory, E. (1994a) 'Cultural assumptions and early years' pedagogy: the effect of the home culture on minority children's interpretation of reading in school', *Language, Culture and Curriculum*, 7.2: 111–24.

—— (1994b) 'The National Curriculum and non-native speakers of English', in G. Blenkin and V. Kelly (eds) *The National Curriculum and Early Learning*, London: Paul Chapman.

—— (1996) *Making Sense of a New World: Learning to Read in a Second Language*, London: Paul Chapman and Sage.

—— (ed.) (1997) *One Child, Many Worlds: Early Learning in Multicultural Communities*, London: David Fulton and New York: Teachers College Press.

—— (1998) 'Siblings as mediators of literacy in linguistic minority communities', *Language and Education*, 12: 33–54.

—— (1999) 'Myths of illiteracy: childhood memories of reading in London's East End', *Written Language and Literacy*, 2: 89–111.

—— (2000) 'Work or play: unofficial literacies in the lives of two East London communities', in M. Martin-Jones and K. Jones (eds) *Multilingual Literacies: Reading and Writing in Different Worlds*, Amsterdam: John Benjamins.

—— (2001) 'Sisters and brothers as language and literacy teachers: synergy between siblings playing and working together', *Journal of Early Childhood Literacy*, 1.3: 301–22.

Gregory, E. and Williams, A. (2000) *City Literacies: Learning to Read across Generations and Cultures*, London: Routledge.

—— (2003) 'Investigating family literacy histories and children's reading practices in London's East End', in S. Goodman, T. Lillis, J. Maybin and N. Mercer (eds) *Language, Literacy and Education: A Reader*, Stoke-on-Trent: Open University.

Gregory, E., Mace, J., Rashid, N. and Williams, A. (1996) *Family Literacy History and Children's Learning Strategies at Home and at School*, ESRC Final Report R000221186.

Guerra, J. C. (1998) *Close to Home: Oral and Literate Traditions in a Transnational Mexicano Community*, New York: Teachers College Press.

Gumperz, J. J. (1982) *Discourse Strategies*, Cambridge: Cambridge University Press.

Gutiérrez, K.D., Baquedano-López, P. and Tejeda, C. (1999) 'Rethinking diversity: hybridity and hybrid language practices in the Third Space', *Mind, Culture, and Activity*, 6.4: 286–303.

Haight, W. (2002) *African-American Children at Church: A Sociocultural Perspective*, New York: Cambridge University Press.

Haight, W. L., Wang, X., Fung, W. H., Williams, K. and Mintz, J. (1999) 'Universal, developmental and variable aspects of young children's play: a cross-cultural comparison of pretending at home', *Child Development*, 70.6: 1477–88.

Haight, W., Rhodes, J. and Nicholson, M. (2001) 'Cross race mentoring: perspectives of mentors over time and strategies for support', *The Mentor: Journal of Mentoring and Field Experience*, 1.1: 8–17.

Hakuta, K. (1986) *Mirror of Language: The Debate on Bilingualism*, New York: Basic Books.

Hale-Benson, J. (1986) *Black Children: Their Roots, Culture, and Learning Styles*, Baltimore, MD: Johns Hopkins University Press.

—— (1987) 'The transmission of faith to young Black children', paper presented at the Conference on Faith Development in Early Childhood, Henderson, NC.

Hall, N. (1987) *The Emergence of Literacy*, Portsmouth, NH: Heinemann.

Halliday, M. (1975) 'Relevant models of language', in M. Halliday, *Explorations in the Functions of Language*, New York: Elsevier.

—— (1984) 'Three aspects of children's language development: learning language, learning through language, learning about language', in Y. Goodman, M. Haussler and D. Strickland (eds) *Oral and Written Language Development Research: Impact on Schools*, Urbana, IL: National Council of Teachers of English.

Hamers, J. F. and Blanc, M. H. (1989) *Bilinguality and Bilingualism*, Cambridge: Cambridge University Press.

Harste, J. (2001) 'Rethinking a balanced curriculum', in K. Egawa and J. Harste (eds) *School Talk*, Urbana, IL: National Council of Teachers of English.

Harste, J., Burke, C. and Woodward, V. (1984) *Language Stories and Literacy Lessons*, Portsmouth, NH: Heinemann.

Haste, H. (1987) 'Growing into rules', in J. Bruner and H. Haste (eds) *Making Sense: The Child's Construction of the World*, London: Methuen.

Hatch, J. A. and Wisniewski, R. (eds) (1995) *Life History and Narrative*, Bristol, PA: Falmer.

Heath, S. B. (1983) *Ways with Words: Language, Life and Work in Communities and Classrooms*, Cambridge: Cambridge University Press.

Hennessey, S. and Murphy, P. (1999) 'The potential for collaborative problem solving in design and technology', *International Journal of Technology and Design Education*, 9.1: 36.

Hicks, D. (2002) *Reading Lives: Working Class Children Learning Literacy*, New York: Teachers College Press.

Hidalgo, N. M. (1994) 'Profile of a Puerto Rican family's support for school achievement', *Equity and Choice*, 10: 14–22.

—— (2000) 'Puerto Rican mothering strategies: the roles of mothers and grandmothers in promoting school success', in S. Nieto (ed.) *Puerto Rican Students in U.S. Schools*, Mahwah, NJ: Lawrence Erlbaum.

Hiebert, E. H., Pearson, P. D., Taylor, B. M., Richardson, V. and Paris, S. G. (1998) *Every Child a Reader: Applying Reading Research in the Classroom*, Ann Arbor, MI: Centre for the Improvement of Early Reading Achievement, University of Michigan.

Hirschler, J. (1994) 'Preschool children's help to second language learners', *Journal of Educational Issues of Language Minority Students*, 14: 227–40.

Hogan, D. M. and Tudge, J. R. H. (1999) 'Implications of Vygotsky's theory for peer learning', in A. M. O'Donnell and A. King (eds) *Cognitive Perspectives on Peer Learning*, Mahwah, NJ: Lawrence Erlbaum.

Holdaway, D. (1979) *The Foundations of Literacy*, Sydney, Australia: Ashton Scholastic.

Howard, A. and Borofsky, R. (eds) (1989) *Development in Polynesian Ethnology*, Honolulu, HI: University of Hawaii Press.

Hudley, E., Haight, W. and Miller, P. (2003) *Raise Up a Child: Human Development in an African-American Family*, Chicago: Lyceum Press.

Huebner, T. (1987) 'A socio-historical approach to literacy development: a comparative case study from the Pacific', in J. Langer (ed.) *Language, Literacy, and Culture: Issues of Society and Schooling*, Norwood, NJ: Ablex.

Hull, G. and Schultz, K. (eds) (2002) *School's Out: Bridging Out-of-School Literacies with Classroom Practice*, New York: Teachers College Press.

Hymes, D. (1974) *Foundations of Sociolinguistics*, Philadelphia, PA: University of Pennsylvania Press.

James, A. (2001) 'Ethnography in the study of children and childhood', in P. Atkinson, A. Coffey, S. Delamont, J. Lofland and L. Lofland (eds) *Handbook of Ethnography*, London: Sage.

Jarrett, R. L. (1995) 'Growing up poor: the family experiences of socially mobile youth in low-income African-American neighbourhoods', *Journal of Adolescent Research*, 10.1: 111–35.

Jennings, C. and Di, X. (1996) 'Collaborative learning and thinking: the Vygotskian approach', in L. Dixon-Krauss (ed.) *Vygotsky in the Classroom: Mediated Literacy Instruction and Assessment*, New York: Longman.

Jessor, R., Colby, A. and Shweder, R. A. (eds) (1996) *Ethnography and Human Development: Context and Meaning in Social Inquiry*, Chicago: University of Chicago Press.

Johns, L. (2000) *The Underground Railroad*, Bothell, WA: Wright Group.

Johnson, F. L. (2000) *Speaking Culturally: Language Diversity in the United States*, Thousand Oaks, CA: Sage.

Johnson, J. E. (1976) 'Relations of divergent thinking and intelligence test scores with social and non-social make-believe play of pre-school children', *Child Development*, 47: 1200–3.

John-Steiner, V. (1985) 'The road to competence in an alien land: a Vygotskian perspective on bilingualism', in J. V. Wertsch (ed.) *Culture, Communication and Cognition: Vygotskian Perspectives*, Cambridge: Cambridge University Press.

Johnstone, R. (1993) 'Research on language and teaching', *Language Teaching*, 26: 131–43.

Joiner, R., Littleton, K., Faulkner, D. and Miell, D. (eds) (2000) *Rethinking Collaborative Learning*, London: Free Association Books.

Karniol, R. (1990) 'Second language acquisition via immersion in daycare', *Journal of Child Language*, 17: 147–70.

Kenner, C. (2000a) 'Biliteracy in a monolingual school system? English and Gujarati in South London', *Language, Culture and Curriculum*, 13.1: 13–30.

—— (2000b) *Home Pages: Literacy Links for Bilingual Children*, London: Trentham.

—— (2003) 'Embodied knowledges: young children's engagement with the act of writing', in G. Kress and C. Jewitt (eds) *Explorations of Learning in a Multimodal Environment*, New York: Peter Lang.

—— (forthcoming) 'Living in simultaneous worlds: difference and integration in bilingual script learning', *International Journal of Bilingual Education and Bilingualism*.

Kincheloe, J. L. and Steinberg, S. R. (1997) *Changing Multiculturalism*, Bristol, PA: Open University Press.

Kindersley, A. and Kindersley, B. (1997) *Celebrations!*, New York: Dorling Kindersley.

Kirch, P. V. (1984) *The Evolution of Polynesian Chiefdoms*, Cambridge: Cambridge University Press.

Kondo, D. (1996) 'The narrative production of "home", community, and identity in Asian American theater', in S. Lavie and T. Swedenberg (eds) *Displacement, Diaspora, and Geographies of Identity*, Durham, NC: Duke University Press.

Krashen, S. (1982) *Principles and Practice in Second Language Acquisition*, Oxford, NY: Pergamon.

—— (1985) *The Input Hypothesis: Issues and Implications*, London: Longman.

Kress, G. (1997) *Before Writing: Rethinking the Paths to Literacy*, London: Routledge.

—— (2000) *Early Spelling: Between Convention and Creativity*, London: Routledge.

Kulick, D. (1992) *Language Shift and Cultural Reproduction: Socialization, Self, and Syncretism in a Papua New Guinean Village*, Cambridge: Cambridge University Press.

Ladson-Billings, G. (1995) 'Multicultural teacher education: research, practice, and policy', in J. A. Banks and C. A. M. Banks (eds) *Handbook of Research on Multicultural Education*, New York: Macmillan.

—— (2001) *Crossing Over to Canaan: The Journey of New Teachers in Diverse Classrooms*, New York: John Wiley.

Lambert, W. (1974) 'Culture and language as factors in learning and education', in F. Aboud and R. Mead (eds) *Cultural Factors in Learning and Education*, Bellingham, WA: 5th Western Symposium on Learning.

Lave, J. and Wenger, E. (1991) *Situated Learning: Legitimate Peripheral Participation*, Cambridge: Cambridge University Press.

LeCompte, M. D. and Schensul, J. J. (1999) *Designing and Conducting Ethnographic Research*, Walnut Creek, CA: Altamira Press.

Leichter, H. J. (ed.) (1974) *The Family as Educator*, New York: Teachers College Press.

—— (1984) 'Families as environments for literacy', in H. Goelman, A. Oberg and F. Smith (eds) *Awakening to Literacy*, Portsmouth, NH: Heinemann.

Lenneberg, E. (1967) *Biological Foundations of Language*, New York: Wiley and Sons.

Levine, J. (1990) *Bilingual Learners and the Mainstream Curriculum*, London: Falmer.

Lewison, M., Flint, A. S. and Van Sluys, K. (2002) 'Taking on critical literacy: the journey of newcomers and novices', *Language Arts*, 79.5: 382–92.

Lincoln, C. E. (1999) *Race, Religion, and the Continuing American Dilemma*, New York: Hill & Wang.

Lincoln, C. E. and Mamiya, L. H. (1990) *The Black Church in the African American Experience*, Durham, NC: Duke University Press.

Lindfors, J. (1999) *Children's Inquiry: Using Language to Make Sense of the World*, New York: Teachers College Press.

Linehan, C. and McCarthy, J. (2001) 'Reviewing the "community of practice" metaphor: an analysis of control relations in a primary school classroom', *Mind, Culture, and Activity*, 8: 129–47.

Linguistic Minorities Project (1985) *The Other Languages of England*, London: Routledge & Kegan Paul.

Littleton, K. (2000) 'Rethinking collaborative learning: an overview', in R. Joiner, K. Littleton, D. Faulkner and D. Miell (eds) *Rethinking Collaborative Learning*, London: Free Association Books.

Long, C. H. (1997) 'Perspective for the study of African-American religion in the United States', in E. Fulop and A. Raboteau (eds) *African-American Religion: Interpretive Essays in History and Culture*, New York: Routledge.

Long, S. (1997) 'Friends as teachers: the impact of peer interaction on the acquisition of a new language', in E. Gregory (ed.) *One Child, Many Worlds: Early Learning in Multicultural Communities*, London: David Fulton and New York: Teachers College Press.

—— (1998a) 'Learning to get along: language acquisition and literacy development in a new cultural setting', *Research in the Teaching of English*, 33: 8–47.

—— (1998b) 'The significance of playmates in the acquisition of a second language: implications from a study of cross-cultural adjustment', in G. Walford and A. Massey (eds) *Studies in Educational Ethnography: Children Learning in Context*, Stamford, CT: JAI Press.

Long, S. and Volk, D. (2004) 'Addressing inequities: ethnographic lessons from Mexican-American and Puerto Rican children at home and at school', *Studies in Educational Ethnography*, Stamford, CT: JAI Press.

Long, S., Volk, D., Gregory, E. and Williams, A. (2001) 'Syncretism and sociodramatic play: language, literacy, and cultural learning in multilingual settings', paper presented at the Ethnography in Education Forum, Philadelphia, PA.

Luke, A. and Kale, J. (1997) 'Learning through difference: cultural practices in early childhood socialization', in E. Gregory (ed.) *One Child, Many Worlds: Early Learning in Multicultural Communities*, London: David Fulton and New York: Teachers College Press.

Luria, A. R. (1976) *Cognitive Development: Its Cultural and Social Foundations*, Cambridge, MA: Harvard University Press.

McCormack, R. (1997) 'Eavesdropping on second graders' peer talk about African Trickster tales', in J. Paratore and R. McCormack (eds) *Peer Talk in the Classroom: Learning from Research*, Newark, DE: International Reading Association.

McDermott, R. P. and Gospodinoff, H. (1981) 'Social contexts for ethnic borders and school failure', in H. Trueba, G. Guthrie and K. Au (eds) *Culture and the Bilingual Classroom: Studies in Classroom Ethnography*, Rowley, MA: Newbury House.

McDermott, R. P., Goldman, S. V. and Varenne, H. (1984) 'When school goes home: some problems in the organization of homework', *Teachers College Record*, 85.3: 391–400.

McInytre, A. (1997) *Making Meaning of Whiteness: Exploring Racial Identity with White Teachers*, Albany, NY: SUNY Press.

McMahon, S. (1997) 'Book clubs: contexts for students to lead their own discussions', in S. McMahon and T. Raphael (eds) *The Book Club Connection: Literacy Learning and Classroom Talk*, New York: Teachers College Press.

McMillon, G. T. and Edwards, P. A. (2000) 'Why does Joshua hate school? . . . but love Sunday School?', *Language Arts*, 78.2: 111–20.

Marsh, J. A. (1999) 'Batman and Batwoman go to school: popular culture in the literacy curriculum', *International Journal of Early Years Education*, 7.2: 117–31.

—— (2003) 'Tightropes, tactics and taboos: an enquiry into the attitudes, beliefs and experiences of pre-service and newly qualified teachers with regard to the use of popular culture in the primary literacy curriculum', unpublished doctoral dissertation, University of Sheffield.

Marsh, J. and Millard, E. (2000) *Literacy and Popular Culture: Using Children's Culture in the Classroom*, London: Paul Chapman.

Marshall, H. R. (1961) 'Relation between home experiences and children's use of language in play interactions with peers', *Psychological Monographs*, 75.5: 509.

Martin-Jones, M. (1995) 'Codeswitching in the classroom: two decades of research', in L. Milroy and P. Muysken (eds) *One Speaker: Two Languages*, Cambridge: Cambridge University Press.

Mason, J. M., McCormick, C. and Bhavnagri, N. (1986) 'How are you going to help me learn? Lesson negotiations between a teacher and preschool children', in D. B. Yaden and S. Templeton (eds) *Metalinguistic Awareness and Beginning Literacy: Conceptualizing What It Means to Read and Write*, Portsmouth, NH: Heinemann.

Massey, A. and Walford, G. (1998) 'Children learning: ethnographers learning', in G. Walford and A. Massey (eds) *Studies in Educational Ethnography: Children Learning in Context*, Stamford, CT: JAI Press.

Meek, M. (1991) *On Being Literate*, London: Bodley Head.

Meek, M., Warlow, A. and Barton, G. (1977) (eds) *The Cool Web: The Pattern of Children's Reading*, London: Bodley Head.

Miller, W. (1998) *The Bus Ride*, New York: Lee & Low.

Mills, D. (2000) *Lima's Red Hot Chilli*, London: Mantra.

Minami, M. (2002) *Culture-Specific Language Styles: The Development of Oral Narrative and Literacy*, Clevedon, UK: Multilingual Matters.

Minns, H. (1990) *Read It to Me Now*, London: Virago.

Mitchell, E. P. (1986) 'Oral tradition: legacy of faith for the Black church', *Religious Education*, 81: 93–112.

Moje, E. B. (2000) 'Circles of kinship, friendship, position, and power: examining the community in community-based literacy research', *Journal of Literacy Research*, 32: 77–112.

Molinari, V. and Reichlin, R. E. (1984) 'Life review reminiscence in the elderly: a review of the literature', *International Journal of Aging and Human Development*, 20.2: 81–92.

Moll, L. C. (1992) 'Literacy research in community and classrooms: a sociocultural approach', in R. Beach, J. L. Green, M. L. Kamil and T. Shanahan (eds) *Multidisciplinary Perspectives on Literacy Research*, Urbana, IL: National Conference on Research in English and National Council of Teachers of English.

—— (2001) 'The diversity of schooling: a cultural-historical approach', in M. de la Luz Reyes and J. Halcón (eds) *The Best for our Children: Critical Perspectives on Literacy for Latino Students*, New York: Teachers College Press.

Moll, L. C. and González, N. (1994) 'Lessons from research with language minority children', *Journal of Reading Behaviour*, 26: 439–56.

Moll, L. C. and Greenberg, J. B. (1990) 'Creating zones of possibilities: combining social contexts for instruction', in L. C. Moll (ed.) *Vygotsky and Education: Instructional Implications and Applications of Sociohistorical Psychology*, Cambridge: Cambridge University Press.

Moll, L. C., Amanti, C., Neff, D. and González, N. (1992) 'Funds of knowledge for teaching: using a qualitative approach to connect homes and classrooms', *Theory into Practice*, 31: 132–41.

Monighan Nourot, P. (1998) 'Sociodramatic play', in D. P. Fromberg and D. Bergen (eds) *Play from Birth to Twelve and Beyond: Contexts, Perspectives and Meanings*, New York: Garland.

Myerhoff, B. (1992) *Remembered Lives: The Work of Ritual, Storytelling and Growing Older*, Ann Arbor, MI: University of Michigan Press.

National Academy of Science, National Research Council (1999) *How People Learn: Brain, Mind, Experience and School*. Washington, DC: National Academies Press.

Nelson, K. (1981) 'Social cognition in a script framework', in J. H. Flavell and L. Ross (eds) *Social Cognitive Development*, Cambridge: Cambridge University Press.

New Mexico Office of Indian Affairs (NMOIA) (2000) *2002 Estimated Population of New Mexico Indians*, Santa Fe, NM: NMOIA.

Nieto, S. (1996) *Affirming Diversity: The Sociopolitical Context of Multicultural Education*, 3rd edn, New York: Longman.

—— (1999) *The Light in their Eyes: Creating Multicultural Learning Communities*, New York: Teachers College Press.

—— (2002) *Language, Culture, and Teaching*, Mahwah, NJ: Lawrence Erlbaum.

Ninio, A. and Bruner, J.S. (1978) 'The achievement and antecedents of labeling', *Journal of Child Language*, 5: 5–15.

Ochs, E. (1988) *Culture and Language Development: Language Acquisition and Language Socialization in a Samoan Village*, Cambridge: Cambridge University Press.

O'Connor, M. C. and Michaels, S. (1996) 'Shifting participant frameworks: orchestrating thinking practices in group discussion', in D. Hicks (ed.) *Discourse, Learning and Schooling*, New York: Cambridge University Press.

Olmedo, I. (1997) 'Voices of our past: using oral history to explore funds of knowledge within a Puerto Rican family', *Anthropology and Education Quarterly*, 28.4: 550–73.

—— (1999) 'Redefining culture through the *memorias* of elderly Latinas', *Qualitative Inquiry*, 5.3: 353–76.

—— (2001) 'Puerto Rican grandmothers share and relive their *memorias*', *Centro Journal*, 13.2: 98–115.

Olson, D. R. (1977) 'From utterance to text: the bias of language in speech and writing', *Harvard Educational Review*, 47: 257–81.

Padmore, S. (1994) 'Guiding lights', in M. Hamilton, D. Barton and R. Ivanic (eds) *Worlds of Literacy*, Clevedon, UK: Multilingual Matters.

Pellegrini, A. D. and Galda, L. (1993) 'Ten years after: a reexamination of symbolic play and literacy research', *Reading Research Quarterly*, 28.2: 163–75.

Philips, S. (1972) 'Participant structures and communicative competence: Warm Springs children in community and classroom', in C. B. Cazden, V. T. John and D. Hymes (eds) *Functions of Language in the Classroom*, New York: Teachers College Press.

—— (1983) *The Invisible Culture: Communication in Classroom and Community on the Warm Springs Indian Reservation*, New York: Longman.

Piaget, J. (1926) *The Language and Thought of the Child*, New York: Harcourt Brace.

Plowden Report (1967) *Children and their Primary Schools*, London: HMSO.

Potts, R. (1996) 'Spirituality and the experience of cancer in an African-American community: implications for psychosocial oncology', *Journal of Psychosocial Oncology*, 14: 1–19.

Pouesi, D. (1994) *An Illustrated History of Samoans in California*, Carson, CA: Kin Publications.

Proctor, S. D. (1995) *The Substance of Things Hoped for: A Memoir of African American Faith*, New York: G. P. Putnam.

Proctor, S. D. and Watley, W. D. (1984) *Sermons from the Black Pulpit*, Valley Forge, NY: Judson Press.

Purcell-Gates, V. (1995) *Other People's Words: The Cycle of Low Literacy*, Cambridge, MA: Harvard University Press.

—— (2002) '. . . As soon as she opened her mouth! Issues of language, literacy, and power', in L. Delpit and J. Dowdy (eds) *The Skin that We Speak: Thoughts on Language and Culture in the Classroom*, New York: The New Press.

Ramirez, J. D. (1992) 'Executive summary of the final report: longitudinal study of structured English immersion strategy, early-exit and late-exit transitional bilingual education programmes for language minority children', *Bilingual Research Journal*, 16: 1–62.

Resnick, L. B. (1990) 'Literacy in school and out', *Daedalus*, 199.2: 169–86.

Riessman, C. K. (1993) *Narrative Analysis*, Thousand Oaks, CA: Sage.

Robertson, L. H. (2002) 'Parallel literacy classes and hidden strengths: learning to read in English, Urdu and classical Arabic', *Reading, Literacy and Language*, 36.3: 119–26.

Robinson, M. (1997) *Children Reading Print and Television*, London: Falmer.

Roediger, D. (1991) *The Wages of Whiteness: Race and the Making of the American Working Class*, London: Verso.

Rogoff, B. (1990) *Apprenticeship in Thinking: Cognitive Development in Social Context*, Oxford: Oxford University Press.

—— (1991) 'US children and their families: current conditions and research trends', *Society for Research in Child Development Newsletter*, Winter: 1–3.

—— (2003) *The Cultural Nature of Human Development*, New York: Oxford University Press.

Rogoff, B., Mosier, C., Mistry, J. and Goncu, A. (1993) 'Toddlers' guided participation with their caregivers in cultural activity', in E. A. Forman, N. Minick and C. A. Stone (eds) *Contexts for Learning: Sociocultural Dynamics in Children's Development*, New York: Oxford University Press.

Rogoff, B., Matusov, E. and White, C. (1996) 'Models of teaching and learning: participation in a community of learners', in D. R. Olson and N. Torrance (eds) *The Handbook of Education and Human Development: New Models of Learning, Teaching and Schooling*, Cambridge, MA: Blackwell.

Rogoff, B., Turkanis, C. G. and Bartlett, L. (2001) *Learning Together: Children and Adults in a School Community*, Oxford: Oxford University Press.

Romero, M. E. (1994) 'Identifying giftedness among Keresan Pueblo Indians: the Keres study', *Journal of American Indian Education*, 34.1: 35–58.

—— (2003) 'Perpetuating the Cochiti way of life: a study of child socialization and language shift in a Pueblo community', unpublished doctoral dissertation, University of California, Berkeley.

Rosaldo, R. (1993) *Culture and Truth: The Remaking of Social Analysis*, Boston, MA: Beacon.

Roskos, K. and Carroll, J. (2001) 'Under the lens: the play–literacy relationship in theory and practice', in S. Reifel (ed.) *Advances in Early Education and Day Care*, Greenwich, CT: JAI Press.

Rowe, D. (1994) *Preschoolers as Authors: Literacy Learning in the Social World of the Classroom*, Cresskill, NJ: Hampton Press.

Rubin, K. H. and Maioni, T. L. (1975) 'Play preference and its relation to egocentrism, popularity and classification skills in preschool', *Merrill-Palmer Quarterly*, 21: 171–9.

Sanders, M. G. (1997) 'Overcoming obstacles: academic achievement as a response to racism and discrimination', *Journal of Negro Education*, 66.1: 83–93.

Sando, J. S. (1998) *Pueblo Nations: Eight Centuries of Pueblo Indian History*, Santa Fe, NM: Clear Light Publishers.

Saville-Troike, M. (1988) 'Private speech: evidence for second language learning strategies during the "silent period"', *Journal of Child Language*, 15: 567–90.

Sawyer, K. (2002) *Improvised Dialogues: Emergence and Creativity in Conversation*, Westport, CT: Ablex.

Schickedanz, J. (1990) *Adam's Righting Revolutions*, Portsmouth, NH: Heinemann.

Schieffelin, B. B. (1995) 'Getting it together: an ethnographic approach to the study of the development of communicative competence', in E. Ochs and B. B. Schieffelin (eds) *Developmental Pragmatics*, New York: Academic Press.

Schieffelin, B. B. and Cochran-Smith, M. (1984) 'Learning to read culturally: literacy before schooling', in H. Goelman, A. Oberg and F. Smith (eds) *Awakening to Literacy*, Portsmouth, NH: Heinemann.

Schieffelin, B. B. and Gilmore, P. (1986) *The Acquisition of Literacy: Ethnographic Perspectives*, Norwood, NJ: Ablex.

School Curriculum and Assessment Authority (1996) *Desirable Outcomes for Children's Learning on Entering Compulsory Education*, London: SCAA.

—— (1997) *Looking at Children's Learning: Desirable Outcomes for Children's Learning on Entering Compulsory Education*, London: SCAA.

Scribner, L. (1985) 'Vygotsky's uses of history', in J. V. Wertsch (ed.) *Culture, Communication, and Cognition: Vygotskian Perspectives*, New York: Cambridge University Press.

Scribner, S. and Cole, M. (1981) *The Psychology of Literacy*, Cambridge, MA: Harvard University Press.

Searfoss, L. W. and Readence, J. E. (1985) *Helping Children Learn to Read*, Englewood Cliffs, NJ: Prentice Hall.

Seixas, P. (1993) 'Historical understanding among adolescents in a multicultural setting', *Curriculum Inquiry*, 23.3: 301–27.

Shankman, P. (1993) 'The Samoan exodus', in V. S. Lockwood, T. G. Harding and B. J. Wallace (eds) *Contemporary Pacific Societies: Studies in Development and Change*, Englewood Cliffs, NJ: Prentice Hall.

Shaw, R. and Stewart, C. (1994) 'Introduction: problematizing syncretism', in C. Stewart and R. Shaw (eds) *Syncretism/Anti-syncretism: The Politics of Synthesis*, London: Routledge.

Shor, I. (1999) 'What is critical literacy?', in I. Shor and C. Pari (eds) *Critical Literacy in Action: Writing Words, Changing Worlds*, Portsmouth, NH: Heinemann.

Shor, I. and Pari, C. (eds) (1999) *Critical Literacy in Action: Writing Words, Changing Worlds*, Portsmouth, NH: Heinemann.

Shore, B. (1982) *Sala'ilua: A Samoan Mystery*, New York: Columbia University Press.

Sitton, T., Mehaffy, G. and Davis, O. L. (1983) *Oral History: A Guide for Teachers and Others*, Austin, TX: University of Texas.

Slavin, R. E. (1987) 'Developmental and motivational perspectives on cooperative learning: a reconciliation', *Child Development*, 58: 1161–7.

Sleeter, C. and Grant, C. A. (1993) *Making Choices for Multicultural Education: Five Approaches to Race, Class, and Gender*, New York: Macmillan.

Smilansky, S. (1990) 'Sociodramatic play: its relevance to behaviour and achievement in school', in E. Klugman and S. Smilansky (eds) *Children's Play and Learning: Perspectives and Policy Implications*, New York: Teachers College Press.

Smilansky, S. and Feldrhan, N. (1980) 'Relationship between sociodramatic play in kindergarten and scholastic achievement in second grade', Tel Aviv: Department of Psychology, Tel Aviv University.

Smith, F. (1985) *Reading*, 2nd edn, Cambridge: Cambridge University Press.

Smitherman, G. (1977) *Talkin and Testifyin: The Language of Black America*, Boston, MA: Houghton Mifflin.

Snow, C. and Ninio, A. (1986) 'The contracts of literacy: what children learn from learning to read books', in W. H. Teale and E. Sulzby (eds) *Emergent Literacy: Reading and Writing*, Norwood, NJ: Ablex.

Sobel, M. (1988) *Trabelin' On: A Slave Journey to an Afro-Baptist Faith*, Princeton, NJ: Princeton University Press.

Solsken, J., Willet, J. and Wilson-Keenan, J. (2000) 'Cultivating hybrid texts in multicultural classrooms: promise and challenge', *Research in the Teaching of English*, 35: 179–212.

Sperry, L. and Sperry, D. (1996) 'Early development of narrative skills', *Cognitive Development*, 11: 443–65.

Spradley, J. (1980) *Participant Observation*, Fort Worth, TX: Harcourt Brace.

Stack, C. B. (1974) *All our Kin: Strategies for Survival in a Black Community*, New York: Harper & Row.

Stone, C. A. (1993) 'What is missing in the metaphor of scaffolding?', in E. A. Forman, N. Minick and C. A. Stone (eds) *Contexts for Learning: Sociocultural Dynamics in Children's Development*, New York: Oxford University Press.

Street, B. V. (ed.) (1984) *Literacy in Theory and Practice*, Cambridge: Cambridge University Press.

—— (1999) *Multiple Literacies and Multi-lingual Society*, NALDIC Literacy Papers, London: National Association for Language Development in the Curriculum.

—— (2003) 'The implications of the "New Literacy Studies" for literacy education', in S. Goodman, T. Lillis, J. Maybin and N. Mercer (eds) *Language, Literacy and Education: A Reader*, Stoke-on-Trent: Trentham.

Street, J. C. and Street, B. V. (1995) 'The schooling of literacy', in P. Murphy, M. Selinger, J. Bourne and M. Briggs (eds) *Subject Learning in the Primary Curriculum*, London: Routledge.

Stuart-Wells, A. and Crain, R. (1997) *Stepping Over the Colour Line: African American Students in White Suburban Schools*, New Haven, CT: Yale University Press.

Suina, J. H. (1994), 'From natal culture to school culture to dominant society culture: supporting transitions for Pueblo Indian students', in P. M. Greenfield and R. R. Cocking (eds) *Cross-Cultural Roots of Minority Child Development*, Hillsdale, NJ: Lawrence Erlbaum.

Suina, J. H. and Smolkin, L. S. (1995) 'The multicultural worlds of Pueblo Indian children's celebrations', *Journal of American Indian Education*, 34.3: 18–27.

Sulzby, E. (1986) 'Writing and reading: signs of oral and written language organization in the young child', in W. Teale and E. Sulzby (eds) *Emergent Literacy: Writing and Reading*, Norwood, NJ: Ablex.

Swann Report (1985) *Education for All* (Report of the Committee of Enquiry into the Education of Children from Ethnic Minority Groups), London: HMSO.

Tabors, P. (1997) *One Child, Two Languages: A Guide for Preschool Educators of Children Learning English as a Second Language*, Baltimore, MD: Paul Brookes.

Tabors, P. and Snow, C. (1994) 'English as a second language in pre-schools', in F. Genessee (ed.) *Educating Second Language Children: The Whole Child, the Whole Curriculum, the Whole Community*, New York: Cambridge University Press.

Tannen, D. (1989) *Talking Voices: Repetition, Dialogue, and Imagery in Conversational Discourse*, New York: Cambridge University Press.

Taylor, D. and Dorsey-Gaines, C. (1988) *Growing Up Literate: Learning from Inner City Families*, Portsmouth, NH: Heinemann.

Teale, W. H. and Sulzby, E. (1986) *Emergent Literacy: Writing and Reading*, Norwood, NJ: Ablex.

Tharp, R. and Gallimore, R. (1988) *Rousing Minds to Life: Teaching and Learning in Social Context*, New York: Cambridge University Press.

Thompson, L. (1996) 'School ties: a social network analysis of friendships in a multilingual kindergarten', *European Early Childhood Education Research Journal*, 4.1: 49–70.

Tizard, B. (1993) 'Early influences on literacy', in R. Beard (ed.) *Teaching Literacy, Balancing Perspectives*, London: Hodder & Stoughton.

Tomlinson, S. (2000) 'Ethnic minorities and education: new disadvantages', in T. Cox (ed.) *Combating Educational Disadvantage*, New York: Falmer.

Toohey, K. (2000) *Learning English at School: Identity, Social Relations and Classroom Practice*, Clevedon, UK: Multilingual Matters.

Townsend, H. (1971) *Immigrant Pupils in England: LEA Response*, Windsor, UK: NFER-Nelson.

Tudge, P. (1990) 'Vygotsky, the zone of proximal development and peer collaboration: implications for classroom practice', in L. Moll (ed.) *Vygotsky and Education: Instructional Implications and Applications of Sociohistorical Psychology*, Cambridge: Cambridge University Press.

Turner, G. (1861) *Nineteen Years in Polynesia: Missionary Life, Travels, and Researches in the Islands of the Pacific*, London: John Snow.

Urzua, C. (1986) 'A children's story', in P. Rigg and D. S. Enright (eds) *Children and ESL: Integrating Perspectives*, Washington, DC: Teachers of English to Speakers of Other Languages.

Vacca, J. L., Vacca, R. T. and Gove, M. K. (1991) *Reading and Learning to Read*, 2nd edn, New York: HarperCollins.

Valdés, G. (1996) *Con Respeto: Bridging the Distance between Culturally Diverse Families and Schools*, New York: Teachers College Press.

Van Dijk, T. A. (ed.) (1997) *Discourse as Social Interaction*, Thousand Oaks, CA: Sage.

Van Manen, M. (1990) *Researching Lived Experience: Human Science for an Action Sensitive Pedagogy*, New York: SUNY Press.

Vélez-Ibáñez, C. and Greenberg, J. B. (1992) 'Formation and transformation of funds of knowledge among U.S.-Mexican households', *Anthropology and Education Quarterly*, 23.4: 313–35.

Verhoeven, L. (1987) *Ethnic Minority Children Acquiring Literacy*, Dordrecht: Foris.

Volk, D. (1997a) 'Continuities and discontinuities: teaching and learning in the home and school of a Puerto Rican five year old', in E. Gregory (ed.) *One Child, Many Worlds: Early Learning in Multicultural Communities*, London: David Fulton and New York: Teachers College Press.

—— (1997b) 'Questions in lessons: activity settings in the homes and school of two Puerto Rican kindergartners', *Anthropology and Education Quarterly*, 28.1: 22–49.

—— (1999). '"The teaching and the enjoyment and being together . . .": sibling teaching in the family of a Puerto Rican kindergartner', *Early Childhood Research Quarterly*, 14: 5–34.

Volk, D. and de Acosta, M. (2001) '"Many differing ladders, many ways to climb . . .": literacy events in the bilingual classroom, homes, and community of three Puerto Rican kindergartners', *Journal of Early Childhood Literacy*, 1: 193–224.

Vygotsky, L. S. (1962) *Thought and Language*, Cambridge, MA: MIT Press.

—— (1978) *Mind in Society: The Development of Higher Psychological Processes* (eds M.Cole, S. Scribner, V. John-Steiner and E. Souberman), Cambridge, MA: Harvard University Press.

—— (1981) 'The genesis of higher mental functions', in J. V. Wertsch (ed.) *The Concept of Activity in Soviet Psychology*, Armonk, NY: Sharpe.

Wade, B. and Moore, M. (1996) 'Children's early book behaviour', *Educational Review*, 48.3: 283–7.

Wallman, S. (1984) *Eight London Households*, London: Tavistock.

Weis, L. (1990) *Working Class without Work: High School Students in a De-industrializing Economy*, New York: Routledge.

Weisner, T. S. (1989) 'Comparing sibling relationships across cultures', in P. G. Zukow (ed.) *Sibling Interactions across Cultures: Theoretical and Methodological Issues*, New York: Springer-Verlag.

Weisner, T., Gallimore, R. and Jordan, C. (1993) 'Unpackaging cultural effects of classroom learning: Hawaiian peer assistance and child-generated activity', in R. Roberts (ed.) *Coming Home to Preschool: The Sociocultural Context of Early Education*, Norwood, NJ: Ablex.

Wells, G. (1985) 'Pre-school literacy related activities and success in school', in D. Olsen, N. Torrance and N. Hildyard (eds) *Literacy Language and Learning*, Cambridge: Cambridge University Press.

—— (1986) *The Meaning Makers: Children Learning Language and Using Language to Learn*, Portsmouth, NH: Heinemann.

—— (1999) *Dialogic Inquiry: Toward a Sociocultural Practice and Theory of Education*, Cambridge: Cambridge University Press.

—— (2001) 'The case for dialogic inquiry', in G. Wells (ed.) *Action, Talk and Text: Learning and Teaching through Inquiry*, New York: Teachers College Press.

Wells, G., Chang, G. L. M. and Maher, A. (1990) 'Creating classroom communities of literate thinkers', in S. Sharan (ed.) *Cooperative Learning: Theory and Research*, New York: Praeger.

Wenger, E. (1998) *Communities of Practice: Learning, Meaning, and Identity*, Cambridge: Cambridge University Press.

Wenger, E., McDermott, R. and Snyder, W. (2001) *Cultivating Communities of Practice*, Boston, MA: Harvard Business Press.

Wertsch, J. V. (1985) *Vygotsky and the Social Formation of Mind*, Cambridge, MA: Harvard University Press.

—— (1994) 'The primacy of mediated action in sociocultural studies', *Mind, Culture and Activity*, 1.4: 202–8.

West, K. F. (2001) 'Hispanic population boom portends change', *Charleston Business Journal*, April 9, Charleston, SC.

Whitehead, M. (1997) *Language and Literacy in the Early Years*, London: Paul Chapman.

—— (2002) 'Dylan's routes to literacy: the first three years with picture books', *Journal of Early Childhood Literacy*, 2.3: 269–89.

Willett, J. (1987) 'Contrasting acculturation patterns in two non-English-speaking preschoolers', in H. Trueba (ed.) *Success or Failure? Learning and the Language Minority Student*, Cambridge, MA: Newbury House.

—— (1995) 'Becoming first graders in an L2 classroom: an ethnographic study of L2 socialisation', *TESOL Quarterly*, 29: 473–503.

Willett, J. and Bloome, D. (1993) 'Literacy, language, school, and community: a community centred view', in A. Carrasquillo and C. Hedley (eds) *Whole Language and the Bilingual Learner*, Norwood, NJ: Ablex.

Williams, A. and Gregory, E. (2001) 'Siblings bridging literacies in multilingual contexts', *Journal of Research in Reading*, 23.3: 248–65.

Williams, J. (1832) *Narrative of a Voyage Performed in the Missionary Schooner 'Olive Branch'*, London: London Missionary Society.

Williams, J. D. and Snipper, G. C. (1990) *Literacy and Bilingualism*, New York: Longman.

Willis, P. (1977) *Learning to Labor: How Working Class Kids Get Working Class Jobs*, New York: Columbia University Press.

Wolfendale, S. and Topping, K. (1996) *Family Involvement in Literacy*, London: Cassell.

Wong Fillmore, L. (1976) 'The second time around: cognitive and social strategies in second language acquisition', unpublished doctoral dissertation, Stanford University, CA.

—— (1979) 'Individual differences in second language acquisition', in C. J. Fillmore, D. Kempler and W. S-Y. Wang (eds) *Individual Differences in Language Ability and Language Behaviour*, New York: Academic Press.

—— (1991) 'When learning a second language means losing the first', *Early Childhood Research Quarterly*, 6.3: 323–46.

Wood, D., Bruner, J. S. and Ross, G. (1976) 'The role of tutoring in problem solving', *Journal of Child Psychology and Psychiatry*, 17: 89–100.

Wynne, J. (2002) 'We don't talk right. You ask him', in L. Delpit and J. Dowdy (eds) *The Skin that We Speak: Thoughts on Language and Culture in the Classroom*, New York: The New Press.

Zinsser, C. (1986) 'For the Bible tells me so: teaching children in a fundamentalist church', in B. Schieffelin and P. Gilmore (eds) *The Acquisition of Literacy: Ethnographic Perspectives*, Norwood, NJ: Ablex.

Zukow, P. G. (1989) 'Siblings as effective socializing agents: evidence from Central Mexico', in P. G. Zukow (ed.) *Sibling Interactions across Cultures: Theoretical and Methodological Issues*, New York: Springer-Verlag.

Index